The Mechanical Fuze and
the Advance of Artillery
in the Civil War

The Mechanical Fuze and the Advance of Artillery in the Civil War

Edward B. McCaul, Jr.

McFarland & Company, Inc., Publishers
Jefferson, North Carolina, and London

LIBRARY OF CONGRESS CATALOGUING-IN-PUBLICATION DATA

McCaul, Edward B., 1951–
 The mechanical fuze and the advance of artillery in the Civil War / by Edward B. McCaul, Jr.
  p. cm.
 Includes bibliographical references and index.

 ISBN: 978-0-7864-4613-1
 softcover : 50# alkaline paper ∞

 1. United States — History — Civil War, 1861–1865 — Artillery operations. 2. Fuzes (Ordnance) — United States — History — 19th century. 3. United States. Army — Artillery — History — 19th century. 4. Military art and science — United States — History — 19th century. I. Title.
 E492.6.M33 2010
 973.7'41— dc22   2010016664

British Library cataloguing data are available

©2010 Edward B. McCaul, Jr. All rights reserved

No part of this book may be reproduced or transmitted in any form or by any means, electronic or mechanical, including photocopying or recording, or by any information storage and retrieval system, without permission in writing from the publisher.

On the cover: Union artillery battery with 10-pounder Parrott rifles conducting drill at Ringgold, Georgia (courtesy National Archives); inset: Parrott Percussion Fuze (author's collection)

Manufactured in the United States of America

McFarland & Company, Inc., Publishers
 Box 611, Jefferson, North Carolina 28640
  www.mcfarlandpub.com

I dedicate this work to Sherri, my wife, and to my family
for their patience while I went on this quest.
Sherri also deserves thanks
for reading numerous drafts without complaint.
I would also like to dedicate it
to my comrades in arms, many of whom are no longer
with us, and others who are still in harm's way.

Table of Contents

Acknowledgments — ix
Preface — 1
Introduction — 3

ONE. United States Military Gunpowder — 11
TWO. Prewar Fuzes — 19
THREE. Smooth-Bore Versus Rifled Artillery — 37
FOUR. The Manufacturing War — 46
FIVE. Artillery During the Civil War — 57
SIX. The New Fuzes — 84
SEVEN. Hotchkiss, Parrott, and Schenkl — 110
EIGHT. Postwar Developments — 122

Appendix A. United States Fuze Related Patents, 1855–1872 — 131
Appendix B. British Fuze Related Patents, 1855–1876 — 173
Appendix C. Short Biographies — 177
*Appendix D. Prewar Armories, Arsenals, Navy Yards,
    Foundries, and Small Arms Manufacturers* — 185
Chapter Notes — 195
Bibliography — 205
Index — 215

Acknowledgments

As with any book there are a number of different people that I need to thank and I can only hope that I have not failed to mention all of them.

I would like to thank my PhD advisor, Dr. Joe Guilmartin, for his support and encouragement that made this book possible. I would also like to thank Dr. Mansel Blackford whose knowledge of business history was invaluable and Dr. Randy Roth who introduced me to the use of statistics for historical analysis. John Biemeck deserves thanks for he first introduced me to the world of Civil War projectiles and fuzes and was kind enough to allow me to read and use his unpublished work on artillery projectiles. Clarke Wilhelm, John Montgomery, Chris Evans, Allan Katzberg, and Ann Christy also need to be thanked for reading and reviewing different versions of this book. Chuck Jones, whose knowledge and collection of Civil War fuzes is probably unsurpassed, needs to be thanked as he was generous enough to share that knowledge with me. Chuck also introduced me to Dean Thomas, of Thomas Publications in Gettysburg, who provided information on the production of paper fuzes during the war.

I also received help from overseas. John Day and Trevor Parker were kind enough to share their vast knowledge of British fuzes with me. Peter Smithurst at the Royal Armouries Museum, also provided valuable information on British fuzes. In addition, Rolf Wirtgen, chief curator for the Bundesant für Wehrtechnik und Beschaffung, kindly responded to my inquiry on Charles Bormann and provided much needed information.

My thanks extends to all of the individuals who work for the federal government who assisted me. Patrick Owens, George Eaton, Carol Lilly, and William Moye, all of whom are historians with the United States Army, were kind enough to respond to my inquiries. The staff at the United States Military Academy Library and Alumni Association was an excellent source of information on all of the academy graduates. In addition, Joe Vann, with the United States Corps of Engineers, provided expert advice based on his research and knowledge of explosive ordnance.

Those individuals at Ohio State University who provided support also need to be thanked: Joby Abernathy, who has helped numerous history graduate students and holds a special place in all of their hearts, Mary Jo Arnold in the Science and Engineering Library provided invaluable assistance with questions on United States patents, and Chris Burton, who helped me negotiate OSU's financial system. In addition, I would like to thank Carolyn Merry and her students Christopher Wells, Mark Seidelmann, David Sanford, and Yeosang Yoon who created the maps and drawings.

My thanks are also extended to the Mershon Center and Professor Emeritus Richard Smith, who sponsors the Henry H. Simms Award. The financial support they provided gave me the necessary monetary resources to travel to different archives and conduct research.

Preface

The rifled artillery used during the Civil War created the need for a new type of artillery fuze. Mechanically ignited fuzes were developed as one possible solution to this problem, but the technology for these fuzes was in its infancy and industry had never manufactured them in large numbers. These new mechanical fuzes made rifled artillery more lethal and the battlefield a much more dangerous place. Being a new technology, fuzes underwent a dramatic and rapid evolution during the war based on knowledge gained from costly battlefield experience. Advances in technical knowledge and industry's new ability to produce large quantities of identical items made this evolution possible. These dramatic technological changes created a new fuze paradigm that, in time, replaced the older fuze designs.

Even with the new fuze paradigm, the military knew what it needed, but translating that need into technical reality and finding companies that could take the concept and produce the necessary equipment was the challenge. In addition, the American military, because of the war, had to change its normal methodical testing and requisition process and quickly encourage the development of this technology. Along with this, the Army's and Navy's Ordnance Departments had to find factories capable of producing massive quantities of fuzes requiring tight tolerances. Northern inventors and industry ably responded to this challenge. In contrast, a similar effort in the South failed. The success of the North and the failure of the South in this endeavor can be explained by the Weapon System Pyramid production triad of military need, technical availability, and industrial capability, for it was during the American Civil War that this production triad came of age.

The combination of rifled artillery and mechanical fuzes changed warfare. While much detailed information has been published on rifled artillery only a limited amount has been written about its actual impact upon Civil

War battles. Fuzes have been largely forgotten and only included in books on Civil War projectiles with the exception of Chuck Jones' book which, while it provides detailed information about Civil War fuzes, does not discuss their impact on the battlefield. An appreciation of the impact that rifled artillery combined with mechanical fuzes had upon the Civil War, and future wars, is important for an understanding of how men fought and tried to survive on an increasingly dangerous battlefield. For the first time battlefields had become so dangerous that, by the middle of the Civil War, if a man could be seen, he could be killed.

Introduction

> *The fuze, insignificant in appearance, long misapplied and still neglected in the ordnance service of several countries, constitutes, as I have stated, the principal element in the projectile, the perfection of which may assure to artillery an importance which this arm hitherto has not attained, the glorious deeds of the Royal British Artillery in the Crimea not excepted.*[1]
> — Charles Bormann, 1862

On Sunday the 19th of June 1864, the USS *Kearsage* and the CSS *Alabama* fought an engagement off Cherbourg, France. Early in the fight, a 6.4-inch, 100-pound Blakely projectile from the *Alabama* struck and lodged in the *Kearsage*'s sternpost but failed to explode because of a faulty fuze.[2] Raphael Semmes, the Captain of the *Alabama*, believed that if this fuze had worked properly, the resulting damage would have mortally wounded the *Kearsage*, allowing the *Alabama* to win the battle.[3] Although a victory by the *Alabama* would not have changed the outcome of the war, the gun crew of the *Alabama* that fired this round experienced the same frustration that other gun crews have experienced for centuries — how to get a projectile to explode where and when it needs to explode. Confederate General and artillery commander E. Porter Alexander stated, "For an unreliable fuse or a rifle-shell which 'tumbles' sickens not only the gunner but the whole battery, more than 'misfires' at large game dishearten a sportsman. There is no encouragement to careful aiming when the ammunition fails, and the men feel handicapped."[4] Fuzes are a crucial but forgotten item that changed warfare before, during, and after the American Civil War.[5]

* * *

Technology created tremendous changes in warfare during the American Civil War, and much has been written about the majority of these changes.

USS *Kearsarge* versus the CSS *Alabama*. The *Alabama* probably would have won the battle if the fuze in the projectile that struck the *Kearsarge*'s sternpost had not been faulty (courtesy Library of Congress).

Changes occurred in a variety of weapon systems as well as auxiliary systems such as the railroad, telegraph, and techniques for food preservation. Artillery was one of the weapon systems that experienced dramatic change, and artillery's impact during the war cannot be overstated. Artillery was still devastating in its traditional role, but the new rifled artillery and larger smooth-bore guns made high, masonry, casemate forts obsolete; created a more lethal battlefield; influenced the results of battles; and began long-range gunnery's domination of naval warfare. These changes were mainly dependent upon two items: improvements in metallurgy, which made rifled artillery and the larger smooth-bore guns practical, and improvements in fuze technology. Historians have written extensively about developments in metallurgy, rifled artillery, and the larger smooth-bore guns, but fuzes are a largely forgotten weapon system.[6] The lethality of modern ordnance is, in a large part, dependent upon the effectiveness of its fuzes. It was during the American Civil War that modern fuzes were extensively used for the first time in combat. The design of these fuzes changed as the military gained experience using them in the hard school of combat. By the end of the war, fuzes had evolved to become more dependable even though they were not as reliable as the military desired. Still, the fuzes created during the war were the basic design of all artillery fuzes until the advent of the variable time fuze during World War II.

The need for a reliable fuze became apparent shortly after the discovery of gunpowder. It is believed that exploding projectiles were in use as early as 1382 and were hand grenades lit by the thrower.[7] Once reliable fuzes were created, it took a number of years before hollow artillery projectiles were manufactured in sufficient quantities to enable artillerists to make full use of the new fuzes. This was due to a number of technical reasons, not lack of interest on the part of the military. One problem was that the earliest artillery projectiles were a continuation of the projectile technology that had been used previously in catapults and trebuchets — solid carved round stones, or an arrow similar to those used in crossbows. While the arrow was a failure, stone projectiles were effective enough that they were still used in 1807, when Turkish forces inflicted severe damage to a British fleet as it passed through the Dardanelles.[8] Another problem was that metal was very expensive during the time period in which artillery was first being introduced. The first metal artillery projectiles were made from lead or bronze, both of which are relatively soft metals and do not have much striking power against solid objects such as stone walls. While it was relatively simple to cast hollow lead or bronze projectiles, they could easily be damaged and become nonfunctional. In addition, lead projectiles are substantially denser than stone ones, resulting in higher internal pressures in the cannon, which can lead to a catastrophic failure. Consequently, when cost and effectiveness were compared, stone projectiles were the better initial choice. However, superior iron cannon balls were introduced around 1350, and they quickly became the dominant material of choice for artillery projectiles.[9] In addition, iron projectiles could be cast hollow, without the fear of them being deformed by rough handling, allowing them to be filled with gunpowder.

When fuzes first started being used in artillery projectiles, gunners lit the fuze before placing the projectile into the cannon or placed the fuze so that it would face the charge. This practice was very dangerous, as premature explosions were common. The procedure became much safer in the middle of the eighteenth century when cannoneers realized that there was enough distance between the projectile and the wall of the cannon, known as windage, to allow the flame created by the burning propelling charge to ignite the fuze even if the fuze faced away from the propelling charge.[10] This discovery led to the invention of the artillery projectile sabot. The sabot was, initially, a concave wooden base that was strapped to the base of the projectile with the purpose of ensuring that the gunner put the projectile into the cannon with the fuze facing out. Unbeknown to those artillerymen, wooden base sabots, while creating a more regular pressure in the cannon, resulted in lower projectile velocities and a more irregular recoil.[11] However, the safety benefit derived from using the sabot negated any loss in velocity and irregularity with the recoil. As with the fuze, the sabot would change with the introduction of rifled artillery.

After fuzes came into use artillerymen quickly discovered that there were three conditions which must be fulfilled.[12] The first condition was that the fuze had to detonate at the point in the projectile's trajectory that best suited the projectile's intended purpose. Then, the flight of the projectile needed to be controlled so that it was brought as near as possible to the desired point of explosion. Finally, the projectile had to explode in a manner that created the best possible shape to the sheaf of fire. Only the first condition depends entirely on the fuze, and it "is the most important of all, as its successful application may render of less consequence and failure arising from that of the others, while the failure of the fuze renders the other conditions unattainable."[13] Creating a reliable fuze was, and is, difficult, as there are a number of conflicting criteria. Compromises must be made, with certain criteria favored over others. As with most design criteria, it is seldom possible to meet all of the goals to everyone's satisfaction. Resolving the conflict among these criteria is a matter of deciding whose criteria are the most important.

Fuzes developed alongside the projectiles they were used in and the cannons from which they were fired. By the nineteenth century artillery had evolved into three main types: guns, mortars, and howitzers. Each of these different types of artillery served a specific purpose. Guns fired on a relatively flat trajectory, and their projectiles were used as a battering force. They were the largest and heaviest pieces in regard to their projectiles and were fired with large charges, sometimes up to half of the weight of the projectile.[14] A mortar was a short-chambered piece that fired projectiles at a very high angle over obstacles such as city walls. Mortars only needed a small charge of gunpowder to propel their projectiles. This small charge gave mortars the advantage of being able to fire thin-walled shells filled with gunpowder, which were the only projectiles used in mortars. Beyond the damage the shells created when they exploded, shells could also crush protective shelters due to the velocity they acquired in falling. Howitzers were neither a gun nor mortar but something in-between. While a howitzer could fire at a greater elevation than a gun it did not have the ability to elevate as high as a mortar. Howitzers fired the lighter exploding projectile and could not fire the heavier solid shot as they were unable to absorb the force required to fire it. As exploding projectiles required less powder to propel them, a howitzer could have thinner walls than a gun thus making it lighter and more maneuverable. Howitzers also differed from guns and mortars as the gunpowder charge used in a howitzer was contained in a small chamber located in its breech.[15] All three types of artillery were required by the military as none of them fulfilled every need.

There is a complicated relationship between artillery pieces and their projectiles. Some of the variables are length and thickness of the barrel, size of the charge, as well as weight and size of projectile. A detailed discussion of these variables is beyond the scope of this book as fuzes are only needed for exploding projectiles. What is key, in relation to fuzes, is that all of these variables affect an artillery piece's performance and thus the missions it is capable of accomplishing. The military wanted an artillery piece that could fire solid shot and explosive projectiles at a flat trajectory and at higher elevations for longer range. Henri-Joseph Paixhan began the solution to this problem when he invented the shell gun in 1822 to counter British naval superiority. The shell gun's advantage was that it could fire an exploding projectile in a flat trajectory. Its development made wooden ships very vulnerable due to the destructive power of the exploding projectiles. However, the shell gun was not able to fire solid shot due to the additional gunpowder that was needed to propel it and the resulting increased internal pressures. Still, the invention of the shell gun made the need for reliable fuzes even more important. The invention of the shell gun helped lead to the invention of the light 12-pounder Napoleon gun in France as well as the heavy Rodman and Dahlgren guns in the United States. All three of these guns were an improvement on the shell gun as they were capable of firing both solid shot and explosive projectiles in a flat trajectory.

The light 12-pounder Napoleon was developed in France in the 1850s under Napoleon III and was the first field artillery piece that could function as both a gun and a howitzer. Table 1.1, 1860 United States Smooth-Bore Field Artillery, summarizes some of the differences listed by John Gibbon in his 1860 *The Artillerist's Manual* between the old style gun, the howitzer, and the new hybrid light 12-pounder Napoleon.

The differences between the three types of cannons are obvious. While the 12-pounder Napoleon weighed less than the 12-pounder gun, it did weigh more than the 12-pounder howitzer. Weight was important, for if a gun was too heavy it was not easily maneuvered, and the Army made sure that the Napoleon gun was maneuverable before it was adopted.[16] Additionally, the Napoleon gun, unlike the old 12-pounder gun and the howitzer, could fire solid shot or case shot without any substantial decrease in range, while the range for shells was increased. The Napoleon gun gave the Army a more versatile cannon, increased the uniformity of the artillery, and made exploding projectiles more desirable because shells could now be fired horizontally. As a result, the 12-pounder Napoleon was the principal field artillery piece for the United States Army when the Civil War began. However, the adoption of rifled artillery forced the Army and Navy to rapidly adopt new mechanical fuzes.

The evolution of fuzes was part of a wider technological innovative movement and dependent upon the need of and acceptance by the military. Although some historians argue that active warfare does not result in the

Table 1*— 1860 United States Smooth-Bore Field Artillery

	12-pound gun	12-pound gun Napoleon	12-pound howitzer
Weight	1,757 lbs	1,220 lbs	788 lbs
Length of bore	74.0 in	63.6 in	46.25 in
Diameter of bore	4.62 in	4.62 in	4.62 in
Projectiles			
Solid shot	Yes	Yes	No
Shell	No	Yes	Yes
Case shot	Yes	Yes	Yes
Canister	Yes	Yes	Yes
Grape shot	Yes	Yes	Yes
Ranges			
5° elev. Solid shot	1663 yds (2.50 lb charge)	1619 yds (2.50 lb charge)	N/A
Shell	N/A	1300 yds (2 lb charge,	1072 yds (1 lb charge, 5° 00' elev.
Case shot with 4 sec fuze	1250 yds (1.50 lb charge, 2° 30' elev.)	1135 yds (2.5 lb charge, 3° 75' elev.)	1050 yds (3° 45' elev., 0.75 lb charge)

*Gibbon, Appendix, pages 40–42.

advancement of technology but rather discourages innovation, research and development do occur during a war. However, most of this research and development could be termed field research and development, as active warfare encourages innovation, especially by those men whose lives are at stake. During the Civil War, fuze design changed based on what was learned from using the fuzes in combat. It is true that the mechanical fuzes used during the initial phase of the war were designed before the war began, but the same could be said about the helicopter before its initial use during World War II, as Leonardo da Vinci had designed one centuries before. Designing an item and making it workable are two completely different arenas, but during wartime, it is workability that counts.

As fuzes became more complex, the manufacturing of these fuzes also became more complex. Consequently, fewer factories could manufacture reliable fuzes. In addition, other inventions, such as mercury fulminate primers, necessary to make mechanical fuzes a reality, could only be manufactured by an industrial base staffed with skilled workmen and supplied with an adequate amount of raw material. During the Civil War, the Union had a vast industrial district on the northeast coast that was capable of producing fuzes that required quality machining and high tolerances. In contrast, the Confederacy was never able to produce reliable mechanical fuzes in any quantity. The military fully realized how complicated it was to manufacture a mechanical fuze, and as a result, the cost of a mechanical fuze was proportionally more than the projectile in which it was placed. This cost differential appears in the order for a large number of projectiles and fuzes placed with Robert J. Parrott's West Point Foundry in March 1864. The projectiles in this order ranged from 10-pound to 200-pound percussion fuze shells. The price of these projectiles varied from $0.70 to $12.00 per projectile, or about six cents per pound. However, each of the percussion fuzes included in the order cost $0.45. A Parrott Percussion Fuze weighs about eight ounces, making its cost about 90 cents per pound or fifteen times more than the projectiles, a substantial difference reflecting the difficulty of manufacturing mechanical fuzes.[17]

The artillery fuze is a small, expensive, forgotten piece of military ordnance. Yet without it, modern warfare would be very different. Its evolution was complex with numerous dead ends, but by the end of the Civil War the modern artillery fuze had been created and fully tested. Other countries were also working on this same technological problem, but the rate of change for their fuzes was relatively flat compared to the rate of change in the United States during the Civil War. The new fuzes, projectiles, and rifled artillery helped change warfare to such an extent that an individual schooled in the older Napoleonic style of warfare would not have understood it. At the same time, the new fuzes were a victim of their own success in that they raised expectations beyond what could be achieved. The future development of effective recoil systems, better communications, and more precise machining of parts helped but did not fully satisfy the needs of the military. Still, the combination of rifled artillery and new fuzes made the Civil War a much deadlier war, one in which there was no safe place on the battlefield.

ONE

United States Military Gunpowder

As gunpowder has become one of the principal agents in modern warfare, it is important to understand the means of collecting and preparing the materials of which it is composed, and the process of its manufacture.[1]
— Edward Simpson, 1862

The creation of reliable fuzes was principally dependent upon two independent factors. First, gunpowder had to be manufactured so that it burned reliably. This involved developing an effective formula that was consistently followed by the manufacturer. Along with this, the proper size of the grains used in the fuzes had to be determined and replicated for each batch. In addition, a reliable means of timing the burning of the fuzes had to be developed. Before the invention of accurate, portable timepieces some artillerymen would say the Apostles' Creed to proof fuzes which, needless to say, can have tremendous variations in the amount of time it takes.[2] Consequently, it was not until the latter part of the seventeenth century that reliable fuzes became a reality. Even then, quality control of the manufacture of gunpowder continued to be closely monitored, and research continued to be conducted.

Gunpowder's importance during the Civil War cannot be overemphasized based on the significance the military placed on its officers' knowledge of gunpowder and the quality it expected manufacturers to meet. In John Gibbon's 1860 *The Artillerist's Manual* gunpowder is the theme of the first chapter of the book. In that chapter, Gibbon covers such information as gunpowder's history, how it was manufactured, its composition, analysis, and storage, and testing of it using such equipment as the Mortar Eprouvette, Gun and Ballistic Pendulum, and Navez's Machine. The Navy put a similar emphasis on gunpowder. Its 1862 ordnance and naval gunnery text book, written by Lieutenant Edward Simpson and used by the Midshipmen at the Naval

Academy, devoted an entire chapter, out of a total of nine, to the subject. An understanding of manufacturing, storing, as well as the various types of gunpowder was crucial knowledge for both Army and Navy officers.

Gunpowder was the first nonnatural force created by man as it is not a naturally occurring phenomenon. While it is accepted that gunpowder was first created in ancient China no one knows exactly who, when, or how it was invented, as initially the secrets of manufacturing gunpowder were closely guarded. However, by the middle of the nineteenth century, gunpowder's properties were known and well publicized with many different formulas being used. In 1860 gunpowder produced for the United States' Army and Navy was composed of "75 or 76 parts, by weight, of nitre, to 15 to 14 of charcoal, and 10 of sulphur."[3] Of the three ingredients, charcoal and nitre, also known as saltpeter, were and are the most difficult to process, as sulphur can be found in an almost pure form in nature. Charcoal provides the means of combustion in gunpowder and when burnt creates the gas that provides necessary propelling force. The charcoal used in the United States' military gunpowder came from light, quick growing wood, with willow and poplar being preferred, as it was the easiest to pulverize through distillation.[4]

Nitre, or saltpeter, is known by chemists as potassium nitrate with a chemical formula of KNO_3. It is an oxidizer, which means that it releases oxygen when it breaks down and thus provides oxygen to a combustion reaction in an atmosphere otherwise void of oxygen. Some of the best nitre used in the nineteenth century was "mined" in India. However, additional deposits could be found in other warm climates. In the United States nitre was found in some of the limestone caves in Virginia, Georgia, Tennessee and Kentucky but all the United States' military gunpowder used nitre that came from India. Nitre could also be created "artificially" by mixing animal and vegetable substances in nitre beds. This method was in common use until nitre "mines" were discovered and continued to be used by countries, to include the Confederacy, who were cut off from these mines. However, creating artificial nitre is a long, time consuming process.

Nitre was a strategic material during the gunpowder era. When the Civil War started the Federal Government feared that the British government would embargo the shipment of all military related equipment to both sides, to include the excellent nitre from India. The potential of this happening was taken so seriously that as the stockpiles of nitre began to run low, Lammot du Pont was sent to England with orders and monetary backing from the Federal government to purchase all of the nitre he could. He was successful but the *Trent* Affair stopped his shipment of nitre to the United States for a period of time. Once the *Trent* Affair was resolved the nitre shipment was allowed to leave England. Beyond the fear of having to fight two wars at one time, the fear of a British embargo, which would have included nitre, had an impact upon the Federal government's decision to release the Confederate commissioners.[5]

Sulphur was included in gunpowder as it added consistency to the mix and intensity to the flame. In addition, since sulfur is insoluble in water, it helps gunpowder resist absorbing moisture. Great care had to, and must, be taken when mixing these three ingredients. If a batch has too much charcoal in proportion to nitre it will not burn, or if there was too little sulfur it would either absorb excess moisture or not burn as intensely.

Once the ingredients for gunpowder were ready they were pulverized, mixed, compressed, granulated, glazed, dried, and dusted. The granulation process broke the pressed gunpowder down into the required grain size. Different size grains were important as smaller grains generate gas more rapidly when burnt than larger grain gunpowder. Thus, small grained gunpowder was used in rifles and pistols as they could withstand higher pressures and wall thickness could be much greater relative to the amount of gas created. Large grain gunpowder was used in cannons to decrease the maximum pressure, yet at the same time the barrel was long enough to allow sufficient propelling gas pressure to build up behind the projectile. (It is interesting to note in Table 1.1 that, while the number of grains varies tremendously between the various types of gunpowder, the total weight by volume does not.)

Table 1.1*— Prewar Types of Gunpowder Used by the Army

Type	No. Grains of Powder in 10 grs. Troy	Weight of 1 Cu. Ft. in ounces (shaken)
Cannon	150	1,039
Musket	1,100	1,012
Rifle	6,000	1,060

*Instruction for Field Artillery, page 10.

In order to understand why the military required different size grains of gunpowder one must understand that the key in the burning rate of gunpowder, consisting of an identical composition, is the size of the grain:

> The larger the grains the more rapid is the ignition, but the slower the combustion. With smaller grains the ignition is slower, but the combustion much faster; and hence, in small-arms, when small grains are used, the projectile gets the full force of the powder in a smaller space than in larger guns.[6]

Given an equal quantity of military cannon and musket powder, the musket powder would have a much faster combustion rate than the cannon powder. This is important to understand because the pressure buildup of the gases produced by the smaller grain powder will be much faster than that produced by larger grain powder. Large artillery pieces need larger grains of powder so that the pressure slowly builds within the tube; a rapid buildup of pressure could result in a catastrophic failure of the piece.

Manufacturing and loading projectiles, as well as storing gunpowder and loaded projectiles, was and is dangerous. The better gunpowder plants were specifically designed and located to lessen the effect of any catastrophic explosion. When explosions occurred loss of life was the norm. At the DuPont gunpowder mill in Brandywine, Delaware, eleven explosions occurred during the Civil War killing 43 men and injuring numerous others.[7] Once the gunpowder had been manufactured it was transported to the various arsenals. However, before the military accepted a shipment the gunpowder had to be inspected and proofed. This process included tests for general qualities, size of the grain, gravimetric density, specific gravity, initial velocity, hygrometric qualities, and strain upon the gun. After the shipment passed inspection and proofing, an inspection report was completed and the barrels were marked.

At the arsenals the gunpowder was used to load cartridges, projectiles, fuzes, and other explosive devices but this work was only done at the arsenals' laboratories. The work conducted in the laboratories was considered so dangerous that it was located away from the rest of the arsenal. Fire prevention and limiting the effect of any explosion were prime considerations in the construction of the laboratories. Admission to the laboratories was strictly controlled and india rubber overshoes were required to be worn in some of the rooms. Still, a number of serious accidents occurred. Three explosions on September 17, 1862, at the Allegheny Arsenal destroyed two of the laboratories and killed 57 workers. Interestingly, many of the workers in the laboratories were women and children due to the perception that they were more skilled at making cartridges. Nevertheless, they were paid lower wages.

Both the Navy and Army had specific, detailed regulations for the storage of gunpowder and loaded projectiles. The Navy's 1864 *Ordnance Instructions* stated that the Powder Regulations were to be "read, and copies placed within the reach of every officer and man connected in the remotest degree with the service of the Magazine and Shell-rooms."[8] In addition, any officer or man who could not answer questions relating to the Powder Regulations within a reasonable period of time was not to work in those areas. Fuzes were given special attention in that they were to be occasionally removed from a loaded shell and examined to determine if they were still serviceable. The Army's 1862 *Ordnance Manual* was equally detailed, stating that neither loaded shells nor fixed ammunition were to be placed into magazines unless absolutely necessary. In addition, the manual stated that when piled the fuzes in the lower tier of shells were to face the vacant spaces between the shells and that the fuzes in all of the other tiers were to face downward.[9] Emphasis was also placed on airing the magazines and rolling the cartridges so that the gunpowder would not become caked. This was important as caked gunpowder would not burn properly potentially causing a misfire.

At the start of the American Civil War, the Union Army used three types of gunpowder (see Table 1.1) but additional types of gunpowder were created as needed. Mammoth gunpowder was created by Captain Thomas Rodman when he was developing a 15-inch gun just prior to the start of the war. His purpose in creating mammoth gunpowder was to ensure "that the pressure of the gas should be uniform throughout the entire length of the bore."[10] Rodman conducted numerous experiments with different forms of gunpowder until he discovered that cakes of gunpowder molded in a hydraulic press were impermeable to gas and, when pierced with a number of uniform holes, fit the criteria. Rodman felt that while less costly large grained gunpowder could be used without creating excessive strain on most cannons "for guns of very large calibre [sic], or when extraordinary velocities are required, the perforated cake should be exclusively used."[11] As shown in Table 1.2 the Army was using four different sizes of gunpowder by the middle of the war. The increase was due to a greater variety in the sizes of artillery gunpowder although there had also been a consolidation of the types of gunpowder used in small arms. The tight tolerances used in determining grain size are an indication of the quality the Ordnance Department expected its suppliers of gunpowder to meet. However, the tolerances did increase as the size of the grain increased.

Table 1.2*— Civil War Types of Gunpowder Used by the Army

Type	Sieve Size All Pass Through	Sieve Size None Pass Through
Musket	0.03 inch	0.06 inch
Mortar	0.06 inch	0.10 inch
Cannon	0.25 inch	0.35 inch
Mammoth	0.6 inch	0.9 inch

*The Ordnance Manual, *third edition, page 242.*

The Navy also used a range of different sizes of gunpowder. The Navy's 1852 *Ordnance Instructions* discussed using six brass sieves having various hole sizes (.12, .10, .09, .06, .05, .035 inches) to separate the grains. The three larger holed sieves were marked "For Cannon Powder" and the three smaller holed sieves were marked "For Small Arms." This method was based on the Army's *Ordnance Manual* as the Navy used the Army's standards for the manufac-

Table 1.3* — Late Civil War Types of
Gunpowder Used by the Navy

Type	Sieve Size Pass Through	Sieve Size Remain On
Musket	0.06 inch	0.02 inch
Cannon	0.15 inch	0.10 inch
Rifle (only used in the 8-inch, 60-pounder, and 100-pounder Parrott Rifles)	0.3 inch	0.15 inch

*Ordnance Instructions for the United States Navy, 1866, Part III, page 48.

ture and inspection of their gunpowder. By late in the war the Navy had developed its own set of instructions for the manufacture and inspection of gunpowder as reflected in its 1866 *Ordnance Instructions*. Those instructions only showed three gunpowder grain sizes, as shown in Table 1.3. Rifle gunpowder was exclusively used in the large caliber Parrott rifled cannons due to a request by Robert Parrott who was attempting to solve the problems associated with premature failures of his large caliber rifled cannon. All other naval guns used cannon gunpowder as the Navy was simplifying its gunpowder logistical system. The Navy recognized that there was a difference in the size of its granules when compared to the Army's and cautioned its ordnance officers to be aware of this difference when using Army gunpowder. In addition, the Navy allowed a 10 percent variation in the size of the grains, something the Army did not. Still, the Navy's tolerances were very tight. The Navy thought so highly of its gunpowder and the quality control associated with it that its 1860, 1864, and 1866 *Ordnance Instructions* stated that officers were allowed to purchase gunpowder overseas for saluting in order to preserve a supply of Navy issued proof gunpowder for action.[12]

The Army and Navy had another variation in their use of gunpowder as the Navy often used a larger amount of gunpowder in the bursting charges of their shells, especially their larger ones. When propelling or bursting a projectile, if too much gunpowder is used (assuming the cannon does not explode) the excess will be discharged along with the projectile or with its fragments. These remnants will normally be on fire. Although no official statement has been found on the Navy's reasoning for doing this, it is safe to assume that their hope was that these burning gunpowder remnants from the exploding shell would start fires wherever they landed. Each service had different needs, and modifications were made so that any piece of ordnance would fit their specific requirements; gunpowder was not an exception.

Two types of gunpowder that the military used in the ignition system of many of their fuzes, but not mentioned in lists of military gunpowder, were mealed powder and fuze composition. Mealed powder was high quality, very finely grained gunpowder but it was not a dust. The physical properties of mealed powder made it desirable in those applications in which an exact rate of combustion was needed. In the Bormann fuze, mealed powder was the powder used in the section of the fuze punched by the gunner that determined the length of time the fuze would burn. The military closely controlled the burning rate of the powder train because the fuze could be punched at quarter-second intervals. The secret was that mealed powder was pressed into the powder train, and compressed mealed powder acts as a single grain of powder. Compressed mealed powder was crucial to the success and reputation of the Bormann fuze even though it was not considered a military powder. In addition, mealed powder was placed in a paste form on the tops of the wooden and paper fuzes although the actual fuze was filled with fuze composition.

The military used fuze composition in its wooden and paper fuzes but the actual composition varied depending on the length of time the fuze was to burn. For the Army's heavy guns, fuzes either burnt 10 seconds per inch, 14 seconds per inch, or 20 seconds per inch. The recommended mixture of nitre, sulphur, and mealed powder for each of these time periods is shown in Table 1.4. As the amount of mealed powder is the only variation between the compositions it is obvious that mealed powder was the determining factor in how fast the fuze burned. However, the mixture was not fixed as the Army's *Ordnance Manual* noted that due to the variation in "the quality of the ingredients and the manipulation in mixing them, the exact proportions must be determined by experiment."[13] In addition, the amount of mealed powder used in light and heavy mortar fuzes also varied. The mixture for the 8 and 10-inch light mortar fuzes consisted of two parts nitre, one part sulphur, and three parts mealed powder while the 10 and 13-inch heavy mortar fuzes consisted of two parts nitre, one part sulphur and 2¼ parts mealed powder.[14]

By the time of the Civil War the science of gunpowder was well developed. The military was well aware of its peculiarities, dangers, and how slightly different mixtures created very different results. As a consequence, gunpowder manufacturing was rigorously controlled. A greater knowledge and control of the manufacture of gunpowder was one of the principle differences

Table 1.4*— Civil War Heavy Gun Fuze Compostion

Burning Time	Parts Nitre	Parts Sulphur	Parts Mealed Powder
10 seconds	26	9	14
14 seconds	26	9	12
20 seconds	26	9	10

*The Ordnance Manual, *third edition, page 295.*

between the military of the mid nineteenth century and its predecessors. This knowledge was what made the time fuzes used during the Civil War far superior to those used in the Napoleonic era and earlier. Unluckily, these improvements also helped artillery become a more deadly, long-range factor during the war.

Two

Prewar Fuzes

> *In view of the progress that has been made in every branch of human industry, it may seem singular that so important an appliance as the fuze should not have advanced beyond the primitive article used in the earlier epochs of explosive projectiles.*[1]
>
> —John Dahlgren, 1856

> *The fuze therefore, is the soul, the groundwork of any system of explosive projectile, it is the criterion of the system.*[2]
>
> —Charles Bormann, 1862

The first fuze used by the United States Army was a fixed composition wooden fuze and is the only fuze discussed in the Army's 1841 *Ordnance Manual*. As with most pieces of equipment made under the supervision of the Ordnance Department, the instructions for its manufacture were very detailed. Ordnance Department instructions stated that "hard, close-grained woods are best adapted for making fuzes: beech or ash is generally used. It should be dry, sound, free from sap, knots, worm-holes, or shakes."[3] Once a piece of wood was selected, cut to the proper length and in the shape of a prism, an employee, known as a turner, placed the piece of wood in a lathe, hollowed it, and cut it into its proper shape. As part of this process, the turner marked the fuze's exterior, starting at the bottom of the fuze, into inches and tenths of an inch using a steel gauge. The markings allowed artillery gunners to cut the fuze to the length that would give the projectile the required time of flight before the fuze detonated. Once the body of the fuze passed inspection, it was filled with fuze composition, a special mixture of nitre, sulphur and mealed gunpowder as explained in Chapter 1.

Filling the fuze with the fuze composition was the most dangerous part of the operation and was accomplished in the arsenal's laboratory, a building safely separated from the rest of the arsenal. Laboratory workers carefully filled each fuze with fuze composition, one ladleful at a time, compacting the composition after each ladle either by hand or screw press. (As explained in Chapter 1 compressed gunpowder is very hard, has a much greater density than loose gunpowder, and, when properly compressed, acts as one grain.) After filling the fuze, a worker placed a mealed gunpowder paste primer on top of the fuze composition. When the primer dried, the next step involved covering the top of the fuze with a piece of waterproof paper and marking the piece of paper with the number of seconds the fuze burned to the inch. Workers determined the burn time of the batch by igniting several of the fuzes and rejecting the batch if too much variation existed. Skilled hand labor was an essential part of the operation as only portions of the manufacturing process were performed by machinery. The use of calibrated gauges throughout the process ensured that the manufacturing process was as uniform as possible, for quality control was an important principle of the Ordnance Department.

Problems existed with the fixed composition fuze. One of the difficulties was that the fuze had a tendency to be thrown out of a spinning projectile by the generated centrifugal force as it was only held in place by friction. There was also a problem with wooden fuzes breaking when the gunpowder composition was driven into the bottom of the fuze by setback forces. By the start of the Civil War, the fixed composition wooden fuze was no longer used in field artillery and heavy gun projectiles because it had been replaced by the paper and Bormann Fuzes. These fuzes were adopted because they solved many of the problems associated with the fixed composition wooden fuze. As a result, only mortar projectiles continued using fixed composition wooden fuzes because they were subjected to smaller setback forces than a projectile fired from a gun. In addition, a fixed composition wooden fuze had a longer burn time than either the paper or Bormann Fuze, and as a mortar projectile normally had a long flight time, this was critical. Fixed composition wooden fuzes also gave a mortar battery the maximum flexibility with a minimum fuze inventory. A gunner could cut a fixed composition wooden fuze to length in the field while other fuzes had a specific burn time, creating the need to have a number of different fuzes on hand. Lastly, mortars had a much slower rate of fire than guns, giving the gunners more time to safely and carefully prepare the fuze.

As with the Army, the Navy initially used fixed composition wooden fuzes, but had a different design and a different method of arming them. Naval fixed composition wooden fuzes were long enough to reach the opposite side of the projectile from the fuze hole, solving the problem of setback forces breaking the fuze. The fuze was armed and its burning time determined by boring a hole into its side rather than a portion of the fuze being cut off. Once armed, a Sailor drove the fuze into the projectile with a wooden mallet then filled the projectile with gunpowder through a filling hole which was immediately plugged. Only a few projectiles aboard a ship were fully armed at all times, and these had their fuzes bored at the longest possible burn time.[4]

However, the Navy had additional problems with fixed composition wooden fuzes not generally experienced by the Army. In storage at sea, wooden fuzes could swell, becoming too large to be driven into the fuze hole. Although the Navy learned how to control this problem in sailing ships, steam ships, due to the hot and moist atmosphere created by the machinery, were frequently found to have ruined fuzes.[5] The Navy also had the problem that during combat, the fuze could be extinguished when the projectile hit the water. This situation was aggravated by the common naval tactic of skipping a projectile across the water. Consequently, the Navy's search for a new fuze without these drawbacks was more intensive than the Army's. The problem with the fuze being extinguished when the projectile hit the water was solved first. In the early 1840s, the Navy began placing a small iron plate that was perforated with four small holes over the top of its fuzes.[6] The plate concentrated the gases created by the burning gunpowder so that water could not enter the fuze. The technique was so successful that projectiles armed with the iron plate could explode underwater. Although this application was successful, the Navy still had problems with fixed composition wooden fuzes that swelled.

In the mid–1840s, Cyrus Alger, owner and operator of the South Boston Foundry and a manufacturer of cannon for the military, developed an improved fuze for the Navy.[7] Alger's fuze slowly evolved from a wire reinforced wooden fuze to a paper fuze inside of a metal socket that was an integral part of the projectile and an extension of the fuze hole. Using a paper fuze inside of a bronze fuze was critical because the Navy had discovered that gunpowder rapidly deteriorated when it was in direct contact with bronze in a sea air atmosphere.[8] The paper fuze also had a lead safety knob on its end. The safety knob prevented the fuze from detonating the main charge until the projectile was fired from a cannon. When the gun was fired, setback forces broke the safety knob off and allowed the flame from the fuze to reach the main charge. One advantage the new fuze had was the elimination of the charging hole as the projectile could now be filled with gunpowder through the fuze hole. However, the Navy was forced to rework all of their older projectiles so that they would accept the new fuze. The start of the Mexican War accentuated the problem because the Navy wanted to use the new fuze in the war.[9]

After the Mexican War, development continued on the Alger Naval Fuze until it became a threaded, metal, waterproof fuze containing a paper fuze with the plate covering the paper fuze having a zigzag pattern of holes drilled through it. The Navy's first published ordnance instructions in 1852 discussed this fuze, and stated that the Washington Navy Yard would prepare all fuzes for shells and limited the variation on the burning time of the fuzes to five, ten and fifteen seconds.[10] In addition, only the ship's captain could give permission to shorten the burning time of the fuzes.[11]

Alger was prepared in 1846 to file three patents based on his invention. However, he did not file the patents, as he was convinced by the Navy that the operation of the fuze should remain a secret. Alger became so secretive about the operation of his fuze that Navy Lieutenant A. A. Harwood commented on Alger's apprehension in his correspondence. However, Lieutenant Harwood reassured Alger that the information was required "to instruct those who must understand the nature of the projectile in order to use it effectively."[12] Consequently, Lieutenant Harwood included as part of his instructions that "officers are particularly enjoined not to explain the character of these fuzes, and the manner of fitting them to persons unconnected with the service of the United States."[13] The Navy further institutionalized this in its 1864 *Ordnance Instructions* which stated, "It is strictly forbidden to show to, or explain, to foreigners or others the construction of any fuzes, except so far as may be necessary for the service of the guns."[14]

Alger's fuze had two major safety features. First, a solid lead cap covered the top of the fuze. The cap kept water out of the fuze while it was in storage, and had the number of seconds the fuze was designed to burn stamped on it. The other safety feature was the previously

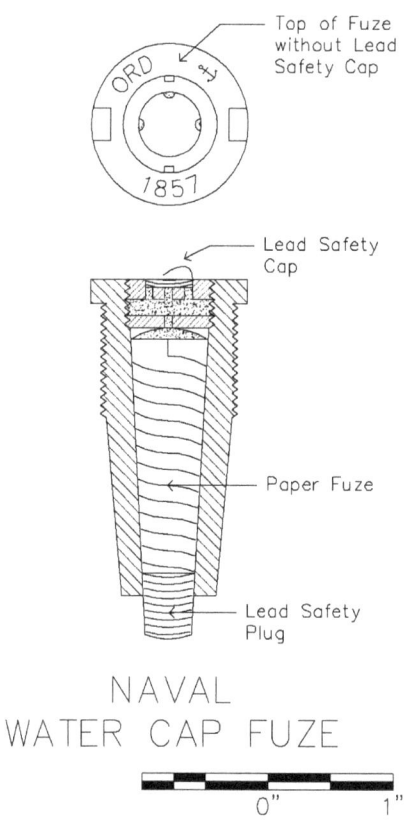

The Navy's secret Water Cap Fuze. Due to the fuze's construction it was able to burn underwater.

mentioned lead safety knob located in the base of the fuze.[15] The Navy conducted tests on whether or not ordinary impacts would break the safety knob off. The tests determined that even if a projectile was dropped 16 to 18 feet onto an iron plate, the safety knob would remain in place.[16] Cyrus Alger continued to make improvements to his fuze until his death in 1856, and after that his son, Francis Alger, continued his work. The Alger Fuze was so reliable that both the Navy and Army used it for many years after the Civil War. In fact, the time fuze described for use by the Army's heavy artillery in the 1880 *Manual of Heavy Artillery Service* was the Alger Fuze.

The Army had also been experimenting with paper fuzes, and in 1846, experiments using paper fuzes were conducted at Fort Monroe by Captain Benjamin Huger. In his report, Huger mentioned four advantages that paper fuzes had over wooden fuzes. First, paper fuzes permitted the attachment of gunpowder cartridges to projectiles, creating a fixed round. This eliminated the possibility of the cartridge turning in the bore. In addition, fixed rounds with ready fuzes allowed shells and case shot to be fired as rapidly as solid shot. Huger also discovered that paper fuzes had a more consistent burn time than wooden fuzes. In addition, because paper fuzes used a smaller wooden plug more case shot balls could be placed in the projectile. More case shot balls meant greater weight and thus a longer range, as well as the possibility of causing a greater number of enemy casualties. Huger included in this report the observation that out of 123 rounds of shell and case shot fired, only seven did not explode, giving the fuze high marks for reliability.[17] Captain Huger concluded by writing, "I see no difficulty in applying these fuses [sic] in service, and I think they will prove a decided improvement."[18]

In 1849, additional experiments were conducted at Fort Monroe to determine "the proper charge, the range & effects, of spherical case shot with new fuzes."[19] Huger reported after those experiments that "the fuzes & fuze plugs stand perfectly well the shock of the highest charge, and the shoulder at the bottom of the fuze plug can be omitted without the fuze being ever driven into the shell." [20] The Army did not create a fuze similar to the Alger Fuze, but rather placed the paper fuze in a wooden plug or, later, a threaded brass plug just prior to firing. A battery of 12-pounder mountain howitzers used the Army paper fuze for the first time in combat during the Mexican War and considered the fuze a great success.[21] Based on all of the tests and the success of the fuze in combat, the Ordnance Board recommended in 1849 to the Secretary of War a revision to the Ordnance Regulations. "The system of fuses in paper cases, to be inserted at the time of firing, answers all the purposes of field service, and [we] recommend, accordingly, that they be adopted for both shells and spherical case shot for field service."[22]

The only machinery used in the manufacture of the Army's paper fuze was the option of using a screw press when compacting the fuze composition. In contrast, the Navy preferred to use the screw press rather than compress the gunpowder by hand. The difference was that a screw press applied about 2,200 pounds of pressure compared to 1,900 pounds of pressure when compressed by hand.[23] Both the Army and Navy used patterns and gauges throughout the process to ensure uniformity and conducted tests, as with the wooden fuzes, on the first few fuzes made in a batch to verify the burning time. The Army's 1862 *Ordnance Manual* stated that all paper fuzes were to be two inches in length and filled with one of three different compositions, one for 10 seconds per inch, one for 14 seconds per inch, and one for 20 seconds per inch.[24] To assist with the identification of the fuzes in the field, each of the three different types were stained with a different color. The Navy also adopted the paper fuze for use with boat howitzers, although the Navy marked the fuzes differently. The Navy marked their paper fuzes with one to five black circles with each circle standing for one second of burn time. The comment made in the 1862 Naval Academy text book for ordnance and naval gunnery was that black circles were used in place of the Army's color coding as color coding required an exercise of memory.[25]

The development of a reliable fuze made explosive projectiles more popular, but did not automatically eliminate the use of solid spherical shot. John Gibbon stated in *The Artillerist's Manual* that "the precise effect of a single ball [spherical solid shot] cannot be accurately stated. Cases are cited where thirty or forty men have been disabled by a single shot; but it is laid down as a principle, that a 6 or 12 pound ball will go through six men at 80 yards' distance."[26] Edmund Rice stated that during the third day at Gettysburg, "A cannon-shot tore a horrible passage through the dense crowd of men in blue, who were gathering outside the trees; instantly another shot followed, and fairly cut a road through the mass."[27] It is easy to imagine the havoc created by a 12-pound solid spherical shot flying or even bouncing through a formation of closely aligned men. In addition, pieces of rock, fragments of soldiers' bodies, and particles from their equipment would become missiles capable of killing or wounding men. Beyond antipersonal use, solid shot continued to be the projectile of choice for destroying fortifications and counter battery fire.

Many of the changes in fuze design depended on improvements in cannon technology. As previously discussed, a major development was the invention of the shell gun by Henri-Joseph Paixhan in 1822. The adoption of shell guns accelerated when, in 1853, during the Battle of Sinope, a Russian naval squadron destroyed a Turkish naval squadron in about two hours using the new shell guns. Solid shot projectiles would only have been able to do this same amount of damage in a much greater length of time, if at all. The creation of the shell gun along with the invention of the light 12-pounder gun changed the artillery paradigm for the military and, by making exploding projectiles more useable, increased the importance of fuzes.

To understand the importance of fuzes, it is necessary to have an understanding of artillery projectiles. Lieutenant Henry Shrapnel of the British Army invented the deadly case shot projectile in 1784, but the British Army did not adopt it until 1804.[28] When the British first used case shot during the Peninsula Campaign, the French detested the projectile due to the casualties it created.[29] In spite of this, not everyone in the British Army wholeheartedly endorsed the new projectile as many of the high-ranking officers in the British Army, including Wellington, did not feel that case shot justified its high reputation, probably due to problems with fuzes and internal friction causing failures and premature explosions.[30] Charles Bormann received a letter in 1848 from Sir Robert Gardiner, a prominent British artillery commander under Wellington, stating:

> I became doubtful as to their [case shot] unqualified merits, at the commencement of the Peninsular war-almost from the beginning of that service, I always preferred making my demands for the replenishment of expended ammunition in round and grape shot, with but a comparatively small proportion of Shrapnel-and this I should certainly do, if I was in the field to-morrow.[31]

However, the reliability and reputation of case shot improved as fuzes evolved and the internal friction problem was solved.

The key difference between Shrapnel's new projectile and the older exploding shell was that his produced many more "fragments." These fragments were not part of the wall of the projectile, but round shot or bullets carried inside the projectile. Shrapnel's projectile had a thin wall (in contrast to the thick-walled exploding shell), an interior filled with bullets (shot), and a very small bursting charge. The charge was small, as it only had to be big enough to shatter the wall of the projectile and allow the bullets to disperse. If the bursting charge was too powerful, the shot would become too dispersed and lose its concentrated killing power. Thus, the dispersion and killing capacity of the fragments was directly based upon the momentum given to the fragments from the projectile rather than the bursting charge. Case shot was, in effect, long range canister and could inflict numerous casualties on troops in close formation. In addition, it could inflict a substantial number of casualties on dispersed troops or troops hidden behind a hill, something that solid shot had difficulty doing. Case shot was so deadly that an 1864 Army of the Potomac general order stated that when properly used case shot "was the most effective and powerful of projectiles."[32]

Case shot did have disadvantages. First, the explosion of the projectile had to be perfectly timed as it had to explode in front of the enemy, but not too far in front of the enemy. James Benton stated in his text book written for cadets at the United States Military Academy in 1867 that "the proper position of the point of rupture varies from 50 to 130 yards in front of, and from 15 to 20 feet above, the object."[33] The difficulty of achieving this becomes obvious when one realizes that all artillery projectiles had initial velocities exceeding 1,000 feet per second and that there was only a 150 to 390 feet effective horizontal bursting zone. In addition, if a case shot projectile landed on the ground without exploding, it was not dangerous due to its small bursting charge. However, when a case shot projectile worked as designed, it could have the same deadly, concentrated effect as canister, but at a much greater range. Case shot had an additional advantage over a shell in that it was heavy enough to be substituted for solid shot when needed.

Problems existed with case shot that required solutions before it could be considered a safe projectile and achieve its full effectiveness. All of these problems revolved around premature explosions. One problem was that if the fuze was driven too far into the projectile, the flame from the propelling charge could gain direct access to the bursting charge. This problem was greatest with wooden and paper fuzes with nontapered wooden plugs. The development of threaded fuzes along with tapered wooden fuzes and supporting lips on the metal fuze cases helped alleviate this problem.

Another problem was that the friction created by the movement of the shot/bullets inside the projectile would, at times, generate sufficient heat to ignite the bursting charge. The problem of keeping the shot from breaking loose was solved with the adoption of an 1854 Ordnance Board recommendation that the shot be kept in place by pouring a bonding agent, melted sulphur, around them.[34] However, different countries developed other solutions, such as the diaphragm developed by the British that separated the shot/bullets from the bursting charge.

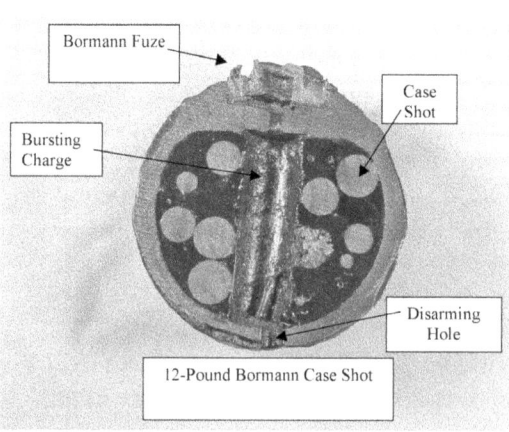

12-Pound Bormann Case Shot. The most deadly artillery projectile when properly employed (author's collection).

Shells presented a different set of problems. One of the limitations for shells was that their range, due to their lighter weight, was substantially less than that for solid shot. John Gibbon stated in *The Artillerist's Manual* that the

a. Represents the projectile bursting when the fuze is good and the elevation is correct.
b. Represents the projectile bursting when the fuze is short and the elevation is correct.
c. Represents the projectile bursting when the fuze is good and the elevation is high.
d. Represents the projectile bursting when the fuze is good and the elevation is low.

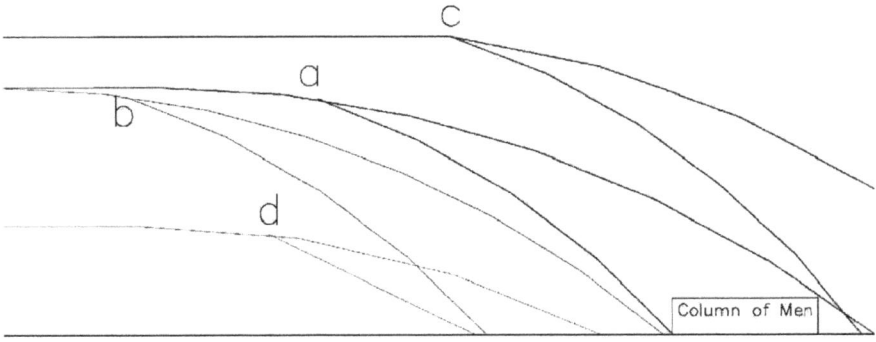

CASESHOT PROJECTILE

NOT TO SCALE

The effectiveness of a Case Shot projectile depended upon its exploding at the proper height and location.

range of shells was "estimated at two thirds that of the corresponding shot."[35] In addition, due to the necessity of a shell being hollow, any irregularity in the thickness of the wall would cause the center of gravity of the projectile to shift from the geometric center of the projectile. When this happened, the flight of the projectile would be even more irregular and would decrease accuracy. The other major limitation of cast iron, black powder filled shells was the limited number of fragments they produced. Gibbon stated that "24 and 32 pound shells break into eighteen or nineteen deadly pieces, which are sometimes thrown 600 yards."[36] While 18 or 19 fragments may seem substantial, a 24-pound case shot had 175 musket balls, while a 32-pound case shot had 225 musket balls.[37] These musket balls were in addition to the fragments from the projectile itself. However, one advantage exploding shells had over case shot was that they were just as deadly even if they exploded on the ground.

While the paper fuze was superior to the wooden fuze, it still had a number of drawbacks, and the military continued looking for a replacement. The replacement for the paper fuze was "discovered" by Brevet Major P. V. Hagner during his trip to Europe in 1848. When he returned and wrote his report in October 1849, he discussed a new fuze known as "Colonel Borman's [sic]" that the Belgians were using. Hagner reported that the fuze was simple, cheap, and considered highly reliable by both Belgian and Dutch officers.[38] Hagner's enthusiastic report on the Bormann Fuze must have been noticed, for in December 1851, case shot projectiles were prepared at the Washington Arsenal with the Bormann Fuze and tested in the summer of 1852.[39] The Chief of Ordnance, Colonel Craig, mentioned in his annual report in November of 1852 that "a new fuse [sic] for spherical case shot has been tried at the Washington and Fort Monroe Arsenals, and the results of these trials indicate a superiority of this kind of fuse, for such projectiles, over that now in use."[40] While this may seem like a long delay, the Mexican War had just ended in the summer of 1848, and the Ordnance Department had to learn how to manufacture the new metallic fuzes.

Further tests of the new metallic fuze were conducted at Fort Monroe in July of 1854 with 24 rounds fired from a 24-pounder gun and twice that amount fired from a 12-pounder gun.[41] The tests indicated that "the new fuzes may be used satisfactorily for all purposes which can be required for field service," but there were a "great number of premature explosions."[42] Major Alfred Mordecai and George Ramsay, the officers in charge of the test, felt that the premature explosions were due to some defect in the manufacture of the fuzes. Due to the number of premature explosions and because not enough rounds were fired to conduct a full trial, they recommended that "a like number be again prepared, with new fuzes, and sent to Fort Monroe for the purpose of repeating the experiment."[43] The subsequent experiment was conducted in August of 1854, and Ramsay reported that "on Major Mordecai's return to Washington Arsenal he had new fuzes prepared and sent to me. The report which, herewith, I now submit, you will find highly satisfactory as to the accuracy of the fuzes."[44] Consequently, the Army adopted the Bormann Fuze and it became the only fuze authorized for use by the field artillery.

The Ordnance Department did not limit itself to testing only the Bormann Fuze, as it did consider other flame-ignited fuzes. In July 1852, Major Alfred Mordecai conducted extensive tests on Böttcher's Fuze. Mordecai's report was favorable, as he reported that "the results of these trials confirm the opinion expressed in my first Report (August 28th, 1851) as to the superiority of these, over our present fuzes, for <u>spherical case shot</u>."[45] (Underlining is in the original report.) Mordecai did not recommend the fuze for exploding shells, for he felt that the tests conducted with exploding shells were not conclusive. Some of the tests were conducted during a drizzling rain, and Mordecai reported that the rain did not interfere with the test, as the gunner was able

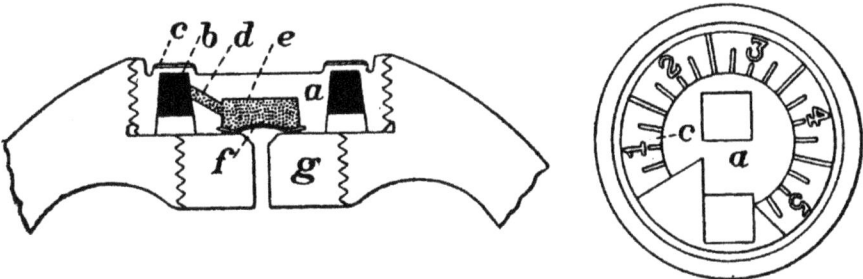

The Bormann Fuze. The figure is from an 1896 text and slightly different types of gunpowder were in use then. During the Civil War channel *d* was filled with rifle powder and chamber *e* was filled with musket powder. (L. Bruff, *Ordnance and Gunnery*, 332).

to cover the fuze with his jacket. This was probably the reason that the Bormann Fuze was selected for the Böttcher Fuze had to be cut before firing and protected from moisture while the Bormann Fuze was completely sealed.

The operation of the Bormann Fuze was simple. The gunner only needed to punch a hole in the pewter case at the spot that indicated how many seconds, down to a quarter of a second, the fuze was to burn before the projectile exploded. The fuze composition in channel *b* would then burn in both directions after it ignited. One direction led to a dead end, and the other led to channel *d*. The fuze composition in channel *d* ignited the quick-match powder in chamber *e*, which ruptured the sheet of tin, *f*, igniting the bursting charge inside of the projectile. Initially, some of the Bormann Fuzes prematurely ignited the bursting charge due to the fuze, made of soft zinc, being driven into the projectile by the setback forces. The Ordnance Department quickly solved the problem by adding a wrought iron disk, *g*, between the fuze and the projectile. However, care had to be taken to ensure that the fuze was tightly screwed down and in contact with the iron disk. This was important enough that instructions stating this and emphasizing that "when practicable, the fuse (Bormann) should always be screwed down just before firing" were included in Special Orders No. 79 issued by the Army of the Potomac in 1863.[46]

The Bormann Fuze differed from previous fuzes in a number of aspects. Primarily, it was fully sealed. This was important, as it eliminated the fear of the fuze becoming unusable due to the gunpowder becoming wet. In contrast to the Bormann Fuze's metal case, the weatherproof seal for other flame-ignited fuzes only consisted of a piece of coated paper, which ruptured easily. In addition, the Bormann Fuze had a greater degree of mechanization in its manufacturing process than either the paper or wooden fuze, although its process was not fully mechanized. The manufacturing process for the Bormann Fuze started with the fuze body being cast in a mold. After casting, different parts of the fuze were filled with three types of gunpowder: meal, rifle, and musket. Once in place, a screw press compressed the gunpowder after which the fuze base was attached by having part of the fuze body pressed over it. The fuze was then placed in a lathe, where its lower surface was smoothed and cut to the proper thickness. Then, a coat of varnish was applied to the fuze. While the manufacturing process for the Bormann Fuze was more mechanized than the process for either the paper or wooden types, it still required a high degree of hand labor.[47]

One key to the reliability of the Bormann Fuze was that its powder train lay horizontally rather than vertically. This was an advantage, as a horizontal powder train burnt more regularly than a vertical powder train due to the fact that the powder was compressed in a single motion and it acted as if it was one grain of gunpowder. In contrast, vertical fuzes had irregular layers created when small amounts of powder were compressed one layer at a time. These irregular layers in the vertical powder train caused it to act as a number of different grains with each one having a different burning rate. Gibbon summed up the other advantages of the Bormann fuze when he stated that "shells can be loaded, all ready for use, and remain so any length of time, perfectly safe from explosion; as the fuze can be screwed into its place, and the composition never exposed to external fire until the metal is cut through."[48]

The Bormann Fuze had one major disadvantage in that the maximum length of burn time was five seconds, which limited its range to about 1,300 yards with a 12-pounder field gun. This limitation became a major problem with large guns. A 10-inch Columbiad had a range of 4,828 yards with a time of flight of 35 seconds, while a 10-inch sea-coast mortar had a range of 4,250 yards with a time of flight of 36 seconds.[49] In both cases the time of flight was far beyond the allocated burning timespan of a Bormann. This limitation of the Bormann created a continued need for both the wooden fuze and the paper fuze, despite the advantages offered by the Bormann Fuze.

One concern with the Bormann that led some countries, specifically England and France, not to adopt it was the small size of the hole that was punched in the fuze to receive the flame. Dahlgren stated that the cut hole in a Bormann was 0.04 square inches.[50] In contrast, the paper fuze had a gunpowder diameter of 0.35 inches or 0.096 square inches, which is substantially larger than the opening for the Bormann.[51] The difference in area was not much of a factor in the reliability of the fuze, considering that the tests conducted by General Henry Abbot during the Siege of Petersburg gave the Bormann fuze a 77 percent success rate.[52] This is in contrast to the lower success rates for the Parrott and Dyer paper time fuzes of 75 percent and 71 percent respectively.[53] It should be noted that Abbot also reported that the wooden fuzes used in the 13-inch, 10-inch, and 8-inch mortars at Petersburg had a success rate of 87 percent while the paper fuzes used in the Coehorn mortar had a 90 percent success rate.[54] (One possible reason for the differences in the success rates between the mortars and the cannons was the slower rate of fire of mortars and the ability of the gunner to take more time in preparing the fuze.) It is interesting to note how small a surface area a flame-ignited fuze required for successful ignition when sufficient windage existed between the projectile and the interior wall of the cannon.

The Bormann Fuze, once adopted for use by the Army, became so well known for its reliability that John Gibbon stated in his 1860 book *The Artillerist's Manual* that the Bormann Fuze "has been subjected to all kinds of trials, and failed in none; and this can be said of no other fuze yet invented."[55] In addition, General Henry Abbot, commander of the Union siege artillery at Petersburg, stated in his 1868 book *Siege Artillery in the Campaigns Against Richmond* that "the Bormann time fuze for smooth-bore guns and howitzers is too well known to require description."[56] As a flame-ignited fuze, the Bormann was never surpassed, but the rifled artillery adopted during the Civil War changed the paradigm, and the Bormann lost its preeminence as it could neither meet nor evolve to meet the new requirements.

While the American military quickly adopted the Bormann Fuze, it did not blindly adopt every European fuze as American requirements were often different from those of other countries. In 1860 John Gibbon wrote in *The Artillerist's Manual,* when he was discussing the various European fuzes, that the flame-ignited British Boxer Fuzes:

> ... are said to have given very satisfactory results in experiments; but they appear entirely too complicated for ordinary use. The parts are numerous and complicated, requiring nice adjustment at the time of use; and no reason is seen why they should burn any more regularly than the paper fuze; whilst the certainty of exploding the shell appears to be much greater in this last, which also must be much the cheapest.[57]

The British Boxer Fuze referred to by Gibbon was invented by Edward M. Boxer of the Royal Artillery and adopted by the British Army in 1850.[58] The first version was a wooden flame-ignited fuze. In 1855, a metal version of the fuze was adopted due to problems with the wooden fuze swelling when it got wet.[59] This was the same problem faced by the United States Army and it switched to the metal Bormann Fuze. The Boxer Fuze continued to evolve as a different version was created for use in rifled artillery. The rifled artillery version was ignited by the concussion of the firing of the gun, which released a slider that struck a percussion cap, which in turn ignited the fuze composition. However, for both types the gunner had to punch a hole in the proper timing hole that corresponded with the desired time of flight of the projectile before placing the fuze in the projectile. Even with these drawbacks, the British used the Boxer fuze for years and considered it very reliable.

It should be noted that Boxer later became the Superintendent of the Royal Laboratory at Woolwich Arsenal from 1855 to 1869.[60] In this position he had tremendous power over what items of ordnance were selected for use by the British Army. This seemed to be an issue in other countries too. In the United States, a number of ordnance related inventions, which included fuzes, were invented by ordnance officers. One example was Alexander Dyer, Chief of Ordnance in 1864, who invented a projectile, cannon, and fuze prior to the war. However, his inventions only saw limited use. While both Boxer and Dyer were very influential, there was a limit to how far they could use their influence even though conflict of interest laws were not as strict during the nineteenth century as they are today.

* * *

All of the fuzes used by the military prior to the Civil War, with the exception of the body of the Alger Naval Fuze, were manufactured by the Army's and Navy's Ordnance Departments. The Army's Ordnance Department, created in 1812, was responsible for "the inspection and proving of all pieces of ordnance, cannon balls, shells and shot, procured for the use of the Army of the United States," as well as other duties.[61] Consequently, it became responsible for the development, manufacturing, and inspection of

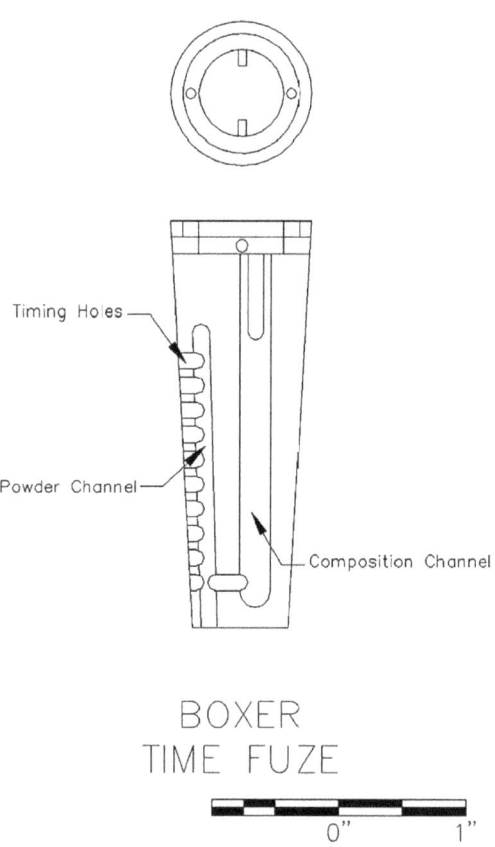

BOXER TIME FUZE

Later version of a Boxer Time Fuze designed for use in a rifled projectile. The correct timing hole had to be punched before the fuze was inserted into the projectile.

artillery fuzes. This was a good match, as the Ordnance Department, along with the Corps of Engineers, were the two most progressive scientific and engineering organizations in the Army and in all likelihood the country. However, the Ordnance Department had problems maintaining a separate identity as the Ordnance Branch was merged with the Artillery Branch in 1821 in a cost-saving measure. As a consequence, ordnance duty was a secondary assignment that was given primarily to artillery and engineer officers. In 1832 the Ordnance Branch was reestablished, and selected artillery and engineer officers transferred to Ordnance. The reputation of the Ordnance Department increased as some of its officers, such as Alfred Mordecai and Thomas Rodman, saw their own reputations spread worldwide. It was a professional organization that prided itself on the quality of the material it produced.

In contrast, the Navy's Bureau of Ordnance and Hydrography was not established until 1842. As a result, it lagged behind the Army's Ordnance Department and did not publish its first manual until 1852, eleven years after the Army's first ordnance manual and two years after the Army's second edition. One advantage the Army's Ordnance Department had was that its officers received a scientific and engineering education at the United States Military Academy. In contrast, the Naval Academy was not established until 1845, over the objections of many of the Navy's senior officers. It was also in 1845 that the *Princeton* disaster led to the creation of a Naval Ordnance Board. This board sent officers to Europe to gather information and advocated increased cooperation with the Army's Ordnance Department. Still, the Navy lagged behind the Army as it concentrated its ordnance operations in the Washington Navy Yard and promotion as a Navy ordnance officer was much slower than for an Army ordnance officer. Later, the Navy's ordnance efforts greatly improved due to the efforts of John Dahlgren, who gained a worldwide reputation, as well as the establishment of the Bureau of Ordnance as a separate bureau in 1862.

Overall, the Army's Ordnance Department and the Navy's Bureau of Ordnance and Hydrography were dedicated, professional organizations capable of providing expert technological guidance. Both organizations tried to ensure that any issued piece of equipment was the best available. However, this desire led to extensive testing and delays. Unfortunately, ordnance officers in both services faced the dual problems of line officers considering themselves superior to "technicians," and Congressional appropriations for needed ordnance not always forthcoming. While both organizations carefully guarded their areas of responsibility, each was responsive to the needs of their service and was willing to make adjustments when convinced the changes were necessary. This included making changes as fuze technology evolved.

The military, especially the Ordnance Departments, was very much aware of the prewar technical advances in fuze technology outside of the United States. Gibbon's *The Artillerist's Manual* discussed in detail 19 different fuzes from around the world. Of the 19 fuzes listed, only three were in use by the United States military, while the fourth, the United States Sea-Coast Fuze, was the Alger Fuze that required the insertion of a paper fuze. The United States military knew about the various types of fuzes around the world but had made a deliberate decision to use only three basic types. Still, innovation was occurring in the United States. Between 1855 and 1861, the Patent Office issued eight fuze-related patents. Out of these, three were for flame-ignited fuzes, while the remaining five were for percussion fuzes. In addition, the Army, through the Ordnance Department, conducted extensive tests prior to the war on a wide range of armaments and equipment including rifled artillery and mechanical fuzes. Many more tests would have been held, but the Ordnance Department was always concerned with cost.

Captain Alexander Dyer conducted some of the first tests on rifled artillery and mechanical fuzes at Fort Monroe in 1854. After the tests, an impressed Dyer stated, "This fuze commends itself not only for the certainty of exploding the shell on direct impact, but from its simplicity and entire safety."[62] The fuze referred to by Dyer was a percussion fuze completely dependent on friction to keep it from prematurely detonating. However, the fuze, with its attached percussion cap, was not inserted into the projectile until just prior to loading the gun. Dyer felt very comfortable with this arrangement and reported that "frequent experiments have also shown that the shell does not explode on being dropped from a height of 20 feet point forward, on a brick pavement, hence it is confidently believed that this percussion arrangement is perfectly safe."[63] The Ordnance Department conducted further tests with this fuze at West Point. Due to these tests, this style of percussion fuze became known as the West Point style.[64] This design, with additional safety devices, became the basic design for most of the percussion fuzes used during the war. However, as the Army only had smoothbore cannon prior to the war, there was no immediate need for this type of fuze. It took the start of the war and the adoption of rifled artillery for the military to embrace this fuze and others like it.

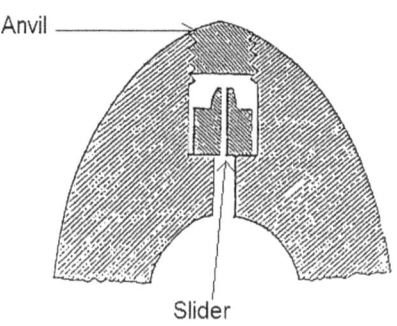

West Point Style Percussion Fuze placed inside a rifled projectile. The friction between the slider and the projectile was its only safety feature (Gibbon, 323).

Adopting new ordnance became more

difficult just prior to the war as Congress handicapped the military when it passed a statute in June 1860 that prohibited the military from purchasing any patented item unless authorized by law.[65] This statue so hampered the military that Secretary of War Floyd felt it necessary to recommend in his 1860 Annual Report to Congress that "the law be so amended as to except from the prohibition such arms or other military supplies as constitute a regular part of the armament or equipment of troops, and also the improved patented mode of casting and cooling for iron cannons."[66] There were some instances where the military was able to skirt the law. Captain William Maynadier wrote to Secretary of War Floyd in December 1860 concerning the need to convert some smooth-bore cannons to rifled guns using the James method. He mentions that "the rifling, not being patentable, could not so be so secured. It does not then, of course, come within the prohibition of the law as respects patented inventions."[67] Nevertheless, the law did have an impact on the military's ability to purchase equipment. Luckily, Congress repealed the law in March of 1861.

Even with these restrictions, the military, especially the Army's Ordnance Department, regularly conducted experiments. The Secretary of War's 1859 Annual Report stated:

> The subject of rifled cannon and projectiles has received much attention, and careful experiments have been instituted to test a variety of such contrivances. It is not deemed advisable to proceed to the manufacture of such cannon, beyond those required for experimental purposes, until full and fair trials shall have demonstrated practically, which of the various inventions possesses most advantages, or whether a combination of the advantages peculiar to several of them may not furnish the best government model.[68]

The military wanted to make sure that it was purchasing a high quality weapon that met all of its needs, as its purpose would have to be justified and authorized by Congress. This objective was an ongoing theme for the Army's Ordnance Department.

John Gibbon stated in 1860 in *The Artillerist's Manual* that the Bormann Fuze "has added immeasurably to the importance and efficiency of the inventions of Generals Schrapnell [sic] and Paixhan; for without a good system of fuzes, schrapnell shot and paixhan guns may well be called 'bodies without souls.'"[69] Although the Bormann Fuze was an excellent fuze, new fuze technology continued to be developed. The military knew about this new fuze technology, and the individuals who had tested it were aware that it had the potential of changing the artillery weapon system. Even though it was willing to make use of the new fuzes, the military had not done so for two main reasons — cost and the need to determine which of the numerous options was best. The war, along with the advent of rifled artillery, created the need for rapid change and thus eliminated those reasons for inaction. Still, the military knew that there was no perfect technological solution. Gibbon restated this when describing the Breithaupt Fuze. "This fuze, like all others, is not devoid of defects."[70]

Three

Smooth-Bore Versus Rifled Artillery

To those readers who may now, or at some future time, conceive the idea of designing some weapon of war, we would give this serious advice: Whatever you may propose, be practical.[1]

—Vivian D. Majendie, 1878

The 1846–1848 Mexican War was the training ground for many of the military leaders during the Civil War, including artillery officers. During the Mexican War, American field artillery was used aggressively, both offensively and defensively, and proved to be a decisive factor in a number of battles. It was mobile, well equipped, well trained, and, arguably, battery for battery, the best in the world. American field artillery demonstrated its superiority with its ability to advance alongside or in front of the infantry and provide continuous, close support. During the Battle of Palo Alto, American field artillery, advancing in front of the infantry, stopped Mexican cavalry attacks and inflicted a large number of casualties among the enemy infantry. At the Battle of Buena Vista, American field artillery successfully maneuvered on the battlefield and stopped a number of determined Mexican attacks. When assaulting Mexico City, American field artillery was often in front of the infantry and successfully breached the gates of the city. However, the ability of the American smooth-bore field artillery to perform these deeds was also a result of smooth-bore artillery's ability to outrange the smooth-bore musket, the poor accuracy of the smooth-bore musket, and the lack of quality Mexican artillery.

Smooth-bore muskets had been used by the military for many years, even though they were inaccurate and short ranged, mainly due to difficulties in manufacturing sufficient quantities of the preferred alternative, rifles.

In his memoirs, President Grant, when discussing his experiences with musketry fire during the Mexican War, wrote, "At the distance of a few hundred yards a man might fire at you all day without your finding it out."[2] In contrast, a 12-pounder gun's effective range for solid shot was 1,000 yards against infantry and 1,200 yards against cavalry.[3] In addition, a 12-pounder howitzer, which could not fire solid shot, had an extreme range of 2,000 yards when firing a shell.[4] Plus, both the 12-pounder gun and howitzer could fire case shot, the most deadly long-range projectile, out to an effective range of 800 yards.[5] In addition, the most deadly close-range projectile fired by field artillery was canister. This projectile could be fired by both a 12-pounder gun and howitzer, and had a range greater than that of a smooth-bore musket. These differences gave artillery a distinct advantage over the infantry and made artillery a decisive force on the battlefield.

Canister projectiles were deadly due to the size and quantity of the shot they contained. Canister fired by a 12-pounder gun consisted of twenty-seven canister shots, while canister fired by a 12-pounder howitzer had forty-eight canister shots.[6] Canister shot varied in size from that of a musket ball (.69 inches during the Mexican War) for a 12-pounder Mountain Howitzer to 2.24 inches in diameter for a 42-pounder gun. Canister was most effective between 400 and 450 yards but could achieve good results from 300 to 600 yards.[7] The reason canister's effectiveness decreased at distances less than 300 yards was that the shot contained inside the canister did not have enough time to disperse. At ranges over 600 yards, effectiveness decreased as the shot became too dispersed, and the individual canister balls lost a substantial amount of momentum.

The advantage in range of smooth-bore artillery over smooth-bore muskets was only part of the advantage held by the field artillery. To fully understand the impact an artillery battery firing in a defensive role could have upon an attacking unit, it is necessary to understand how fast a unit could travel across a battlefield. In one minute, an infantry soldier could travel 70 yards in common time, 86 yards in quick time, or 109 yards in double-quick time.[8] Assuming a relatively flat field of 500 yards in length, it would take an infantry unit at least 5 minutes to move that distance. A 12-pounder gun could fire an average of one round per minute, but when firing at close targets the crew could increase the rate of fire to two or three rounds per minute.[9] The average rate of fire for a 12-pounder howitzer was slower, at one round every 1 1/2 minutes, but, as with the 12-pounder gun, its rate of fire increased when necessary. Thus, one field artillery piece could fire from four to twelve canister projectiles at an attacking infantry unit before the infantry unit would get close enough, within 200 yards, to effectively mass its smooth-bore musket fire. If the infantry unit continued its advance, an artillery piece could fire an additional two to six canister projectiles, although these projectiles would be less effective. Thus, an eight-piece smooth-bore mixed artillery battery (six 12-pounder guns and two 12-pounder howitzers) could average 96 rounds of canister during those five minutes. These canister rounds would contain 3,096 canister shot, with each shot being larger in diameter than the musket ball fired by the infantry's musket.

Using this situation, a full strength artillery battery would decimate an attacking full strength infantry regiment (878 men, based upon pre Civil War army regulations[10]). The casualties would result from the three-and-a-half canister shot per man fired at the unit, even if the artillery battery did not double-load its guns. It is easy to understand why infantry considered attacking an undamaged artillery battery as either a very risky or suicidal maneuver. These calculations do not consider the physical exhaustion of the attacking infantry unit that had just marched 500 yards at double-quick time, its vulnerability to counterattack, nor any losses than may have occurred by long-range artillery fire from solid or case shot.

Cavalry charging the same unbroken mixed smooth-bore battery would also suffer heavy casualties. Cooke's 1861 *Cavalry Tactics* states that "circumstances permitting, the line approaches within 200 paces of the enemy at the trot, then galloping with increasing speed, the charge is commanded at 50 or 60 yards."[11] Since one pace equals three feet, the gallop that would lead into the charge would start about 200 yards from the battery.[12] A cavalry regiment could cover this distance in less than one minute since at a gallop cavalry traveled about 300 paces per minute. However, the previous 300 yards, assuming the attack started 500 yards from the battery, would be covered at a trot, and at a trot, a cavalry unit traveled at 200 to 220 paces per minute.[13] At a minimum, it would take a cavalry regiment two minutes to travel the 500 yards. During that time, the regiment would have had 32 to 48 rounds of canister fired at it without the battery resorting to using a double load of canister. For a full strength cavalry regiment (890 men, based upon pre–Civil War army regulations[14]), this would be slightly over one-and-a-half canister shot per man and horse. However, a mounted cavalryman is a substantially larger target than a man on the ground because a man on a horse is about one-and-a-half times taller.[15] In addition, if a horse was hit and went down, the rider was also lost, along with any other horses and riders that may have tripped over the fallen horse. It would be a very costly affair for a cavalry regiment to charge an undamaged artillery battery.

The arming of infantry with rifled muskets changed this inequity for at least the infantry. The rifled musket increased the effective killing range from 400 yards for a smooth-bore musket to 1,000 yards for a rifled musket when used by marksmen.[16] Although a Soldier firing a rifled musket could not reasonably expect to hit a man at 1,000 yards, he had a very good chance of placing accurate fire onto the relatively large target of an artillery battery at 600 yards, the effective range of canister, even with the smoke created by the black powder. Consequently, artillerymen feared that if even a small group of men got within effective rifle range of an artillery battery, they would create havoc in the battery.

The problem artillerymen faced was that solid shot was relatively ineffective against dispersed troops and exploding shells only created a small number of fragments. Case shot was the key long-range weapon for artillery against infantry. Alfred Mordecai wrote in 1852 that "I am of opinion that the use and practice of spherical case shot has assumed recently a new importance, in reference to enabling field artillery to contend successfully with the rifle-musket of long range, and that we should therefore use every endeavor to perfect this projectile."[17] Artillerymen desperately wanted an effective case shot fuze and the Bormann Fuze filled that need.

However, the advent of rifled artillery and percussion caps changed the paradigm. The Bormann Fuze, like all flame-ignited fuzes, was ignited by the flames created by the exploding propelling charge that came around the projectile due to windage. (Windage was the distance between the projectile and the interior wall of the bore.) Although a difference in diameter between the projectile and the bore of the gun was still necessary to muzzle load a projectile ideally, windage in rifled artillery reduced to zero as the projectile traveled down the tube. The windage disappeared once the soft metal ring, or similar device, that circled the rifled projectile expanded to fill the rifling grooves in the gun.[18] With a windage that only lasted moments and a greater distance between the fuze and the powder bag, the odds of the fuze being lit dramatically decreased. Thus, to take full advantage of the benefits that rifled artillery could give, another means of igniting the fuze had to be found.

The military recognized the potential advantages of rifled artillery over smooth-bore artillery well before the Civil War, even though rifled artillery was more difficult to manufacture. As early as 1851, Captain Alfred Mordecai of the Ordnance Department conducted experiments with rifled artillery at Fort Monroe. The potential advantages were substantial, for a three-inch rifled gun with a one-pound charge and an elevation of 12 degrees firing a Dyer shell weighing nine pounds had a range of 3,114 yards.[19] In contrast, a smooth-bore 12-pounder field gun with a two-and-a-half-pound charge and an elevation of 12 degrees firing a shell weighing nine pounds only had a range of 1,979 yards.[20] It should also be noted that the three-inch rifled gun could achieve an elevation of 20 degrees, and at that elevation had a range of 3,972 yards.[21] In addition, rifled artillery could achieve greater penetration and accuracy than smooth-bore artillery. Experiments conducted in Great Britain determined that at a distance of 1,032 yards, an Armstrong rifled gun firing an 80-pound projectile with a 10-pound charge had an average penetration of seven and a half feet into a masonry wall.[22] At the same range, a 68-pound smooth-bore gun firing a 68-pound projectile with a sixteen-pound charge only achieved an average penetration of one and two-thirds feet,[23] a difference of 352 percent. Other experiments conducted in Great Britain showed that at a range of 800 yards, a smooth-bore 18-pounder had a 50 percent probability of hitting a ninety-two-by-seven-yard (644 square yards) rectangular target. In comparison, an Armstrong rifled 18-pounder, at the same range, had a 50 percent probability of hitting a seventeen-yard-by-two-and-a-half-feet (14 square yards) rectangular target.[24] For range, accuracy, and penetrating power, smooth-bore artillery could not compare to rifled artillery.

Rifled artillery allowed artillerymen to use a new shape of projectile. The projectiles used in rifled artillery were conical rather than spherical and designed to develop a spin as they "took" the rifling. The spin imparted by rifling, along with a more efficient aerodynamic shape, gives conical projectiles greater accuracy and range when compared to spherical projectiles fired at the same initial velocity. In addition, a conical shape also allows projectiles to be longer for a set diameter, enabling them to carry a greater bursting charge than spherical projectiles of the same diameter. Artillery and ordnance officers also knew that a projectile fired from a rifled gun would impact on the front point of the projectile, assuming it did not tumble. In contrast it was not possible to predict how a projectile fired from a smooth-bore gun would impact. Knowing the point of impact allowed a rifled projectile to be armed with a percussion fuze. However, spherical projectiles did have at least one advantage over conical projectiles. This advantage was that on solid ground a spherical projectile would bounce and inflict numerous casualties as it ricocheted through a formation even if its fuze did not ignite. A conical projectile, on the other hand, did not bounce as easily across the ground and through a formation.

There are a number of variables, beyond rifling, that affect a projectile's range. Some of these variables are elevation of the gun, weather conditions, initial propelling charge, aerodynamics of the projectile, and whether the projectile is perfectly concentric. Nineteenth century artillerists were well aware of these variables as well as two additional ones they used to their advantage. These two additional variables were the diameter and density of the projectile. Diameter was critical, for in the case of Civil War artillery projectiles, air resistance can be directly related to the exposed surface area of the projectile.[25] Area increases by a power of two (squared) while volume increases by a power of three (cubed). Consequently, a larger projectile had a greater range assuming that both had the same density (i.e., made out of the same material) and initial velocity. This is the reason that a 32-pound smooth-bore projectile had a greater range than a 24-pound smooth-bore projectile with the same initial velocity. This relationship was also one of the reasons a cylindrical rifled projectile had a greater range than a spherical projectile of equal weight as it presented a much smaller surface area for the air to develop drag friction. In addition, due to its shape, a cylindrical rifled projectile could weigh more than a larger diameter spherical projectile. For example, a 12-pound smooth-bore projectile had a diameter of 4.52 inches but a 20-pound Parrot rifled projectile was 3.63 inches in diameter — an increase of eight pounds with a substantially smaller diameter. Of course, all of this was negated if the rifled projectile failed to take the rifling and tumbled, which occurred all too often during the Civil War.

The Potomac River Blockade of Washington by the Confederacy in 1861 illustrates the inaccuracy and limited range of smooth-bore artillery. During the blockade, Confederate artillery fired upon a number of ships, hitting some but not sinking any, even though the Confederates used large-caliber Columbian smooth-bore guns. General Hooker stated, "Of all the rebel firing since I have been on the river, and it has been immense, but two of their shot have taken effect, and that was the wood schooner anchored in the middle of the river."[26] The Confederates faced the dual problems of the Potomac River being one-and-a-half to two miles across where the Confederate batteries were located and the fact that the navigable channel was on the opposite side of the river. Still, at short ranges, smooth-bore artillery was deadly, and a stationary or very slow ship could quickly be destroyed by shells exploding within it.

The inaccuracy of smooth-bore artillery can be contrasted with the range and accuracy of rifled artillery observed by Colonel Charles Wainwright during the Battle of Fredericksburg. During that battle a Confederate Whitworth gun enfiladed a number of Union infantry units and brought effective fire upon them at about three miles. Wainwright personally aimed a three-inch Ordnance Rifle using a telescope and returned fire at a distance that he estimated to be 2,700 yards. Wainwright noted that his first shell "flew and burst beautifully," and that after his second shot, which was equally effective, the Confederate gun limbered up and moved away.[27]

The overall importance of rifled artillery must be questioned when the Artillery Headquarters for the Army of the Potomac wrote in 1864 that "the value of the rifled cannon consists principally in its accuracy."[28] Also, at the beginning of the war, Captain M. C. Meigs, future Quartermaster of the Federal Armies, sent a message to William Seward, Secretary of State, saying, "Major Hunt is with us, somewhat depressed at going into the field without his horses. His battery of Napoleon guns, probably the best field guns in our service, is to follow in the *Illinois*."²⁹ Later, Major General Bormann stated in his 1862 book *The Shrapnel Shell in England and in Belgium* that the destructive power of the smooth-bore Dahlgrens employed during the American Civil War proved that no State should put aside smooth-bore artillery while adopting rifled artillery.³⁰ However, the Union Army reported that for the quarter ending December 1862, there were 448 smooth-bore cannon and 542 rifled cannon in the inventory. Then, over two years later for the quarter ending March 1864, there were 622 smooth-bore cannon and 755 rifled cannon in the inventory.³¹ In both cases, the percentages were 45 percent smooth-bore and 55 percent rifled. If the Army as a whole had 45 percent smooth-bore artillery and 45 percent rifled artillery, how did the percentage break down for the two of the major Union armies whose commanders could dictate the type of artillery in their command? Table 3.1 gives a good indication of how these two armies viewed the relative importance of these two types of artillery. The Army of the Potomac's average, from its four samples, shows that it had 42 percent smooth-bore artillery and 48 percent rifled artillery while the armies under Sherman during their March to the Sea, where he specifically chose the type of artillery to take with them, took an equal mix of smooth-bore and rifled artillery.

Table 3.1*— Percent Smooth-Bore and Rifled Artillery in the Army of the Potomac and Sherman's March to the Sea (excluding mortars)

		July 1861 1st Bull Run	Oct. 1862 Army of the Potomac	July 1863 Gettysburg	March 1864 Army of the Potomac	Nov. 1864 Sherman's March to the Sea
Percentages	Smooth-Bore	41%	42%	40%	47%	50%
	Rifled	59%	58%	60%	53%	50%

O.R.A. Series I, Volume II, pages 345–346; Volume XIX, page 407; Volume XXVII, page 241; Volume XXXVI, pages 284–286; Volume XXXIX, page 713.

Both smooth-bore artillery and rifled artillery had their place on the battlefield. General William F. Barry, Sherman's Chief of Artillery, wrote highly of rifled artillery and reported that "the 10 and 20 pounder Parrots and the 3-inch wrought-iron guns have fully maintained their reputation for endurance and for the superior accuracy and range expected from rifled guns."³² General Barry did not disregard smooth-bore artillery for he stated, "The light 12-pounder has more than ever proved itself to be the gun for the line of battle, where facility of service and effectiveness of solid shot, spherical case, and canister is most required."³³ The key capability of the 12-pounder light gun was its superiority when firing canister. Canister was important, as it was the best projectile for creating large numbers of casualties among attacking troops that were between 300 to 600 yards from the guns.[34] Canister fired from a 12-pounder Napoleon was so deadly that Union Brigadier General John Corse stated, "No column can stand a concentrated fire of six Napoleons by volley or battery, double shotted with canister."[35] The 12-pounder light gun was superior to a three-inch rifled gun when firing canister due to a number of factors. One factor was that when canister was fired from a rifled gun, it tended to have a greater spread because of the spin created by the rifling. This aspect would have decreased the maximum effective range of canister fired from a rifled gun. Another aspect was that, although both projectiles held the same number of shot, the 12-pounder's canister projectile's shot were in four tiers while a three-inch rifled canister projectile's shot were in seven tiers due to its smaller bore.[36] This difference would have allowed the 12-pounder light gun canister shot to stay in a tighter group longer, while the three-inch rifled canister shot would have a greater and quicker dispersion. Canister fire from a three-inch rifled gun was considered so inferior that Union Captain Hubert Dilger's report on his battery's actions during the first day of Gettysburg stated, "The two rifled guns had to retire first, because I would not expose them too much at this short range, at which they commenced to become useless."[37]

Another method of determining the importance of rifled artillery and consequently the importance of mechanical fuzes to the major field armies is to consider how much ammunition each type of gun used. After the long Atlanta Campaign during which the Union Army conducted offensive, defensive, and siege operations, Brigadier General Barry reported that ammunition for both the field and siege guns was always abundant. The total expenditures of ammunition are shown in Table 3.2. Considering that almost two-thirds of the artillery ammunition used during the Atlanta Campaign was fired from rifled guns, the importance of and need for reliable fuzes in rifled artillery projectiles becomes even more apparent. Once reason for the difference in the amount of ammunition used was that the Union army was on the offensive more than they were on the defensive during this campaign, and the long-range ability of rifled artillery would have been more valuable than the short-range defensive capability of the smooth-bore guns.

Armies had to adapt to the new paradigm presented by the increased range of both infantry weapons and artillery during the Civil War. The advent of the rifled musket put smooth-bore artillery at a disadvantage it had not previously experienced. However, long-range rifled artillery fire counteracted this effect and enabled field artillery gunners to bring effective fire upon enemy units at distances that were up to that time inconceivable. In addition,

Table 3.2* — Ammunition Expended/Rounds Fired

	Smooth-bore				Rifled			
	12-pdr light	12-pdr howitzer	24-pdr howitzer	3-inch	10-pdr Parrott	20-pdr Parrott	4½-in gun	Total
Army of the Cumb'land	29,643	—	201	35,321	14,786	5,059	3,368	88,378
Army of the Tennessee	14,095	1,853	543	17,385	4,182	8,951	1,158	48,167
Army of the Ohio	4,327	—	—	2,742	1,709	—	—	8,778
Total	48,065	1,853	744	55,448	20,677	14,010	4,526	145,323
Percent	33.1%	1.3%	0.5%	38.2%	14.2%	9.6%	3.1%	
	34.9%				65.1%			

*O.R.A., Series I, Volume XXXVIII, Part I, page 123.

masonry forts became obsolete, and wooden ships became even more vulnerable. So great were the changes that an artillery officer of the Mexican War would have found little with which he was familiar in the artillery of 1865. These changes resulted from a combination of imaginative inventors and manufacturers, as well as technically proficient ordnance and artillery officers in the Army and Navy. Military officers, especially artillery officers, had great expectations of the effect the new long-range fire from rifled artillery would have on the battlefield. While many of their hopes were realized, others would not be, as rifled artillery came with its own set of unique limitations. Still, the American Civil War can be said to be the first war in which if you could be seen, you could be killed. Ultimately, the effectiveness of deadly long-range fire was dependent upon a new generation of artillery fuzes. However, the new fuzes were largely untested, and many failed when first used in combat. To be successful, the fuze had to rapidly evolve, for it had truly become "the soul, the groundwork of any system of explosive projectile, ... the criterion of the system."[38]

Four

The Manufacturing War

The production of weapons more so than the conscription of men was the deciding factor in battle. God had marched with the biggest industries rather than with the biggest battalion[1]

—J.F.C. Fuller, 1946

The dramatic changes in warfare during the Civil War were made possible by advances in technical knowledge and industry's revolutionary ability to produce large quantities of identical items. This transformation, although revolutionary in its effect, was evolutionary in that the changes were based on previous technology and in development well before the start of the war. The military adapted to this transformation because the men who led it grew up with industrialization and were, for the most part, technologically adept. The Union's victory depended as much upon its industrial superiority as upon its battlefield victories for many of them were a direct result of superiority in both quantity and quality of equipment.

Fuzes figured into this equation as they required an extensive industrial base for production along with quality machine tools and materials. Even the simplest fuze, if it is to function properly, requires strict manufacturing tolerances. Prior to 1794, the United States purchased all of its military arms from private manufacturers or importers.[2] Numerous difficulties occurred with this system and on the April 2, 1794, Congress approved "an act to provide for the erecting and repairing of arsenals and magazines, and for other purposes."[3] Based on this act, President George Washington selected the existing government arsenal at Springfield, Massachusetts, as one site and Harpers Ferry, Virginia, with the plan to build a new armory there, as the second. Harpers Ferry Armory became the birthplace of the manufacture of interchangeable parts through the use of machinery. This concept so impressed the British that they named it the American System. However, the quality of work done at the Ordnance Department's armories did not surprise the Ordnance Department for Brevet Major P.V. Hagner had previously reported in 1849 that based on his observations of the European armories, United States armories and arsenals were superior. Hagner stated that he could not "refrain from expressing the gratification derived from comparing the general condition of our arsenals and armories (as well in the machinery used and the character of the work done as in the comfort and well being of the workmen and the cleanliness and neatness of the establishments) with the most advanced of those abroad."[4]

The professionalism and progressiveness of the Ordnance Department was tested when, well before the European discovery of the American System, a number of additional arsenals and depots joined the two armories and original arsenals. Need was the primary driving force behind this expansion as the War of 1812 highlighted the country's inability to produce adequate military ordnance. By 1841, there were a total of two armories, nineteen arsenals, and four depots,[5] all of which made the Ordnance Department one of the country's major manufacturers. The primary mission of the two armories was to manufacture small arms, but they also functioned as sites for the deposit and accumulation of military stores as well as points of supply and issue. Depots, on the other hand, were only used for the storage and issue of equipment, and many were temporary facilities. Arsenals were more complex and varied than either the armories or depots since they manufactured a variety of equipment. As a result, there were three different types of arsenals.

The most important arsenals were the first-class arsenals of construction. Besides being a depository and issue point for equipment, these arsenals manufactured many different types of ordnance supplies, excluding small arms. The Allegheny Arsenal, located near Pittsburgh, Pennsylvania, exemplifies a first-class arsenal. The permanent stone or brick buildings in the complex included a three-story storehouse, officers' quarters, barracks, harness shops, a timber shed, a machine shop, a smith shop, a depot, powder magazines, laboratories, offices, and a large number of storage buildings along with a number of temporary wooden buildings. It was one of the largest factory complexes in the Pittsburgh area, becoming the center of an industrial district with a workforce of 1,200 during the Civil War. During the war the arsenal manufactured artillery equipment, accouterments, horse equipment, and artillery and bullet cartridges, as well as producing 50,000 rifle bullets of various calibers per day.[6]

Second-class arsenals of repair were storage, repair, and issue sites. One advantage many second-class arsenals possessed was that they could quickly be converted into first-class arsenals because the buildings necessary for manufacturing already existed. A number of second-class arsenals, especially the Fort Monroe Arsenal, also had a major role in experiments conducted by the Ordnance Department on proposed equipment. The Frankford Arsenal, located just outside of Philadelphia, exemplifies a second-class arsenal. At the beginning of the war, the arsenal's permanent stone or brick buildings consisted of officers' quarters, four warehouses, an arsenal building, a percussion cap factory, and a laboratory. By the end of the Civil War, three additional permanent buildings had been added — a machine shop, experimental laboratory, and rolling mill — as well as a number of temporary wooden buildings. In addition, the workforce increased to over 1,200 workers. Production at the Frankford Arsenal was impressive as by the middle of 1862 the arsenal produced 180,000 percussion caps per day. In addition, it was responsible for inspecting all of the three-inch Ordnance Rifles produced by the nearby Phoenix Iron Company.[7]

Third-class arsenals were only used as places of storage and issue and were not much different from an ordinary depot. As a consequence, these arsenals only contained a limited number of buildings and manufacturing equipment as well as a limited number of personnel. In 1828, the permanent stone or brick buildings of the third-class arsenal located in Champlain, Vermont, consisted of a three-story arsenal building, officers' quarters, a magazine, a gun house, an armorer's and carpenter's shop, a laboratory, and a blacksmith shop. This arsenal never expanded beyond these buildings until the Civil War and, just prior to the war, the arsenal's staff consisted of three civilians whose main job was to safeguard the installation. When the war started, Congress allocated money to repair the facilities at the arsenal and it began producing military equipment. In addition, some temporary wooden buildings were erected during the war.[8]

Laboratories deserve special mention as they were an integral and essential part of the arsenal system and were located at all of the major arsenals, although sited away from the main arsenal buildings. Laboratories were located away from the rest of the buildings as they were used to load cartridges, projectiles, fuzes, and other explosive devices in addition to making the fulminate of mercury. The Ordnance Department considered laboratories so dangerous that additional rules beyond those for the arsenal were enforced there. In addition to the rules discussed in Chapter 1, lanterns and candles were not permitted in the laboratory and, if night work was required, the lanterns were to be hung outside of the windows. Other rules included ensuring that the nails used in the floors were sunk below the surface and puttied over as well as a recommendation to cover the floor with a stout oil cloth. Every effort was made to keep the laboratories safe and to limit the effect of a fire or explosion.

As with any manufacturing system the machine shops and the workers who operated the machinery were the keys to the quality and quantity of production. The armories, as well as the first-class and second-class arsenals, were well equipped and staffed. For example, the machine shop at the Frankford Arsenal included presses, drills, lathes, planers, and a 150-horsepower steam engine.[9] The operators of these machines at both the armories and arsenals were highly skilled and highly paid. In addition, private industry paid a premium wage for these workers if they left the arsenal and worked for them. All of this was a direct result of the work begun at the Harpers Ferry Armory with machine-produced interchangeable parts which the Springfield Armory continued and expanded upon.

In October 1855 the Ordnance Department had the armories and arsenals shown in Table 4.1. Of the eighteen arsenals listed, only five would come under Confederate control during the war. Of those five, none were first class arsenals, two were second-class arsenals, and three were third-class arsenals. Although the Confederacy captured the valuable Harper's Ferry Armory and transferred its machinery to Richmond, the amount of manufacturing capability it obtained could not compare to Union manufacturing capability.

By 1860 there were more than eighteen arsenals as some had not been closed and new ones had been created. However, these additional arsenals were, for the most part, third-class arsenals with very little manufacturing equipment. The San Antonio Arsenal, which was seized by Texas troops, only had 1,301 converted muskets and 260 rifles on hand in 1859. This can be compared to the 46,721 converted muskets and 9,688 rifles on hand at the first-class Watervliet Arsenal.[10] Creating a major arsenal took a number of years and a substantial amount of money, and Congress was reluctant to make large appropriations for the Ordnance Department before the war. The location of the major arsenals helps explain why the Confederacy was limited in its ability to manufacture many articles of ordnance in sufficient quality and quantity when compared to the Union. It is interesting to speculate what the impact would have been on the war if both armories as well as additional first- and second-class arsenals had been located deep within Confederate territory.

One type of manufacturing unit the Ordnance Department did not possess was a foundry, although it had repeatedly tried to get Congress to authorize and fund one. Lieutenant Colonel George Talcott, Chief of Ordnance, wrote in response to an inquiry from Representative A. Yell, a member of the House of Representatives Military Committee, that the Ordnance Department wanted a foundry for the fabrication of cannon based on three reasons. Principally, the military wanted absolute control over the production of heavy ordnance. The other two reasons were to allow the military the opportunity to conduct experiments on heavy ordnance and on different methods of pro-

Workers filling cartridges at the Watertown Arsenal laboratory. The laboratory is the most dangerous place to work in an arsenal. A high percentage of the laboratory's workers were women (*Harper's Weekly*, volume 5, July 20, 1861, page 449. Library of Congress).

Table 4.1* — Ordnanace Department Armories and Arsenals, October 1855

Armories	First-Class Arsenals of Construction	Second-Class Arsenals of Repair	Third-Class Arsenals of Deposit
Harpers Ferry, VA	Allegheny, PA	Baton Rouge, LA	Augusta, GA
Springfield, MA	Washington, D.C.	Fayetteville, NC	Champlain, VT
	Watervliet, NY	Fort Monroe, VA	Charleston, SC
	Benicia, CA (under construction)	Frankford, PA	Detroit, MI
		Watertown, MA	Kennebec, ME
	Saint Louis, MO (being converted from an Arsenal of Repair)		Little Rock, AR
			Mount Vernon, AL
			New York, NY
			Five other third-class arsenals existed but were recommended to be sold.

* Benét, Volume II, pages 561–562.

ducing and casting iron and brass.[11] Talcott went on to say, in reference to the economics of creating a national foundry, that the military expected to "derive from the foundry the same benefits as are experienced from the armories, in both the standard of the work received from private contractors and the prices to be paid to them."[12] However, Congress did not view the Ordnance Department's initial nor subsequent request favorably and never authorized the construction of a national foundry. In retrospect, this was advantageous to the Union's war effort. If Congress had approved the Ordnance Department's request, a dominant ordnance foundry may have discouraged privately owned foundries from getting into the business of casting cannons. This would have made it much more difficult for the Union to expand its production of cannons when the war began as too few foundries would have been familiar with the necessary techniques.

Given Congress' refusal to approve a national foundry, the Army used private foundries to manufacture cannons. By the late 1850s there were six private foundries doing contract work for the army. The following four foundries only manufactured iron cannons: West Point foundry, West Point, NY; Fort Pitt foundry, Pittsburgh, PA; Tredegar foundry, Richmond, VA; and Bellona foundry on the James River, 12 miles above Richmond, VA. One foundry (Chicopee foundry, Chicopee, MA) only manufactured brass cannon while the South Boston foundry in Boston manufactured both iron and brass cannon.[13] Of the six foundries, only three (South Boston, West Point, and Tredegar) were equipped to produce heavy artillery.[14] As with the location of the arsenals, it is worth noting that of the six foundries, only two were located in the future Confederacy and of the three that could manufacture heavy artillery, only one was located there. Knowing the location of prewar foundries is important for these foundries produced many of the artillery projectiles and fuzes used during the war. However, by 1860 neither Tredegar nor Bellona were authorized federal foundries. The reason was that both foundries refused to use the Rodman method of casting guns, in which the gun was cooled from the inside out rather than the older method of cooling the gun from the outside in.

Other major producers of armaments also remained in Union control. Most of these manufacturers, E. Remington & Sons, James T. Ames, S. Colt, and North & Savage, were located in the vicinity of an Ordnance Department armory or arsenal, with the exception of Harper's Ferry Armory, which did not have any other major manufacturers in its vicinity. The Springfield Armory and the arsenals located in the northeast were the nuclei of a critical mass of local arms manufacturers. This critical mass created an environment that allowed related industries to flourish by improving their product and means of production through conversations between and movement of managers and workers.

The Navy was also a major manufacturer through its shipyards which were located around the nation, although the capabilities of the yards varied considerably. The navy yards at the beginning of the Civil War were in Boston, MA; Mare Island (San Francisco, CA); New York, NY; Norfolk, VA; Pensacola, FL; Philadelphia, PA; Portsmouth, NH; and Washington, D.C.. In addition, a naval facility, constructed during the War of 1812, existed at Sackets Harbor, New York. A navy yard had also been located in Memphis, Tennessee, from 1844 to 1853. Confederate forces made use of this yard when the war began, and when the Union river fleet captured it in 1862 the Union Navy proceeded to use it. Navy yards were, as were the army's armories and arsenals, centers of manufacturing. Around many of these facilities, ship building industrial districts existed. While many of these ship building industrial districts would have existed without the presence of the navy yards, the navy yards gave an extra dimension to the districts since the skills needed to construct and supply a warship were different from those required for a commercial vessel.

While the majority of the navy yards built and repaired ships in addition to storing supplies, the Washington Navy Yard became the center of the Navy's ordnance efforts through the hard work of John Dahlgren. Because it was the ordnance center for the Navy, the Washington Navy Yard was as well equipped as any of the Army's armories or arsenals. One item that the Washington Navy Yard had that none of the Army's facilities possessed was a foundry. It was possible to cast, machine, and test a large-caliber cannon at the yard. The Washington Navy Yard became vital to the Navy's ordnance efforts due to the experiments conducted there, the equipment to manufacture the ordnance, and the skilled workmen to operate the machinery.

The majority of government manufacturing facilities were located in the northeastern part of the country. Their close proximity to each other was one of the factors that assisted in the development of the northeastern industrial districts. The main part of this industrial district was located in a broad arc from Boston through New York City to Philadelphia, and included one armory, two second-class arsenals, one third-class arsenal, three navy yards, two foundries, and two small arms manufacturers. Based on the 1860 census, the combined value of the industrial production in the grand industrial district of Massachusetts, Connecticut, Rhode Island, New York City, and Philadelphia was over $673 million. This total is more than four times greater than the combined value of the industrial production in all eleven states that seceded and joined the Confederacy. This grand district produced a wide range of manufactured items, beyond the military related ones of ship building and small arms production, such as textiles, metal working (which included mills), machine tools, and leather working. One key to the success of this grand industrial district was the ability of skilled individuals to leave one industry or company and transfer their manufacturing knowledge to a completely different one while staying in a relatively limited geographical area. The location of military-related industries, especially the armory, arsenals, and navy yards, provided a location where workers could learn the newest manufacturing techniques due to the manufacturing innovations that the military developed in machining, the use of gauges, and metallurgy.

The future Confederacy was in a very different situation from the Union with respect to armament manufacturing. The South did not have the manufacturing base to produce adequate quantities of ordnance that required high tolerances to work successfully. One reason for this shortage was that the states in the future Confederacy never developed the critical masses of co-located manufacturing firms. J. W. Mallet, Superintendent of Confederate Ordnance Laboratories, wrote after the war, "To produce on a large scale even such equipment as this (armament and warlike munitions) involved in the Southern States, shut out from free commerce with the rest of the world, most formidable difficulties arising from dearth of materials, machinery, and skilled labor."[15] Lieutenant Colonel William Le Roy Broun, Commander of the Richmond Arsenal, supported Mallet's statement when Broun wrote after the war that Confederate inventors "were prevented from accomplishing what they planned by reason of the want of machinery to do the necessary work."[16] The lack of sufficient industrial districts and the subsequent lack of a grand industrial district put the South at a distinct manufacturing disadvantage compared to the North especially when precision manufacturing was required.

The value of the industrial production of the 20 greatest manufacturing cities in the United States, based on the 1860 census, highlights even more differences in the industrial capabilities of the two regions. Of the 102 cities with a population of 10,000 or greater in the United States, the top 20 cities produced 72 percent of the total value of products manufactured. Of these 20 cities, only two, Richmond and New Orleans, were situated in states that would secede. Although Louisville and Saint Louis could be considered southern, they were in border states and never controlled by the Confederacy. What is even more telling is that the value of the items produced in Manchester, New Hampshire (18th on the list), was worth almost as much as the items produced in New Orleans (17th on the list), a city eight times its size.

The District of Columbia deserves special mention, even though it is not listed as one of the 20 greatest manufacturing cities in the United States in 1860. Although the District of Columbia only had a population of 75,080 in the 1860 census, smaller than any of the states, the census showed that it had an annual value of $5,412,102 from its manufactured goods. This total is more than the combined manufacturing value of the goods produced in the southern states of Arkansas ($2,880,578) and Florida ($2,447,969). In fact, the value of manufactured goods from Mississippi ($6,590,687) and Texas ($6,577,202) was only slightly above the District of Columbia's. Moreover, the production of manufactured goods by the military was not included in the census totals.[17] Had the census included the value of the manufactured goods from the first-class Washington Arsenal and the Washington Navy Yard, the District of Columbia's total would have been much greater. During the Civil War the District was more than the center of government, it was also a major manufacturing center. Manufacturers located there produced a variety of military equipment and part of the District's industrial production included $97,859 worth of mainly large artillery projectiles manufactured by private foundries, all in addition to what was manufactured at the Washington Arsenal and the Washington Navy Yard.[18] If Confederate forces had captured the District of Columbia, its manufacturing capability would have been a great addition to the South and its loss, beyond the political ramifications, as great a disaster as the loss of the Harpers Ferry Armory and the Norfolk Navy Yard.

The future Confederacy's industrial disadvantage extended beyond individual cities as nine of the ten greatest manufacturing states in the United States, based on the 1860 census, were states that did not leave the Union. Of these ten states, only Virginia would be in the future Confederacy, and its statistical data included that of the future state of West Virginia. The disparity between the industrial capacity of the North and South can be illustrated by the difference between Connecticut and Virginia. The value of the manufacturing in Connecticut was 1.6 times greater than that of Virginia's even though its population was less than one-third that of Virginia's. In addition, the value of manufacturing production in Massachusetts, where the population was a little less than Virginia's, was five times that of Virginia's. The connection between armories, arsenals, navy yards, and federally contracted foundries and private industry probably helped put Virginia on this list, as it had the Harpers Ferry Armory, the Fort Monroe Arsenal, the Norfolk Navy Yard, the Tredegar Foundry, and the Bellona Foundry within its state boundaries. In addition, the Washington Arsenal and Washington Navy Yard were in the adjacent District of Columbia. No other state in the future Confederacy had that many federally connected industries within its boundaries.

This detailed information explains why the Confederacy was not capable of producing reliable copies of the excellent Bormann Fuze and was unable to produce the same quality of mechanical fuzes as the North. At the beginning of the war, southern artillery used ammunition seized from Federal arsenals located in Confederate territory. These artillery rounds, armed with Bormann Fuzes manufactured prior to the war, had relatively few complaints. Confederate manufacturers tried to manufacture the Bormann Fuze but with very poor results. General E.P. Alexander, Chief of Artillery for Longstreet's Corps, noted that:

> ... complaints of its bad quality were immediately made. Careful test being made of it, it was found that fully four-fifths of the shell exploded prematurely, and very many of them in the gun. The machinery for their manufacture was overhauled, and a fresh supply made and sent to the field, where the old ones were removed and the new were substituted, but no improvements was [sic] discernable. The trouble was found to be in the hermetical sealing of the under-side of the horse-shoe channel containing the fuse composition. Although this was seemingly accomplished at the factory, the shock of the discharge would unseat the horse-shoe-shaped plug which closed this channel, and allow the flame from the composition to reach the charge of the shell without burning around to the magazine of the fuse. Attempts were made to correct the evil by the use of white-lead, putty and leather under the fuse, and in the winter of 1861 these correctives were applied to every shell in the army with partial but not universal success. Repeated attempts were made to improve the manufacture, but they accomplished nothing, and until after the battle of Chancellorsville the Bormann fuse continued in use, and premature explosions of shell were so frequent that the artillery could only be used over the heads of the infantry with such danger and demoralization to the latter that it was seldom attempted.[19]

The Confederacy lacked the precision machining equipment and trained operators necessary to manufacture either the more advanced flame-ignited fuzes or the mechanical fuzes needed to make rifled artillery truly effective. The Union Army understood this deficiency, as Brevet Brigadier General Henry Abbot, Commander of the Federal Siege Train during the 1864–1865 Campaign against Richmond, commented: "We had little to learn from the confederates in the matter of rifled gun fuzes, which were inferior in their service to our own. Their standards were paper time fuzes and percussion fuzes, both closely resembling our patterns."[20]

While the Confederacy unquestionably needed reliable artillery fuzes and had the technical knowledge to create advanced mechanical fuzes, it did not have the industrial capability to do so. As a consequence, Confederate long-range artillery fire was inadequate. It was so inadequate that Porter Alexander stated that one reason the Confederate bombardment of the Union Army at Chattanooga was unsuccessful was because "when it came to extreme ranges, a considerable percentage of our rifle shell would tumble, or explode prematurely, or not explode at all."[21] Major Edward Manigault also continually complained about the poor quality of the fuzes he was issued while commanding the South Carolina Siege Train at Charleston. During one attempt to bombard the Union guns located on Morris Island Manigault stated in his diary that of the 27 shells fired from an eight-inch Columbiad that "all the shells failed to burst except about three."[22] The Confederacy lacked one of the supporting legs of the Weapon System Pyramid. As a consequence, their artillery weapon system never developed to the same level as the Union's artillery.

The states remaining under Union control throughout the war were well-prepared for the difficult task of manufacturing military equipment that required high-precision machining, to include fuzes, due to the industrial districts centered on the arsenals, Springfield Armory, and the navy yards. As a result, in November 1862, 20 months after the fall of Fort Sumter, Brigadier General James W. Ripley, Chief of Ordnance, wrote Secretary of War Stanton that production of arms and equipment had reached such a point that his department could "replace every arm in service, not of the first class, by one of the best quality and kind, and to place in store enough arms of the same description to meet the probable losses and damages from all causes."[23] This is in contrast to the Confederacy as the Army of Northern Virginia still had men armed with smooth-bore muskets until Gettysburg, and even then many of their rifles had been captured.[24] The Civil War was as much a manufacturing war as a physical war, and the Union's superior industrial capability allowed it to produce fuzes and other items needed to make artillery a truly effective weapon.

Five

Artillery During the Civil War

> *Whether in the form of invention, or as an act of diffusion, a new technical device becomes incorporated into an already established system of organized behavior, and produces gradually a complete remolding of that institution.*[1]
> — Bronislaw Malinowski, 1960

Artillery labored under some distinct technical disadvantages during the Civil War, and these deficiencies adversely impacted its effectiveness. First, there was no recoil system to automatically bring the cannon back to its original position. Thus, every time a cannon was fired, the crew had to manually wrestle it back to its position and re-aim it. Next, artillery could effectively fire farther than observers could effectively judge the results. The smoke generated by the black powder used in the guns worsened this shortcoming, and the forests that covered large parts of the country further limited the artillerymen's field of vision. Other limitations artillery officers faced resulted from industry's inability to properly manufacture many items, such as firmly connecting the new metal sabots to the projectiles. The military also had a negative impact on the problem due to its antiquated tactical doctrine, its inability to implement a cohesive effort to develop future military weapons, and an inadequate research program.

Even with these tactical and technological disadvantages, artillery was not relegated to a secondary role during the war. In fact, it played a critical role in a number of battles, and long-range artillery, along with the rifled musket, was responsible for the extensive trench warfare that figured so prominently at the war's end. The extensive trench systems and bomb proofs constructed by both sides went far beyond what was necessary to protect men from rifle fire. The men and officers knew the danger long-range artillery fire presented and acted accordingly. Captain Charles Mattocks, Commander of Company A, 17th Maine, wrote that during the Battle of Chancellorsville his company came under accurate artillery fire as they occupied some breastworks. While there, three projectiles struck the breastworks, and others went overhead without injuring any of his men. Mattocks compared this to an incident a few days earlier in which one projectile wounded five of his men, two mortally. Mattocks stated that due to these experiences, he was "strongly in favor of fortifying now."[2] Given artillery's inability to inflict significant casualties on men protected by these fortifications, as well as terrain limitations, its offensive role steadily decreased as the war progressed.

Artillery had a major impact upon the war from the very beginning as a long-range artillery bombardment, mainly by smooth-bore artillery and mortars, was used to force Fort Sumter to surrender. However, the bombardment of Fort Sumter was not considered to be the principle reason for its surrender. Captain (later Major General) J. G. Foster, an Engineer officer assigned to the fort, felt that the rubble created by the bombardment could have been used to put the fort in a more defensible condition than it was before the bombardment began. Foster wrote in his report that the weakness of the defense principally lay with the lack of cartridge bags for the guns and a lack of men to serve the guns, in addition to the lack of provisions. Foster went on to state:

> I do not think that a breach could have been effected in the gorge at the distance of the battery on Cummings Point, within a week or ten days; and even then, with the small garrison to defend it, and means for obstructing it, at our disposal, the operation of assaulting it, with even vastly superior numbers, would have been very doubtful in its results.[3]

The bombardment and capture of Fort Sumter did not change the masonry fort paradigm in the minds of the military.[4]

In contrast, the reduction of Fort Pulaski by heavy rifled artillery changed how the military viewed masonry forts. Both the Confederates and Federals knew that Fort Pulaski, even with its seven-and-a-half-feet thick walls and large amount of ordnance, could be reduced by a long sustained siege. However, no one imagined that it would be forced to surrender within two days, especially since it was fully manned and well supplied with food and ammunition. The siege was so short that Confederate forces never had an opportunity to even attempt a relief of the fort. General Hunter reported after Fort Pulaski had surrendered that "the result of this bombardment must cause, I am convinced, a change in the construction of fortifications as radical as that forshadowed [sic] in naval architecture by the conflict between the Monitor and Merrimac. No works of stone or brick can resist the impact of rifled artillery of heavy caliber."[5] What made the reduction of Fort Pulaski so surprising was that military manuals stated that large caliber smooth-bore artillery

A distant photographic view of the breach made by rifled artillery at Fort Pulaski. The capability of rifled artillery to create such breaches ended the reign of high masonry forts (photographed by Timothy O'Sullivan in April 1862. Library of Congress).

had to be within 400 to 600 yards to breach fortifications.[6] However, at Fort Pulaski rifled artillery was used to bombard the fort. Because they were using rifled artillery, the Union breaching batteries were placed about 1,700 yards from the fort, a distance that no one had previously considered possible.[7]

The new mechanical fuzes used with rifled projectiles played an important role in the quick reduction of Fort Pulaski. After the fort surrendered, General Gillmore, the engineer in charge of the siege, conducted a detailed study of the results of the bombardment and observed that against brick walls percussion shells created a much greater crater than a solid shot projectile. However, he doubted if percussion shells would be effective against granite

A close up photographic view of the breach made by rifled artillery at Fort Pulaski (photographed by Timothy O'Sullivan in April 1862. Library of Congress).

walls as they would doubtless break upon impact. Consequently, Gillmore recommended that when rifled guns were used against brick walls that at least half of the projectiles should be percussion shells.[8] At Fort Pulaski the new mechanical fuzes clearly demonstrated their superiority over the older flame-ignited fuzes in their ability to detonate a projectile upon impact and thus create more damage to the walls of a masonry fort.

Still, the reduction of Fort Pulaski by land based siege artillery did not make casemated forts obsolete as a means of harbor defense. While ironclad ships could run past them, no casemated fort was taken by naval forces alone

Interior view of Fort Pulaski's front parapet. Almost all of the Confederate guns that could fire at the Union batteries were disabled by during the bombardment (photographed by Timothy O'Sullivan in April 1862. Library of Congress).

during the war, and it was "generally conceded that a force must be landed, and siege batteries (armed with heavy guns) erected."[9] Fort Sumter, even though it was a total wreck by the end of the war due to continual bombardment by the Union Army and Navy, held out until its garrison abandoned it when the Confederate forces left the city. Casemate forts were powerful enough that the Union fleet's attack upon the Charleston Harbor by ironclads under Admiral DuPont in April 1863 was a disaster for the Union Navy. Heavy rifled artillery made masonry forts more vulnerable but not untenable if properly sited, constructed, and supported.

Field artillery was used much differently from the less mobile siege artillery, and on the battlefield it was normally placed in the line of battle for a number of reasons. First, during most Civil War battles, the terrain was hilly and wooded, which limited visibility. Consequently, officers placed artillery batteries where they could most effectively fire upon the enemy which, in most cases, was alongside the infantry. In addition, artillery's most effective round against attacking infantry or advancing cavalry was canister, but given its lethal characteristics, these projectiles could not be fired over friendly units. Beyond canister the Army restricted long-range fire from behind friendly units due to problems with premature projectile explosions and the new metal sabots separating from rifled projectiles.[10] The Artillery Headquarters of the Army of the Potomac formalized this policy by issuing an order in January 1864 stating that "as a rule that artillery should not fire over our own troops."[11] The order explained that there were three good reasons not to fire over friendly units. Primary was that accidents were liable to happen to the troops from the projectiles. In addition, firing over the head of friendly units slowed down their advance by tearing up the ground in front of them as well as forcing them to hold back until the artillery fire could be stopped or its range extended. Lastly, it made the men over whom the projectiles passed uneasy, and could potentially demoralize them. The order stated, "When it becomes necessary to fire over troops, solid shot and, in rare cases, shell should be used, and not canister nor shrapnel; the latter projectile being liable to burst too soon, and to carry destruction among those over whose heads it was intended to pass."[12] Colonel Theodore Lyman, a member of General Meade's staff, explained this problem to his wife in an August 1864 letter in which he wrote:

> You see that cannon-shot must rise high in the air to go any distance; so tey [sic] fire over each other's heads. In practice this system is not without its dangers, owing to the imperfections of shells. In spite of the great advances, much remains to be done in the fuses of shells; as it is, not a battle is fought that some of our men are not killed by shells exploding short and hitting our troops instead of the enemy's, beyond. Sometimes it is the fuse that is imperfect, sometimes the artillerists lose their heads and make wrong estimates of distance. From these blunders very valuable officers have lost their lives. Prudent commanders, when there is any doubt, fire only solid shot, which do not explode, and do excellent service in bounding over the ground.[13]

All of these issues limited the placement of artillery throughout the war to the infantry battle line and at a location where it could bring effective fire on the enemy. Consequently, there were many battles where it was impossible to effectively deploy all of the available artillery batteries.

Even with these precautions fratricide from artillery fire did occur during the war. During one instance, on the Union right flank during the second day of the Battle of Gettysburg, a Union artillery battery on a low hill was ordered by Major General Slocum to fire over friendly units due to the dangerous tactical situation. This action led to casualties in the 145th New York Infantry and the 46th Pennsylvania Infantry. Because of the casualties both regimental commanders went to the battery to "discuss" the problem. When they arrived, their arguments were disregarded by the battery commander as Major General Slocum was present, the very individual who had ordered the battery to fire over the heads of the friendly troops. Fortunately, the situation resolved itself when the tactical situation stabilized and the infantry regiments withdrew.[14]

Confederate forces were not immune to fratricide from their own artillery. During the Battle of Perryville, General Cleburne reported that when his brigade moved into a location from which Union infantry had just been forced to retreat, his men received fire from Confederate artillery. This fire killed and wounded some of his men and forced his brigade to fall back. Only after one of his aides went to the battery and got them to stop firing at his brigade was Cleburne able to continue his advance.[15]

While the Army discouraged artillery from firing over their own troops, there are examples in which it was done with good effect. The times that it did occur, the batteries were located at a substantially higher elevation than the friendly troops over whom they were firing. At the Battle of Fredericksburg in December 1862, Union batteries located on Stafford Heights on the east side of the Rappahannock River and Confederate batteries located on Marye's Heights both fired over their own troops. On the third day of the Battle of Gettysburg, Union batteries located on Little Roundtop fired over their own troops at the attacking Confederate infantry. In contrast, Confederate artillery had to cease firing at Union positions when the Confederate infantry began their advance on the Union line as they were on the same elevation.

During the Civil War the offensive use of artillery was limited for a variety of reasons. First, there were the restrictions on firing over friendly units. Then, artillery found it very difficult to keep up with infantry or cavalry as they advanced on the battlefield. Although there were notable exceptions to this, such as General Bedford Forrest's order to his artillery at the Battle of Brice's Cross Roads in June 1864 to advance unsupported when the attack began, this tactic was not very common. However, when the right opportunity presented itself, artillery could be a decisive element in an attack. During the Battle of Chancellorsville in May 1863, Confederate artillery was used aggressively and played a significant role in the Confederate victory. The artillery that supported Jackson's flank attack succeeded in obtaining a commanding position on Hazel Grove on the second day of the attack. At Hazel

Grove the Confederates were able to mass a large number of guns and inflicted tremendous damage on the Union artillery as well as significant casualties to the Union infantry. After the Union forces again retreated, the Confederate artillery advanced to the positions just abandoned by those Union units and continued their supporting fire. This achievement was one of the major reasons Confederate infantry attacks on the second day of the flank attack succeeded. The successful offensive use of artillery during this attack was probably one of the reasons Lee felt that the Confederate attack on the third day of Gettysburg would succeed as he had directed that the batteries were "to be pushed forward as the infantry progressed" with the mission of protecting their flanks and closely supporting their attacks.[16]

One of the most important offensive uses of artillery was the destruction of enemy fortifications, as demonstrated at Fort Pulaski. Consequently, all new fortifications built during the war were earthen with some massive earthworks, such as Fort Fisher, being built entirely out of sand. (It should be noted that time constraints were another major factor as the construction of massive masonry or stone forts took years to complete. In addition, concrete forts were constructed throughout the world after the war, although with a much lower profile.) Nevertheless, artillery fire could destroy earthen fortifications, if not constructed properly. Rifled artillery made this easier because the percussion fuzes used in rifled artillery were superior to flame-ignited fuzes when fired against earthen fortifications. Benton noted in his book *A Course of Instruction in Ordnance and Gunnery* that time fuzes, when used against earthen forts, "[are] liable to be extinguished by the pressure of the earth, are inferior to percussion fuzes, which produce explosion when the projectile has made about three-fourths of its proper penetration."[17] During the Siege of Vicksburg, Confederate fortifications were made from the local silty soil, which is loess, and has different characteristics from the sandy soil used for the experiments that were the basis of the construction of earthworks in military manuals.[18] As a result, Union rifled artillery, due to its superior penetrating power, demolished Confederate fortifications to such an extent that they were open to assault. The knowledge that his fortifications could now be successfully assaulted because of this damage directly impacted General Pemberton's decision to surrender.

The Union Army also used artillery as a terror weapon against civilians during the war. During the Siege of Charleston, the Union army sent a message to General Beauregard that they would start bombarding the City of Charleston unless the Confederates evacuated Morris Island and Fort Sumter.[19] General Gillmore later stated, "No military results of great value were ever expected from this firing. As an experiment with heavy guns to test their endurance under the severest trial to which they could possibly be subjected in service, the results were not only highly interesting and novel, but very instructive."[20] As part of the bombardment, projectiles filled with flammable "Greek Fire" were fired at the city from rifled cannon with the hopes of starting fires, but with limited success.[21] Although General Gillmore did not think that any military results of great value would be gained, by the end of the war the sustained bombardment resulted in the destruction of the lower part of Charleston through a combination of fire and damage from exploding shells. Photographs from that time period show damage which could have easily resulted from a World War II aerial bombing.

Indirect fire was an artillery tactic that could be used either offensively or defensively. However, results were less than satisfactory due to the relative

Ruins of Charleston, South Carolina, as viewed from the Circular Church in April 1865. During World War II other cities would experience similar destruction from aerial bombardment (Library of Congress).

A 200-pounder Parrott Rifle in Fort Gregg on Morris Island, South Carolina. This is the type of gun that bombarded Charleston (photographed by Samuel Cooley in 1865. National Archives).

ineffectiveness of black powder as an explosive in an artillery projectile and the problem of achieving accurate indirect fire. Also, the type of projectile available to artillerymen for effective indirect fire was limited. Neither case shot nor solid shot were effective as the timing for case shot had to be exact and solid shot lost its accuracy and momentum at extreme ranges. Consequently, shells, projectiles completely filled with gunpowder, would have been the preferred projectile.

Still, Union gunboats sometimes used indirect fire in support of Army units. During the Battle of Shiloh, at the end of the first day's fighting, the USS *Tyler*, followed by the USS *Lexington,* fired a shell blindly at the Confederate camp about every ten to 15 minutes starting at 9:00 P.M. and continuing until daylight.[22] However, based on Confederate reports this shelling, although annoying, did little damage.[23] Interestingly, earlier in the battle indirect fire from the *Tyler* severed the branches of the trees and hurled them into the ranks of Colonel Geddes' Eighth U.S. Iowa Infantry.[24] Another indirect fire mission for the Union Mississippi River Fleet occurred during the Battle of Milliken's Bend, Louisiana, in June 1863. Confederate forces attacked the Union camp there and forced the defending troops to retreat to the Mississippi River with only one levee between them and the enemy. Two Union gunboats came to their aid, and even though the Naval officers could not see the Confederates because of the levee they brought effective artillery fire upon the enemy from signals they received from Union troops on the levee.[25] The fire from the gunboats stabilized the situation, and in the end the Confederates retreated. Union ships also used indirect fire in support of the Army of the Potomac. One incident occurred during the Battle of Malvern Hill in June 1862, when indirect fire from Union gunboats was "directed and regulated almost entirely by the signal officer from the battle-field and from ship to ship."[26] Confederate artillery also used indirect fire when the opportunity presented itself. In August 1863, during the Siege of Charleston, Major Edward Manigault arranged for a signaler from the Signal Corps to let him know whether their mortar shells were short, over, or hitting the Union batteries located on Morris Island.[27]

The most effective use of artillery during the Civil War was defensive long-range and short-range fire. Confederate artillery was instrumental in keeping Confederate ports open and the Mississippi River closed to Union shipping. Heavy artillery in earthen forts protected Washington, D.C., so successfully that General Lee never seriously considered attacking it. General Early did probe the defenses of Washington in July 1864, and reported that the fortifications consisted "of a circle of inclosed [sic] forts, connected by breast-works, with ditches, palisades, and abatis in front, and every approach swept by a cross-fire of artillery, including some heavy guns."[28] Even though Early was considering an assault he decided against it when he realized the forts were strongly manned and Union forces were cutting off his line of retreat to Virginia.

On the battlefield, artillery proved its worth helping to repel attacks in numerous battles. At the end of the first day's fighting at Shiloh, the Confederates attempted to turn the Union's left flank, which was anchored on the river. The attempt failed due to a combination of well-placed Union artillery batteries, firing from the USS *Tyler* and *Lexington*, difficult terrain, and exhaustion on the part of the Confederates. During the Battle of Malvern Hill in 1862, the Union Army created a grand artillery battery that was strongly positioned with long, open fields of fire and supported by artillery fire from the Union Navy. The fire from this grand battery was so deadly that it has been estimated that about 50 percent of the over 5,000 Confederate casualties during the battle resulted from its fire. During the last day of the Battle of Stones River, Captain John Mendenhall created a grand battery of 58 artillery pieces on the Union left flank, where Confederate General Breckinridge directed his attack.[29] Captain Mendenhall's efforts were so effective that General Breckinridge wrote in his after action report that the Union Army had enough artillery to "sweep the whole position from the front, the left, and the right, and to render it wholly untenable by our present force of artillery and infantry."[30]

The most effective offensive or defensive tactic was enfilade fire. Enfilade fire was possible when a unit could be fired at along its long axis. When achieved, the unit being enfiladed, in most cases, could not respond rapidly as the fire would be striking its flank and its guns would be aimed in a different direction. A mounted six-gun artillery battery had a frontage of seventy feet and a depth of forty-seven feet, with a horse battery having an even larger frontage due to the extra space needed for the horses.[31] Thus, if a mounted battery received enfilading fire, it presented a target that was 50 percent longer, giving a bounding solid shot or an exploding case shot a greater opportunity to hit the target. Three Confederate artillery batteries under the command of Lieutenant Colonel Stephen Lee, along with a number of Confederate infantry regiments, experienced the deadly effects of enfilading fire

Union artillery battery with 10-pounder Parrott rifles conducting drill at Ringgold, Georgia. The space occupied by an artillery battery was quite large with the horses being an easy and tempting target (National Archives).

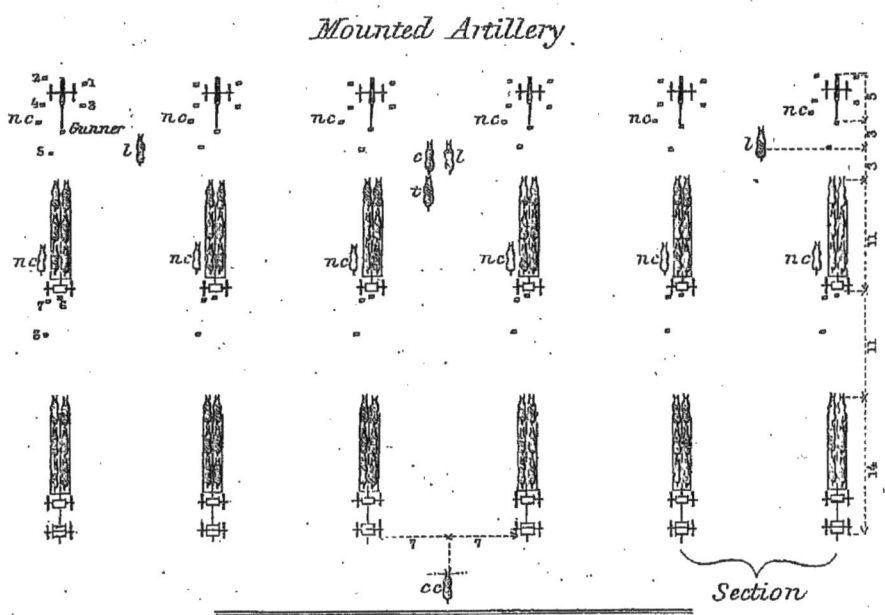

Diagram of a mounted artillery battery ready for action showing the location of the guns, caissons, horses, men, noncommissioned officers, and officers as well as the distances between each. Due to the large area an artillery battery occupied and how it was oriented, it made a tempting target for enfilade fire (distances are shown in feet) (French et al., *Instruction for Field Artillery*, plate 29).

during the Battle of Antietam. During that battle, 20 Union 20-pounder Parrott rifled cannons firing from hills behind the Union front line enfiladed these units and inflicted heavy casualties upon them.[32] The artillery fire was so heavy that Lee called Antietam "Artillery Hell."[33] Infantry and cavalry units were also susceptible to enfilading fire as their frontages far exceeded their depth when in a linear formation. However, infantry and cavalry units had the advantage of being able to move easier and open up their formation compared to an artillery battery. Still, when subjected to enfilading fire from an artillery battery, infantry and cavalry units could expect to take heavy casualties.

* * *

The use of artillery during the war's early battles was limited, although effective, due to the lack of equipment, organization, and training. The organizational problems faced by the armies are obvious when one considers that in July 1861, the artillery of the future Army of the Potomac consisted of "no more than parts of nine batteries, or thirty pieces of various, and, in some instances, unusual and unserviceable calibers."[34] Less than a year later, during the Peninsula Campaign, the Army of the Potomac had with it a total of "60 batteries of 343 guns."[35] This tremendous expansion placed significant stress on the Army's organization and the ability of the Ordnance Department to provide necessary equipment. However, as late as 1864 two British officers, Lieutenant Colonel T. L. Gallwey, Royal Engineers, and Captain H.J. Alderson, Royal Artillery, commented in their report to the British War Department that the United States "artillery were tolerably well drilled, the infantry badly drilled, and the cavalry not drilled at all."[36]

Gallwey's and Alderson's report is interesting in many areas. The two men had been sent to the United States by the British Secretary of State for War to "gain information on professional subjects, and to study the development of Artillery science which has taken place during the last two or three years in that country, affording matter for instruction and comparison."[37] During their six-month visit they visited a number of forts, including those surrounding Washington as well as the forts protecting Portland, Boston, New York and Baltimore; the Army of the South located at Port Royal; the Union camp at Charleston; foundries at Pittsburgh, West Point, and Philadelphia; and the Watertown Arsenal. In addition, they obtained a number of reports and plans. However, Secretary of War Stanton refused their request to accompany the Army of the Potomac during its spring campaign. This was a good decision as their report to the British War Department was classified "confidential," and in their report they discussed the weak points in the United States' harbor defense system. In their report they also recommended that special investigation and experiments be conducted on:

1. Wrought-iron artillery carriages.
2. The question of "no preponderance" in very heavy guns. (The lighter weight of these U.S. guns impressed the two British officers especially when compared to their heavy guns.)
3. Iron embrasures and masonry surrounding, as constructed in the Federal works, to be fired at by such guns as will be carried by our ironclad vessels.[38]

Gallwey and Alderson also recommended that further progress in heavy gun manufacture in the United States be watched. American artillery during the Civil War was technologically progressive although the professionalism of the branch had been compromised by the rapid expansion.

The need for better organization of the artillery branch was recognized by Union commanders. General George B. McClellan, as part of his overall organizational efforts in October 1861, ordered the creation of a Board of

Officers "to examine into and report upon the various kinds of Rifled Cannon and Ammunition therefore, now in use in this Army."³⁹ General McClellan also directed the board to "examine any new projectiles &c. which may be presented to them for the purpose, and will report fully what substitutions if any, should in their opinion be made for those now in use for the different kinds of Ordnance."⁴⁰ The board conducted extensive tests on a number of different guns, projectiles, and fuzes. Schenkl's percussion fuze, Hotchkiss's percussion fuze, Parrott's new percussion fuze, and the new paper time fuze favorably impressed the board. However, they were not able to test the new Schenkl combined time and concussion fuze as it had not arrived, although they had heard good reports about it. The board concluded "that the Rifled Guns now in use in this Army with the improved projectiles for them, appear to answer the purpose very well excepting always the James projectile old pattern, with which they have not experimented, but respecting which all the reports are unfavorable."⁴¹

The report of the board assembled by General McClellan points out at least two very important facts. First, the complaints from artillerymen had been heard and the Army had responded to them. The universally condemned paper time fuze had been changed, although numerous complaints regarding it would continue. The board noted that "it [the paper fuze] is made like the old one, but to prevent injury by dampness, the end of the fuze, as soon as made is covered with gum or varnish, and then immediately dipped in fine powder, which adheres to the gum the grains forming a rough coating. The fuze is thus kept dry and the chances of ignition much increased."⁴² The board continued in its report with, "If the improvement above described in its preparation stands the test of time the fuze may be considered a very good one."⁴³ The report also stated that Robert Parrott sent one of his men to assist the board in the preparation of his new-style projectile. Since Robert Parrott was an inventor and manufacturer, his willingness to send a knowledgeable representative from Cold Springs, New York, to Washington demonstrates the close coordination that was occurring between the manufacturers and the military.

Another example of the close coordination between the military and industry was when the Army experienced problems with the Schenkl percussion fuze during the Peninsula Campaign. Brigadier General Ripley, Chief of Ordnance, wrote to Major General McClellan stating, "The fuses used are Schenkl's, the best of their kind. It is suggested that the failures may arise from an omission to reverse the screw cap, the operation of which General Barry or Major Webb understands. Mr. Schenkl, the inventor, will leave tonight for Yorktown to investigate the matter."⁴⁴ Beyond the fact that the Army of the Potomac was having trouble with the Schenkl Percussion Fuze, what is interesting to note is that John Schenkl was going to go to the front lines to investigate the problem.[45] Schenkl must have solved the problem because in June 1862, Ripley wrote to Robert Parrott requesting 8,500 30-pound projectiles and stated, "One-half of the projectiles should be prepared with Schenkl's percussion fuzes, as these seem to be the only fuzes that give perfect satisfaction at this point."[46]

Criticism of a fuze by the military did not mean that the fuze would be taken out of the inventory. Parrott's fuze had also been severely criticized but he responded to the criticism, made the necessary improvements, and his fuze remained in use. However, the military was careful to not include Parrott's older-style fuze in any future orders. A requisition from the Ordnance Office in the spring of 1863 specified that the percussion shells Parrott was supplying were to be armed with the new pattern fuze.[47] Parrott's reputation remained positive with some artillery officers, such as Colonel Henry Abbot, future commander of the siege artillery for the Army of the Potomac, who wrote to Captain Alfred Mordecai,[48] the Chief Ordnance Officer for the Virginia and North Carolina Department, in June 1864:

> Several days ago I made a requisition for the proper Parrott percussion, but the supply forwarded consists of the Schenkl or Hotchkiss, neither fit for my guns. If I am to use my guns upon the rebel fleet, I must have the proper percussion shells to be able to produce satisfactory results.[49]

After the 1862 Seven Days Campaign, both armies in the east underwent major reorganizations. By the end of the summer, the artillery in both armies had gained tremendous experience, and this experience was put to devastating use at the Battle of Antietam. Antietam was one of the most important Union victories during the Civil War. It is very possible that the placement of strong Union artillery batteries on the army's right flank allowed the Union Army to win the battle. During the afternoon, after the Union assaults had ended on the Confederate left flank, General Lee instructed General Jackson to investigate the possibility of turning the right flank of the Union army. General Jackson wrote in his report:

> ... I moved to the left with a view of turning the Federal right, but I found his numerous artillery so judiciously established in their front and extending so near to the Potomac, which here makes a remarkable bend, as will be seen by reference to the map (map not found) herewith annexed, as to render it inexpedient to hazard the attempt.[50]

It is interesting to note that even though numerous Union infantry regiments were on that flank, they did not dissuade Jackson, just the Union artillery did. If the Union artillery had not been present and Jackson had made a successful attack, it is very likely that General McClellan, considering his fear of being outnumbered and defeated, would have believed that certain disaster was imminent and retreated into the Washington defenses. McClellan's fear was so great that the he wrote in his post battle report:

> The army of the Union, inferior in numbers, wearied by long marches, deficient in various supplies, worn out by numerous battles, the last of which had not been successful, first covered by its movements the important cities of Washington and Baltimore, then boldly attacked the victorious enemy in their chosen strong position and drove them back, with all their superior numbers....[51]

McClellan wrote this even though his army had slightly over a two-to-one advantage on the battlefield and was far better supplied. If Antietam had turned into a Confederate victory, the Emancipation Proclamation would not have been issued when it was, and it is very likely that Great Britain and France would have recognized the Confederacy. Either result would have changed the future course of the war. This little-known event demonstrates the power of long- and short-range artillery fire during the war.

Later that same year, during the Battle of Fredericksburg in December, the Confederate artillery placed on Marye's Heights played a major role in stopping the Union attack on General Longstreet's position with short-range defensive fire. On the Union side, their numerous artillery batteries on Stafford Heights fully demonstrated the power of long-range artillery fire during the Civil War. After the initial attempts by the Union Army to cross the Rappahannock River failed, the Union artillery was ordered to shell Fredericksburg for the purpose of driving the Confederates away from the river. In this they succeeded, as Confederate General McLaws stated in his after action report that "the fire was so severe that the men could not use their rifles, and the different places occupied by them becoming untenable, the troops were withdrawn from the river bank back to Caroline street at 4:30 P.M."[52] Later in the battle, after the failure of the Union's main attack, their heavy siege artillery located on the east side of the river was able to sweep the plain on the west side of the river and protect the left flank of the army. Major Thomas Trumbull, commander of the First Connecticut Heavy Artillery, stated in his after action report that Confederate units were "unable to move across it or approach in any considerable numbers the pontoons on our left."[53] He also reported that when several large Confederate units appeared, his battery opened fire "with such effect that one brigade, at the extreme distance of over 2 miles, broke ranks in great disorder, while several other bodies moved off at double-quick."[54] In all likelihood Major Trumbull's battery broke up General Jackson's counterattack, as Jackson stated in his report:

> Repulsed on the right, left, and center, the enemy soon after reformed his lines, and gave some indications of a purpose to renew the attack. I waited some time to receive it; but he making no forward movement, I

determined, if prudent, to do so myself. The artillery of the enemy was so judiciously posted as to make an advance of our troops across the plain very hazardous; yet it was so promising of good results, if successfully executed, as to induce me to make preparations for the attempt. In order to guard against disaster, the infantry was to be preceded by artillery, and the movement postponed until late in the evening, so that, if compelled to retire, it would be under the cover of night. Owing to unexpected delays, the movement could not be gotten ready until late in the evening. The first gun had hardly moved forward from the wood 100 yards when the enemy's artillery reopened, and so completely swept our front as to satisfy me that the proposed movement should be abandoned.[55]

Again, as at Antietam, the Union artillery with its long-range fire stopped an attack by General Jackson. It is very possible the deadly fire from Major Trumbull's battery had prevented the Union defeat from turning into a disaster with a panic-stricken army trying to get back across the Rappahannock River. It is interesting to speculate whether the Battle of Fredericksburg would have ever occurred if the Confederacy had been able to produce artillery and all of its associated equipment in the quantity and quality the Union did. If so, the battle would probably never have happened, as the Army of the Potomac would not have been able to cross the Rappahannock River against that much concentrated artillery fire. The lack of an adequate industrial base hurt the Confederacy in both artillery guns and fuzes.

The power of long-range artillery fire reached its pinnacle by mid-war, and at Gettysburg, the destructiveness and limitations of long-range artillery fire were fully demonstrated during the Confederate grand assault, known as Pickett's Charge, on the third day of the battle. For the Army of Northern Virginia, the initial phase of Pickett's Charge was the placement of the Confederate artillery. The Confederate artillery had to be placed where various types of guns would attain the best position, ideally an enfilading position, to fire at the Union line. Not all of the Confederate guns were properly placed, and as a consequence, not all of the guns participated in the bombardment. In addition, some batteries were designated to accompany the attacking units to provide support. As these batteries and attacking infantry advanced in front of all of the static batteries, the latter had to cease firing so as not to cause friendly casualties. Overall, the bombardment failed because it did not disable the Union artillery or maul Union infantry, although Union units behind Cemetery Ridge did sustain tremendous damage. The failure to achieve either objective resulted from projectiles overshooting the Union front line due to a combination of bad fuzes, improper actions on the part of the gun crews (not cutting the fuzes for the proper length of time or poor aiming), and/or lack of visibility due to the smoke produced by the black powder. Confederate General Porter Alexander summed up the Confederate artillery effort at

Gettysburg in comparison to the Union effort when he wrote, "For they had superiority in number, & caliber of guns, &, of even greater importance, in quality and quantity of ammunition."[56]

In contrast to the offensive failure of Confederate artillery, Union artillery was much more successful defensively. Except for the artillery units under General Hancock, all of the batteries followed General Hunt's orders not to engage in counter-battery fire. His main reason for the order was to conserve ammunition so that batteries would have enough long-range ammunition to use against the attacking Confederate infantry. Hunt wrote after the war that the most important object for the artillery was "to subject the enemy's infantry, from the first moment of their advance, to such a cross-fire of our artillery as would break their formations, check their impulse, and drive them back, or at least bring them to our lines in such a condition as to make them an easy prey."[57] Hunt went on to state that "the steady fire from McGilvery and Rittenhouse, on their right, caused Pickett's men to drift in the opposite direction, so that the weight of the assault fell upon the positions occupied by Hazard's batteries."[58] Lieutenant Colonel McGilvery, in his official report, had an even more graphic and detailed description of the effects of his enfilading fire.

> At about 3 P.M. a line of battle of about 3,000 or 4,000 men appeared, advancing directly upon our front, which was completely broken up and scattered by our fire before coming within musket range of our lines. Immediately after, appeared three extended lines of battle, of at least 35,000 men, advancing upon our center. These three lines of battle presented an oblique front to the guns under my command, and by training the whole line of guns obliquely to the right, we had a raking fire through all three of these lines. The execution of the fire must have been terrible, as it was over a level plain, and the effect was plain to be seen. In a few minutes, instead of a well-ordered line of battle, there were broken and confused masses, and fugitives fleeing in every direction.[59]

McGilvery's counterpart on the Union right flank of the attack, Major Osborn, had an equally worthy opinion of the effect of his batteries' enfilading fire and reported:

> The left of the charging column rested on a line perpendicular to our front, then stretching away to the right beyond our view, thus offering an excellent front for our artillery fire. We used, according to distance, all descriptions of projectiles. The whole force of our artillery was brought to bear upon this column, and the havoc produced upon their ranks was truly surprising. The enemy's advance was most splendid, and for a considerable distance the only hinderance offered it was by the artillery, which broke their lines fearfully, as every moment showed that their advance under this concentrated artillery fire was most difficult; and though they made desperate efforts to advance in good order, were unable to do so, and I am

convinced that the fire from the hill was one of the main auxiliaries in breaking the force of this grand charge.⁶⁰

Few Confederate unit reports mention the devastating effects of the long-range artillery fire, and most that do state that it did not disrupt their formations and that the men continued to gallantly advance. However, the report from Davis' Brigade on the left flank of the Confederate attack stated that:

> Not a gun was fired at us until we reached a strong post and rail fence about three-quarters of a mile from the enemy's position, when we were met by a heavy fire of grape, canister, and shell, which told sadly upon our ranks. Under this destructive fire, which commanded our front and left with fatal effect, the troops displayed great coolness, were well in hand, and moved steadily forward, regularly closing up the gaps made in their ranks.⁶¹ [Author's note: Three-quarters of a mile is well beyond the effective range of canister. In all likelihood the Union artillery was firing case shot at this unit, but the mistake is understandable as case shot is long-range canister. In addition, field artillery units very seldom used grape.]

General Lee had a slightly different perspective as he wrote that the left flank was "already wavering under a concentrated fire of artillery from the ridge in front, and from Cemetery Hill" and that it gave way when attacked on its flank by Union infantry.⁶²

The significant difference between the Union and Confederate reports is due to each of the reporting commanders wanting to make their commands appear as successful as possible. Still, the fact remains that both flanks of the Confederate attack collapsed inward onto the center units well before they were within effective range of the infantry's rifles. The left flank units collapsed more as they were exposed to heavier artillery fire due to the terrain. In contrast, the center Confederate units were offered a degree of protection from the intense artillery fire as the center Union batteries had fired all of their long-range projectiles prior to the start of the infantry attack. If the Union artillery, with their fuze-dependent, long-range fire, had not inflicted a significant number of casualties upon the attacking Confederate units, these units would have reached Cemetery Ridge in much better condition. This additional force would have made the penetration of the Union line much larger. It is possible that the course of the battle may have changed if this had occurred.

The Army of the Tennessee under General Hood also launched a grand charge during the Battle of Franklin in November 1864. This grand charge involved more men and covered a greater distance than the Confederate grand charge at Gettysburg. It was more successful than the attack at Gettysburg as Confederate units broke into the Union lines and maintained their presence there for a much longer period of time, although casualties were much greater.

Two of the major differences that led to the relative success of this charge were that far less Union artillery was available, and the two Union brigades in front of the main Union lines blocked long-range fire from some of the Union batteries. Consequently, many of the Confederate units suffered few casualties until they reached the Union lines. However, Battery D, First Ohio Light Artillery, armed with three-inch rifled guns placed across the Harpeth River at Fort Granger, provided long-range enfilading fire against the attacking Confederate right flank. Although there were too few guns to have a major impact across the entire Confederate front, these guns had a major impact on the Confederate right flank as they fired 160 shells (armed with percussion fuzes) and three case shot shells (armed with timed fuzes) at those units.[63] Colonel Ellison Capers, Commander of the 24th South Carolina Infantry, stated in his after action report that when reinforcements tried to move to their assistance "the enemy's fire from the houses in rear of the line and from his reserves, thrown rapidly forward, and from guns posted on the far side of the river so as to enfilade the field, tore their line to pieces before it reached the locust abatis."[64]

Long-range artillery fire was so deadly during the Civil War that it was the first war in which anyone who could be seen could be killed. During the Battle for Atlanta, Confederate General Polk, along with other officers, rode into view of the Union lines. Union officers, even though they could not distinguish the individuals' identities, suspected they were high-ranking officers and decided to engage them with artillery as they were well out of rifle range. When the artillery fired, everyone in the group except General Polk quickly took cover. General Polk moved much slower than the others, as he did not want to appear cowardly, and was killed. During the Siege of Petersburg, long-range fire by the Union Army's heavy rifled siege artillery was normal. General Abbot, the commander of the siege artillery, repeatedly used a telescope to locate Confederate targets invisible to the eye and would then aim his heavy, rifled siege guns at the targets by using large objects surrounding them.[65] The combination of accurate long-range fire from rifled artillery and the fuzes developed for this purpose made the Civil War battlefield a more deadly place by extending the kill zone.

Another artillery organizational fact worth noting is the decrease in the number of different types of artillery as the war progressed. During the Battle of First Bull Run, the Union Army had eight different types of artillery, four types of smooth-bore and four types of rifled. By March of 1864, this number had decreased to five types, one type of smooth-bore and four types of rifles, with two of the rifled types being siege artillery. Sherman's armies in their March to the Sea limited their variations to three, one smooth-bore and two rifled. Major Thomas W. Osborn, the Chief of Artillery for the Army

Death of General Polk by a fragment from a rifled projectile. General Polk was killed by long-range artillery fire deliberately aimed at the group he was with (Library of Congress).

of the Tennessee, commented in September 1864 that "the armament was by far too varied for an army in the field, consisting of four calibers of rifled guns and three of smooth-bore...."[66] Major Osborn later wrote in the same report, "The armament of the artillery is reduced to two calibers of rifled and one of smooth-bore, and each battery has orders to complete the equipment of its battery in every particular."[67] One exception to this decreasing trend was Gettysburg, where the desperate Union Army used any artillery available, even if it was no longer a standard size or obsolete.

If the main field armies limited the types of cannons in their inventory, the question remains — what happened to the less desirable types? Less desirable cannons were assigned to secondary theaters of operation. The secondary theaters of operation were forced to deal with a large variety of different caliber and substandard-quality cannons. For example, the field artillery in the Union's Department of the Gulf in January 1863 consisted of 34 rifled and 32 smooth-bore guns. Of the rifled guns, 18 were obsolete rebored and rifled six-pounder guns.[68] Still, the department had a greater percentage of rifled artillery than smooth-bore artillery. Consequently, the need for reliable fuzes for rifled artillery did not dramatically decrease even in secondary theaters of operation. Military Departments in closer proximity to the means of production did not fare any better. In June 1863, the Union's Department of the Cumberland had 113 rifled and 99 smooth-bore guns. The variety of artillery pieces was substantially more than that contained in the major field armies. In addition, many were older, obsolete guns.[69]

The Confederacy faced the same problems the secondary Union theaters did — an increase in variety and use of obsolete ordnance. General Porter Alexander, at that time an ordnance officer in the Army of Northern Virginia, commented that in 1861:

> We had great trouble from the great variety of arms with which our troops were equipped both in small arms & artillery. Every regiment & every battery would have some apparently of all possible calibres & would want every possible variety of ammunition. They objected always to swapping, & the matter only got better materially in the fall of 1862 when we captured enough rifled muskets from the enemy & enough good guns to supply all our deficiencies. [We] first got [a] full supply after Chancellorsville.[70]

While the situation improved for the Confederacy, it was a relative improvement as immediately following Gettysburg, the Army of Northern Virginia had 12 20-pounder Parrots, 39 ten-pounder Parrots, 64 three-inch Rifles, two Whitworth Rifles, ninety-eight light 12-pounders, five 24-pounder howitzers, and twenty-one 12-pounder Howitzers.[71] There was probably an even greater variety of guns in the Confederate artillery as the report did not mention the six-pounder lost during the battle nor that the Confederate Army had 2.9-inch rifled guns mixed in with their three-inch rifled guns.

Another problem faced by commanders and artillerymen was the impact terrain had on the deployment of artillery batteries. In many battles visibility was limited due to vegetation and/or rolling terrain. One result of this was the continued need for large amounts of smooth-bore artillery due to its superiority with the close-range canister round. This aspect was noticed by the two visiting British officers, Gallwey and Alderson, who reported that the "large proportion of smooth bores is due to the fact that the latter is the best gun of the two for canister, and therefore better adapted to the nature of the country in which the fighting is carried on."[72] Brigadier General William Barry, Sherman's Chief of Artillery, also noted how vegetation and terrain limited the use of artillery especially in the western theater "where large tracts of uncleared land and dense forest materially circumscribe its field of usefulness and often force it into positions of hazard and risk."[73] General Grant went so far as to reduce the amount of artillery in the Army of the Potomac after the Wilderness and Spotsylvania as those two battles convinced him that the army had more artillery than could effectively be brought into action. Even when terrain allowed for artillery to fire at its longest effective range it was all too often very difficult, if not impossible, to determine where the projectile impacted.

As with the Army, the Navy's adoption of rifled artillery was not smooth. The Navy's 1860 *Ordnance Instructions* only gave ranges for smooth-bore guns because no United States ship was armed with rifled guns at that time. The start of the war and the need for rifled guns changed the armament ships carried. As an example, in 1861, the USS *Brooklyn's* armament consisted of 22 nine-inch Dahlgren smooth-bore guns, but by June of 1863, her armament was augmented by one 100-pounder Parrott rifle and one 30-pounder Parrott rifle. By the middle of the war, a mix of smooth-bore and rifled guns could be found aboard the vast majority of the Navy's ships and even some of the monitors. As a result of these changes, the Navy's 1864 *Ordnance Instructions* gave ranges for 13 different types of smooth-bore guns and seven different types of rifled guns.[74] After the war ended, the Navy continued arming most ships with a combination of smooth-bore and rifled guns for a number of years. Rifled artillery did not have as great an impact on the Navy due to severe technical difficulties associated with placing large-caliber, rifled guns onboard ships. The principle reason for this was that rifled artillery, especially large caliber rifled artillery, had a tendency for catastrophic failure. The problem was so serious that in 1864, the Joint Committee on the Conduct of the War conducted hearings on "the character and efficiency of the heavy ordnance."[75] While the catastrophic failure of a gun onboard a ship or in a fort

Gun crew of a Dahlgren gun at drill aboard the gunboat USS *Mendota* in 1864. The range of the new naval guns along with the destructiveness of exploding projectiles made wooden ships obsolete (National Archives).

would result in numerous deaths and injuries, a similar failure inside of a turret would completely disable that turret and potentially sink the ship.

An additional reason for the Navy not to use more rifled artillery was that the projectiles fired from them did not have a large enough advantage over smooth-bore projectiles when smashing iron plates. This was especially true at ranges in which a hit on a target would be certain from a gun being fired from onboard a moving ship. In 1863 the British Navy conducted experiments comparing the penetrating power of a 15-inch Rodman smooth-bore gun to various Woolwich rifled guns. The estimated striking power of the 15-inch Rodman compared to a nine-inch Woolwich rifled gun is shown in Table 5.1. On paper, the Rodman gun compared quite well to the Woolwich rifled gun, especially considering that battles between ironclad ships during the Civil War were at very close ranges. A correspondent of the *London Standard*, while not conceding any superiority of the American 15-inch gun, noted that "it is essential to know that the American 450-pounder smooth-bore guns

Table 5.1*— Total Energy Comparison between a Rodman
15-inch Smoothbore and a Woolwich 9-inch Rifled Gun

Range	Total Energy in Foot-tons	
	Rodman 15-inch Smoothbore	Woolwich 9-inch Rifled Gun
200 yards	4,215	2,943
500 yards	3,668	2,717
1,000 yards	2,967	2,393

*Report on a Naval Mission to Europe, especially devoted to the Material and Construction of Artillery, *Volume I, Appendix VI, page 259.*

could certainly hull our iron-cased vessels at 100 yards."[76] Although their future was limited, large smooth-bore guns still had their place during the Civil War considering the close ranges of that war's naval battles. In the end, safety and the ability to smash through iron plate helped convince the Navy that large smooth-bore guns were more desirable than large rifled guns.

Because the Navy had fewer rifled guns they needed fewer types of fuzes and, excluding the 24- and 12-pounder howitzer and all shrapnel (case shot) projectiles, every spherical shell projectile was armed with the Navy's Water Proof Time Fuze.[77] Still, problems with fuzes, especially paper fuzes, extended to the Navy. Lieutenant Commander Greer commented that "the fuzes used in the 42-pounder rifle shell are the army fuze and are not reliable."[78] He went on to criticize the Navy's time fuze when he said, "The 15-second navy fuze used in 9-inch shell, which we had, were not good, a number of them not bursting, although every precaution was taken in loading."[79] One problem was quality control, even though the Navy had always been careful in how and where they manufactured naval timed fuzes. In fact, the Navy's first *Ordnance Instructions* in 1852 through their fourth edition in 1866 stated that, "the fuzes for shell will be prepared at the laboratory in the navy yard at Washington, and distributed to other navy yards as they may be required."[80] In addition, the Navy's 1860 *Ordnance Instructions* specifically made each ship's captain responsible for his ship's fuzes by stating, "He (the captain) is to take care that special attention is paid to the fuzes, whether spare or in the shell; and if there be reason to suspect injury from dampness or any other cause, he will have one or more fuzes burned for trial."[81] Nevertheless, the Navy had problems with this fuze when it was used with rifled artillery. The Navy's 1866 manual stated that "the safety-plug should be removed when the Navy timefuze is used in rifled cannon, as recent experiments show that it is a probable cause of premature explosions of shells."[82] This procedure must have been used during the war as the safety-plug has not been found in any Navy projectiles disarmed by Civil War projectile collectors. This includes some spherical projectiles as well as projectiles used in rifled artillery.[83]

Defeating ironclad ships became a priority for the Navy as the war progressed, creating an interest in the development of a delayed fuze. The idea was that a projectile would punch through the iron protection and then explode once it was inside the ship. This was the same principle the Navy had been using for years with their time fuzes against wooden ships. Getting a mechanical fuze to have a delayed function was very difficult. Only two fuze-related patents, 28,084 and 37,557, state that the fuze was designed to explode after penetration. The Navy used neither of these patents, and no records have been found to show that the Navy even tested them. Creating a mechanical timing mechanism that had the proper delay was beyond mid–nineteenth century technology. Also, penetration of the armor plating was not guaranteed. In addition, both of these fuzes were designed for rifled projectiles, which the Navy made limited use of.

The fuze is a very small piece of equipment when compared to the totality of the artillery system. It is, however, a major contributor to artillery's overall effectiveness. By the time of the Civil War it had become, as stated by Charles Bormann, "the soul, the groundwork of any system of explosive projectile, ... the criterion of the system."[84] The mechanical fuze made it possible for rifled artillery to fire a projectile that would dependably explode at a longer range than the older flame-ignited fuzes. Inventors made numerous attempts to increase the range of the older flame-ignited fuzes by increasing their maximum burn time, but the problem of accurately determining the time of flight of the projectile at long ranges still existed. The mechanical fuze was the key to making rifled artillery a truly effective weapon, for without it the resulting increase in capability would have been much less. The American Civil War was the proving ground for these new mechanical fuzes. By the end of the war, fuzes had finished a period of rapid growth, but had yet to reach their full potential. The creation of the new fuzes depended upon the production triad of military need, technical availability, and industrial capability, but it was not a smooth process. Problems existed in manufacturing fuzes as well as problems in communication between the military, the inventors, and the manufacturers. In addition, unsuccessful designs outnumbered successful ones during this evolutionary process. Still, the new fuzes were crucial as the increased range of infantry rifles made long-range, explosive projectiles vital to the success and survivability of the artillery during the war. When combined with rifled artillery, fuzes changed warfare and increased the effective killing zone.

Six

The New Fuzes

The concept of failure is central to the design process, and it is by thinking in terms of obviating failure that successful designs are achieved.[1]
— Henry Petroski, 1994, Professor of Civil Engineering and History, Duke University

During the Civil War there was an exponential growth in fuze technology. Between January 1861 and December 1864, the United States issued 83 fuze-related patents compared to just eight for the five prior years. This growth was part of an increase in the number of artillery systems. In fact, the number of artillery systems increased to such an extent that the Army went back to the confusion of the pre–1849 publication of *Artillery for the United States Land Service*, which it published for the purpose of establishing a uniform artillery system. Henry Hunt, Artillery Commander for the Army of the Potomac, summed up the problems the Army faced during the war when he wrote, "The complication from which the Napoleon gun had relieved us — a great variety of ammunition — was brought back with the rifle-gun, for which different systems of experimental projectiles, Parrott, James, Schenkl, Hotchkiss, and 'Ordnance,' were supplied, which gave different ranges with the same charges of powder."[2] This complication extended to fuzes as different projectiles would only take certain fuzes.

In retrospect, order can be imposed on the 115 fuze-related patents issued by the United States between 1855 and 1872. (A list of all 115 patents along with detailed information on each patent can be found in Appendix A.) These patents can be broken down into seven major ignited/activated categories as shown in Table 6.1 and explained below.

- Flame-ignited fuzes were ignited by the flames created by the burning propelling charge and flashed after a set period of time;

Table 6.1—Fuze Related Patents 1855–1872

	Flame-Ignited Time	Concussion Time	Friction Time	Percussion Impact	Concussion Impact	Combination	Accessory
Number of Patents	17	8	1	43	13	29	4
Percent	14.8%	7.0%	0.9%	37.4%	11.3%	25.2%	3.5%

- concussion time fuzes were activated by the setback forces created when the gun was fired and flashed after a set period of time;
- friction time fuzes flashed when the friction wire was pulled;
- percussion impact fuzes flashed when the nose of the fuze impacted with a solid object;
- concussion impact fuzes flashed when the projectile hit an object no matter what the angle of impact;
- combination fuzes used at least two of the previous four methods; and
- fuze accessory patents, while dealing with fuzes, were not fuzes.

Percussion fuzes were the most popular type of fuze to patent, followed by combination, flame-ignited, concussion impact, concussion timed, and friction timed. Percussion fuzes were the most common type of fuze patent, as they were relatively easy to design. An individual with mechanical skills but no real knowledge of artillery projectiles and fuzes could design and patent one. However, many of the designs were unrealistic and never tested, much less used, by the military. Combination fuzes were the second most common type of fuze patent, even though they were much more difficult to design, because they provided multiple means of allowing the fuze to flash and explode the projectile. Unluckily, combination fuzes had a very poor success rate relative to other fuzes. The Schenkl Combination Fuze, one of the most common, only had a 55 percent success rate.[3] Still, at least one, the Sawyer Combination Fuze, was very reliable with a success rate of 85 percent.[4] Flame-ignited fuzes were well established and relatively reliable when the war started. Most of the flame-ignited fuze patents dealt with methods of improving existing ones, such as increasing the burning time of the Bormann Fuze. The Patent Office did not issue any flame-ignited artillery fuze patents between 1865 and 1872, probably due to the maturity of the technology and the realization that these fuzes were obsolete. Most accessory patents dealt with methods to improve a fuze's manufacturing process although one, Patent No. 34,040, was a hood that went on top of a flame-ignited fuze with the hope of better directing the flames to the fuze. Friction time fuzes were only used with hand grenades and are included as the inventor, John Adams, stated that the fuze could be used with other projectiles.[5]

A non-smoothed growth graph of the 115 fuze-related United States patents has the same shape as a Standard Logistic Pattern of Growth Curve. However, the 54 British fuze-related patents issued during the same time period do not as there was no traumatic disturbance to initiate a rapid change. The reason that the growth in United States fuze-related patents has this shape is that the start of the Civil War gave inventors the prospect of selling new fuze designs to the military due to its adoption of rifled artillery. As a result, a period of rapid acceleration in fuze design occurred. The growth curve levels out when the war ended as the Ordnance Department reasserted a systematic approach to weapon design and damped out the perceived opportunity for most inventors. In addition, the funds allocated to the military by Congress also decreased, especially for new weapons. The rapid increase in the number of fuze-related patents shortly after the start of the war was not unusual, as other nations have experienced this same phenomena during wartime. In Great Britain during the Crimean War time period, the number of patents relating to firearms doubled compared to the amount granted in the previous 250 years.[6]

Two dates stand out on the graph of United States fuze-related patents. The first, October–December 1861, is the quarter in which the rapid acceleration begins. The second, April–June 1865, is the quarter in which the rapid acceleration begins to slow. There was a time lag between the time an inven-

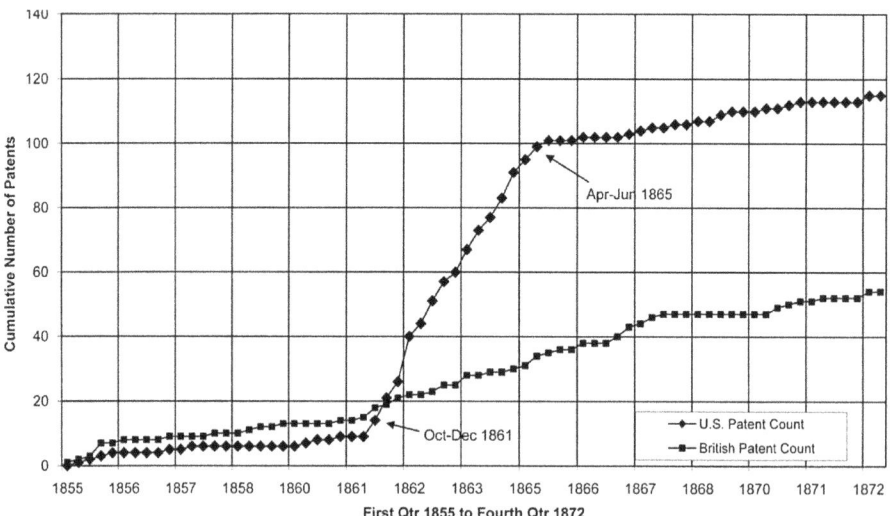

Cumulative number of United States and British fuze-related patents from 1855 to 1872. The rapid rise in the number of United States fuze-related patents was due to the war.

tor submitted a patent proposal and the Patent Office issuing the patent. Unfortunately, only a few of the fuze-related patents show the date when the inventor submitted the patent proposal. Consequently, a time lag of six months is the best possible estimate. Thus, rapid acceleration probably began in the spring of 1861, and the deceleration began in the autumn of 1864, with the leveling off occurring about two quarters, or six months, later. These dates coincide with the start of the war in April 1861 and with the realization that the South would lose the war by January 1865. In addition, by January 1865, the fuze weapon system had stabilized and the military was no longer adopting new fuzes.

A detailed study of fuze-related patents shows some common themes. Foremost, the locations of all the fuze-related patents issued between 1855 and 1872 highlights the concentration of patents in the industrial corridor between Boston and Washington. This is the same corridor in which most of the armories, arsenals, foundries, small arms manufacturers, and navy yards were located. There is a distinct interrelationship between fuze-related patents and the military industry located in this corridor. From this information it becomes obvious that a critical mass of both technical knowledge and industrial capability had developed in this region of the country. It was the combination of these two factors that made the rapid evolution of the artillery fuze possible.

Many of the patentees included in their proposals as many technical concepts as they could conceive, such as using the fuze with either muzzle or breech loading artillery as well as smooth-bore or rifled artillery. Along with this, some patentees applied for a number of patents simultaneously with only slight differences between each application. One person who used this technique was Benjamin Sturtevant. The Patent Office issued Sturtevant Patent Nos. 36,037, 36,038, and 36,039 all on the same day. Although there are differences between each patent, the differences are relatively minor. In addition, cost was of interest to the patentees, and in many of the patents statements were included on how much cheaper it was to manufacture their fuze than others of a similar design. As an example, W. S. Smoot stated in Patent No. 36,806 that "this fuse can be made cheaper than any other approximating to these advantages."[7] Safety was also a major issue, as many patentees implied that their fuze was safe no matter what the circumstance. Samuel R. Russell stated in Patent No. 37,200 that his fuze was "entirely safe from fire, as the fuse might ignite and burn out without exploding the shell, unless accompanied by a concussion so violent as it can receive by nothing less than contact with a powerfully-resisting object upon being discharged from a gun."[8] Russell later stated that a projectile "cannot fail to explode by means of my apparatus."[9] Many of the patentees, beyond Russell, gave unrealistic assur-

All United States fuze-related patents from 1855 to 1872. To simplify viewing, all of the patents within a 22-mile radius were consolidated in each dot. The largest concentration was in the arc between Boston and Philadelphia, the location of a large percentage of the prewar military industry.

ances that their fuzes would work every time. J. D. Henry stated in Patent No. 35,821 that "it is apparent from the foregoing that accidental explosion of a shell is avoided beyond peradventure, and on striking a target, its explosion is certain."[10] For many inventors, new fuze designs were only part of the patent with the other part being a projectile. They would imply that their fuze and projectile were a unique unit. Although many inventors understood the value of a good aerodynamically designed fuze, the vast majority of the fuzes were flat and thus not aerodynamically efficient. This attribute probably resulted from spherical projectile fuze design, where a flat fuze that did not protrude from the projectile was the optimum aeronautical design.

6. The New Fuzes

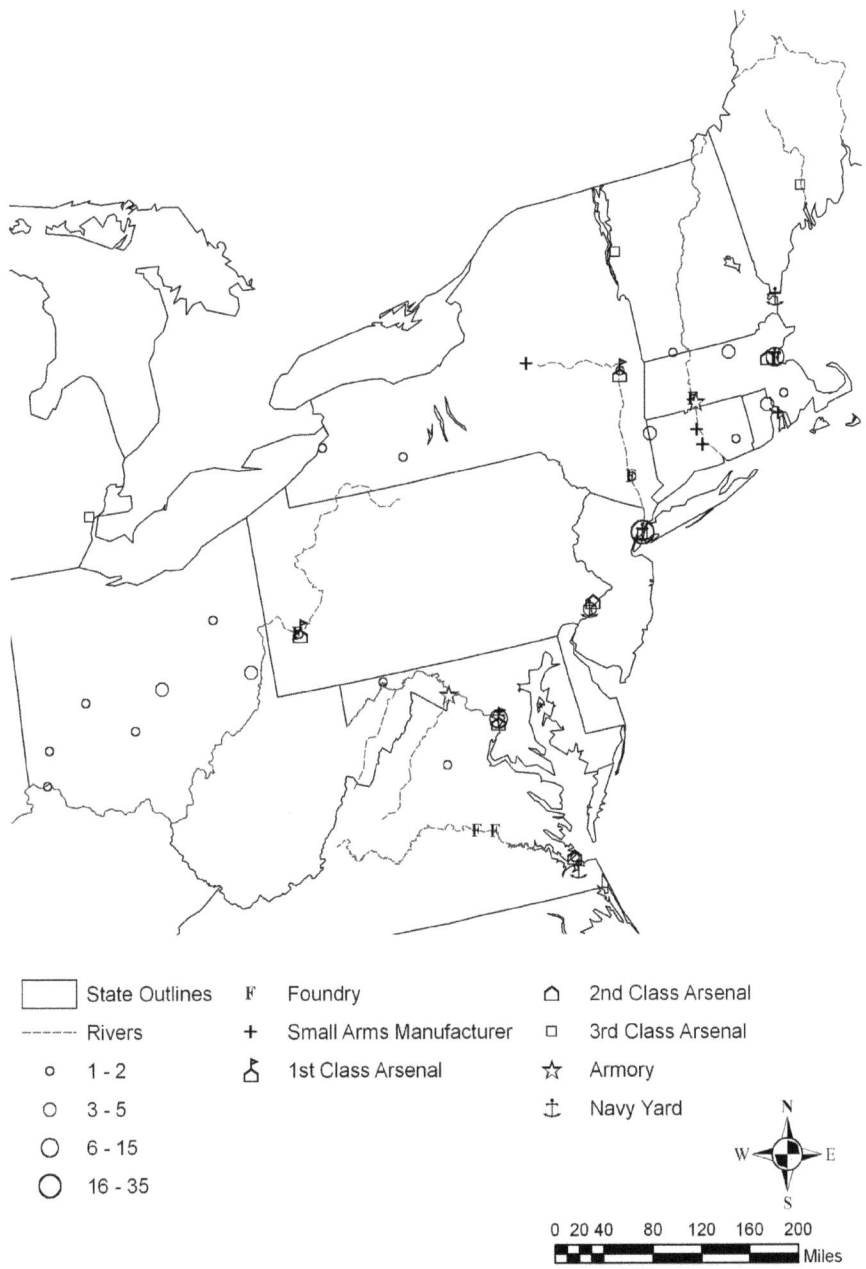

United States fuze-related patents from 1855 to 1872 and the Northeastern Military Industrial District. There was a close relationship between the number of fuze patents and the Northeast Military Industrial District.

As with any evolutionary path, there were dead-end designs. While each patent presented some new use of technology, all too often, individuals who designed the fuzes were not very knowledgeable about fuze technology. They also had limited if any contact with the men who would have to use or manufacture their invention. J.P. Rollins' Patent No. 34,268 was such a dangerous design that it is easy to understand why the military never tested it, much less used it. Rollins, trying to cover all possibilities, stated that the projectile "may be inserted at the muzzle or breech of the gun."[11] Rollins later stated in the patent "that ring C must be rammed by a hollow or concave rammer," which is an obvious requirement when the protruding rod is seen.[12] Although Rollins used a spring as a safety device, it is hard to imagine that any sane artilleryman would want to ram Rollins' projectile, even with a concaved rammer, knowing that if he depressed the projectile's protruding rod the fuze would detonate.

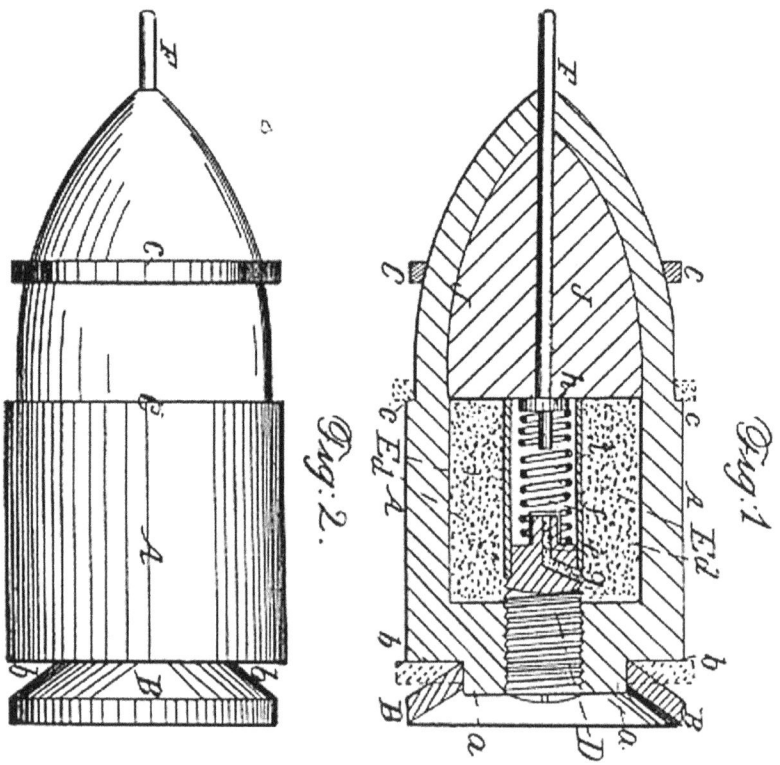

U.S. Patent No. 34,268 with its extremely dangerous protruding rod. No sane artilleryman would ever consider using such a projectile and fuze.

The military never tested most of the 115 patents issued between 1855 and 1872. Individuals with the right industrial connections designed most of the potentially promising fuzes. Still, this did not keep other inventors from trying various methods to gain the attention of government officials and decision makers. One of the most common methods was to send a letter requesting assistance to the President, Secretary of War, Chief of Ordnance, senators, congressmen, governors, ambassadors, or generals, and to include testimonials with the letter. Major Laidley, Commander of the Frankford Arsenal, responded to one letter by telling the individual that the Ordnance Department received so many requests to manufacture new inventions for testing that to do so would "require millions of dollars, and the services of more officers than it has got, to conduct the experiments."[13] Major Laidley informed the inventor that

> the Government depends more on the enterprize of its individual members, believing it to be the most economical to pay for inventions completed or perfected; leaving it to the enterprize of men of wealth to aid inventors instead of doing it itself. Whether this be good policy or not, it is the course it invariable pursues, and saves itself trouble at least by the adoption of this policy.[14]

General Barry, while Inspector of Artillery, received a model of a rifled artillery projectile from a friend of his brother. He wrote a very blunt letter to this person stating that he did not like the model, as it was nothing new. General Barry went on to say that one of his objections to the idea was that the "method of exploding the projectile by percussion is dangerous and uncertain."[15] The letters from Laidley and Barry must have discouraged these two would-be inventors, because neither received a fuze-related patent.

Only a limited number of inventors succeeded in getting their fuzes used by the military. Most of them were well-established inventors prior to the war with excellent connections to industry. John Bartleson in his *A Field Guide for Civil War Explosive Ordnance*, written for the U.S. Navy Explosive Ordnance Disposal School, lists fuzes by nine American inventors, while Charles Jones in his *Artillery Fuses of the Civil War* lists 12.[16] The difference in the number of inventors listed in the two books is due to Jones including John Cochran, John Dahlgren, and Sylvanus Sawyer. Cochran's original fuzes was a West Point style fuze, a percussion fuze that used friction as its only safety device, although he later patented one that substituted wires. Very few of these fuzes were produced, and they are rare battlefield finds.[17] Dahlgren's fuze was experimental, and only one has been found at the Washington Navy Yard's testing range.[18] Sylvanus Sawyer, brother of Addison Sawyer, invented a percussion fuze that did not function very well if the projectile struck its target with a glancing blow. This fuze is considered rare because the Sawyer designed projectile in which it was used is itself relatively rare.

Both Bartleson and Jones listed fuzes invented by John Absterdam, Francis Alger, George Ganster, Benjamin Hotchkiss, Charles James, Robert Parrott, Addison Sawyer, John Schenkl, and Issac Tice. John Absterdam manufactured projectiles and fuzes in New York City. Francis Alger owned the South Boston Iron Company, one of the two companies authorized to manufacture heavy artillery just prior to the war. It seems this was a family affair, as his father, Cyrus Alger, was the inventor of the Naval Water Cap Fuze. Benjamin Hotchkiss was the owner of Hotchkiss & Sons, which manufactured the Hotchkiss rifled projectile. Charles James was a manufacturer and politician who invented a method to convert smooth-bore cannons to rifled cannons, along with the necessary projectile. Interestingly, his firm did not do the work. Robert Parrott was the manager and part owner of the West Point Foundry, which also made Parrott projectiles and rifled artillery. Addison Sawyer and his brother Sylvanus Sawyer invented and manufactured a rifled artillery piece and projectiles, along with fuzes. John Schenkl was the inventor of the Schenkl projectile and fuze, and the South Boston Iron Company manufactured all of his projectiles and fuzes. George Ganster and Issac Tice do not seem to have any direct connection with an artillery projectile or gun manufacturer. While the military made limited use of Tice's fuze during the war, the Ganster Fuze does not appear to have been used during the war, and the photo in Jones' book is of the original patent model. The individuals who manufactured fuzes, projectiles, and cannon had the best chance of having their fuzes accepted into service.[19]

Just because an inventor had a strong manufacturing or military connection did not automatically mean that the military accepted and used his design. Some designs, such as the James Fuze, fell out of favor although they were initially well received. In addition, military officers, even though they were high-ranking Ordnance officers, were not guaranteed that their fuze would become widely used. General Alexander B. Dyer, future Chief of the Ordnance Department, designed a flame-ignited paper fuze adapter along with a rifled projectile before the war. However, his projectile fell out of favor due to its unreliability. Others, such as John Absterdam, had their fuzes tested but rejected because of poor results. Lieutenant Stockton tested some of Absterdam's projectiles and fuzes at the Washington Arsenal in January 1865 and reported that "the fuze plug in these are of soft metal and from their appearance have evidently been cast in a cold iron mould. The screw thread is very defective both in the plug and in the projectile."[20] Test firing of the projectiles was also a failure, as Stockton reported that "8 shots were fired. Three burst at the muzzle, in one case the shell itself being broken, but in the other two only the fuze plug was blown out and the shells proceeded on their course with a diminished velocity."[21]

Many inventors did not accept rejection and filed lawsuits over the rights to various fuze inventions. The longest legal battle was fought by lawyer and inventor William Hubbell and his heirs against the military to the rights of the Naval Water Cap Fuze. Hubbell claimed that the military made use of three of his patents without compensating him and requested that the government pay him $882,500. Congress referred his claim to the Court of Claims. In 1870, the court upheld his claims for Patents 26,904 and 34,059 and found that he was entitled to $66,666.66. Then, in 1874, Hubbell appealed to Congress for additional money and was awarded $33,333.33. These judgments occurred even though the military and the Alger family disputed Hubbell's claims to the Naval Water Cap Fuze.[22] Finally, in 1938, Hubbell's heirs appealed to Congress for an additional payment of $100,000. The Patent Subcommittee conducted a hearing on the matter, but took no action.

Numerous inventors relied on self-promotional pamphlets to extol the virtues of their projectiles and fuzes. In 1860, J. Webster Cochran published *Improvements in Ordnance, Firearms, and Projectiles*; in 1861, Hotchkiss and Sons published *Hotchkiss' Patent Projectiles for Rifled Ordnance*; and in 1862, John Schenkl published *Description of the Combination and the Concussion Fuze*. Beyond pamphlets, inventors attacked their competitors or defended their own inventions in their patent applications. John Schenkl, in Patent No. 33,495, and Benjamin Sturtevant, in Patent No. 36,039, criticized Armstrong's concussion fuze. Schenkl, comparing his method of securing the slider to the method patented by Armstrong, stated the latter's method "is seriously defective, as I have found by practical experience."[23] Sturtevant stated that his invention dispensed with Armstrong's "rotary head or screw-cap, and thus avoid all its disadvantages."[24] Sturtevant went on to say that Armstrong's rotary screw was expensive, implying that without it, a fuze would be cheaper to manufacture. William Hubbell, who had the long legal battle with the Alger family, attempted to assert a claim against other potential rivals in Patent No. 36,566 when he stated,

> I do not claim a central stem of plaster-of-paris cast into the composition and enlarged toward the inner end, as in Splingard's fuse, although the central fracturing-stem of metal was invented by me as early as 1848, as said Splingard's will not ricochet, is too large, and necessarily so, and is liable to premature fracture both in making and in flight, as it is formed in the composition, and consists of nothing but plaster-of-paris; nor a friable metallic fuse-stock, such as is exhibited in the Snoeck fuze.[25]

John Cochran believed his idea to eliminate the slider rebound problem in Patent No. 37,675 was superior to similar ideas because,

> All these devices in which non elastic or plastic material is relied on to prevent the rebound of the striker — as Lancaster's, Smith and Stetson's,

and Hotchkiss'—are liable to so spread and disfigure some part at the time of the discharge of the gun as to very seriously impair or absolutely prevent its action in striking, and this is especially the case in firing with heavy charges at very long ranges — the place where percussion shells are frequently most wanted.[26]

Smith and Steton's Patent No. 34,788, referred to by Cochran, appears to be the first attempt to solve the striker rebound problem, a problem that could result in a premature detonation of the fuze. Hotchkiss' Patent No. 35,611, also referred to by Cochran, stated that the safety wire that runs between the plunger (striker) and plug will act as a buffer and not allow the plunger to rebound. However, Hotchkiss later came to the defense of his patent. In Patent No. 37,756 Hotchkiss stated that it was an improvement upon his Patent No. 35,611 and criticized Smith and Steton's patent stating that since their striker was made of soft metal, it was liable to become deformed and wedged in the fuze plug. Hotchkiss continued by stating that his "improved hammer is very simple and cheap."[27] Despite this bickering, Hotchkiss and Smith remained friendly competitors, as evidenced by the fact that Smith was later one of the four co-holders of Patent No. 38,359, with Benjamin and Charles Hotchkiss, and G. Babcock.

Critical comments made by various inventors in their patents demonstrate the knowledge they had of European fuzes. For example, inventors claimed that their technological advances made their fuze superior to the British Armstrong and Lancaster fuzes. In contrast, the criticism of American patented inventions was relatively limited. This difference can probably be attributed to the Patent Office, because it is unlikely that it would allow an inventor to claim that the Patent Office supported his claim of superiority over another American patented invention. Along with technical superiority, many inventors perceived cost as being important. These inventors stressed the cost advantage of making their fuze when compared to similar fuzes. The Patent Office most likely viewed comments on the cost of an invention differently from negative comments on other inventions and allowed them to be included in the patent.

Inventors also used at least one other method to ensure that the military used their fuzes over their competitors. Prior to the war, the standard number of threads per inch for the Bormann, Navy Water Cap, and paper fuze adaptors was 12 threads per inch.[28] Some inventors, such as Parrott and Hotchkiss, stayed with this number, while Schenkl, Ganster, and Absterdam used a different standard. Schenkl's percussion fuze used 9, 10, or 12 threads per inch, and his early combination fuze used 14 threads per inch.[29] Ganster went to even finer threads and used 16 threads per inch on his fuze, and Absterdam utilized 11, 14, or 16 threads per inch.[30] Although the Army's and

Navy's Ordnance Departments had specifications for most military equipment, no written record has been found on specifications for mechanical fuzes. One possible explanation as to why inventors used different numbers of threads is because it was impossible to put a fuze threaded differently from the projectile into that projectile. This, of course, forced the military to use their fuze or, at a minimum, increased the cost of their competitor's fuze.

Even though the Patent Office issued 115 fuze-related patents between 1855 and 1872 to 86 people, Sylvanus Sawyer and the nine individuals listed by both Bartleson and Jones stand out. The Patent Office issued these 10 inventors 28 of the patents or roughly one quarter of the total. John Absterdam was issued one, Francis Alger three, George Ganster five, Benjamin Hotchkiss seven, Robert Parrott two, Addison and Sylvanus Sawyer four, John Schenkl five, and Issac Tice one. Only Charles James, who died in 1862, had no fuze-related patents. Thus, 11.6 percent of the patent holders controlled 24 percent of the patents during this 17-year span. The impact on fuze technology of these 10 inventors becomes even more obvious when the period between January 1861 and December 1864 is considered. During these years the Patent Office issued 83 fuze-related patents and the 10 individuals listed above controlled 25 of them. Thus, during the period of rapid change, a small group of people controlled 30 percent of the fuze-related patents. General Henry Abbot, Commander of the Union Siege Train during the Siege of Petersburg, confirmed the influence of these few people when he stated that, besides the wooden fuzes used in mortars and the adaptors used with the paper time fuzes, the siege train only used the Parrott, Schenkl, and Absterdam percussion fuzes, the Tice concussion fuze, and the Schenkl and Sawyer combination fuzes.[31] This handful of inventors controlled the fuze technology of the time and charted its rapid growth.[32]

As previously discussed, prior to the war, there were four main types of smooth-bore artillery projectiles — solid shot, case shot, shell, and canister. Only case shot and shell needed fuzes, and they both used timed fuzes. With the advent of rifled artillery, the number of types of projectiles did not increase, but variety in fuzes did. While case shot projectiles still needed a time fuze, a shell could now use either a time fuze or a fuze that flashed on impact. A delayed fuze was also needed for use in armor penetrating projectiles, but little progress was made in this area. In addition, there were combination fuzes that utilized one or more methods. Although Table 6.1 shows seven categories of fuze-related patents, it is possible to view the evolution of artillery fuzes during the Civil War as two major categories — time and impact.

Time Fuzes

The Bormann fuze, as previously described, was arguably the best flame-ignited, time, black powder fuze ever invented. The horizontal gunpowder layering aspect of the Bormann Fuze still remains in use as it eliminates the uneven burn rate of vertically packed gunpowder. Nevertheless, rifled projectiles did not commonly use the Bormann Fuze for two main reasons. The principle reason was that its design limited it to a five-second delay, far too short for the maximum range of rifled projectiles.[33] Also, the hole used to ignite the fuze was substantially smaller than the exposed powder on the paper time fuzes, making it much less likely to ignite in a rifled artillery tube, considering the reduced windage in a rifled piece. However, the paper time fuzes used in rifled projectiles had serious problems. Colonel Charles S. Wainwright, Commander of the 1st New York Artillery, noted in May of 1862 near Williamsburg: "The paper fuses did not work well with them (Confederate artillery) or us either, it being almost impossible to drive them without wetting the powder."[34] The Navy discovered that timed fuzes burnt with greater rapidity in a rifled projectile than in a smooth-bore projectile.[35] The Navy felt that this was caused by the air being forced onto the burning fuze as the projectile flew through the air. The Navy reasoned that this forced air had the same effect upon the fuze as if it was a hot ember and air was being blown upon it. Spherical projectiles did not experience this effect as they spun when they flew through the air, and the fuze was not subject to a continuous, direct flow of air.

Beyond the technical problems with the Bormann and paper fuzes, there were problems with their manufacture and employment. The Bormann Fuze was difficult to manufacture, because it required precision machining and high-quality workmanship, as the Confederacy discovered. Many times, it was difficult to determine whether poor manufacturing or poor employment caused the failure. The most common complaint with the Bormann Fuze was premature explosion of the projectile. It appears that at least some of the premature explosions were due to faulty employment of the fuzes by both Army and Navy cannoneers. One specific problem that the Navy had during the war was that their Sailors would cut too deeply when cutting into the fuze's powder train and slice through to the main charge. As a result, Admiral Porter issued General Order Number 55 to his fleet in May 1863 addressing the issue.[36] The problem was addressed Navy-wide in the Navy's 1864 *Ordnance Instructions*, which stated, "This fuze (the Bormann) should be carefully explained, as shells have been taken from guns with the cut made into the priming magazine, which would explode them at the muzzle."[37] In all probability, Army gunners were doing the same thing, but Army officers were not considering it a potential cause of premature explosions due to the Army's greater familiarity with the fuze. Another problem addressed by an Army of the Potomac Special Order was the need to ensure the Bormann fuze was tightly screwed down. If it was not, the possibility of a dangerous premature explosion existed.[38] As with any technical device, operator error can easily defeat the best design.

The other non-technical problems associated with the Bormann Fuze came from either how it was manufactured or assembled with a projectile. One regulation (which was not followed very well during the war) required arsenals to send samples of ammunition to the Washington Arsenal for testing. James Benton, while Commander of the Washington Arsenal, endorsed a report on projectiles and fuzes from the Watervleit Arsenal in July 1864 with the note, "As the enforcement of this regulation may be the means of correcting defects and avoiding complaints from Artillery Officers. I would call the attention of the Bureau to those omitting."[39] Benton further stated, "I would call the attention of the Dept to the importance of having all Bormann fuzes made alike at all the Arsenals. It seems from Lt. Prince's report that there is considerable difference between those made at this arsenal and those made at the Watervliet Arsenal."[40]

When inspectors at the Washington Arsenal were able to test ammunition from other arsenals, all aspects of the fuzes and projectiles were examined. Lieutenant William Prince's 4 May, 1864, report on a test conducted on some projectiles and fuzes from the Watervliet Arsenal demonstrates some of the manufacturing problems that could lead to a projectile's premature explosion.

> The casting was found defective, air holes and depressions existing which should instantly condemn a fuze in inspection and it appeared evident that the mold in some instances had not been sufficiently hot at the moment of casting. The india rubber washer inserted between the soft metal and the iron plug is not more than a quarter the thickness of that used at this arsenal and the iron plug was loosely inserted. It will be observed that the burning compound in these fuzes must have been correctly proportioned and well inserted for, unless the projectile burst in 1 or 2 seconds from defect in the plug it invariably exploded on time at 5 seconds. There were no intermediate explosions.[41]

The feedback these reports gave to the Watervliet Arsenal and the Ordnance Department did result in improvement. Lt. Prince's report on a later batch of 12-pound projectiles from the Watervliet Arsenal stated,

> The Bormann Fuzes had apparently under gone a more rigid inspection than the former ones as no defective castings were observed. It is to be remarked however that neither the fuze itself nor the iron plug underneath

> are as thick as the corresponding parts used at this post making an aggregate difference of about 1/8." The whole thickness of metal is thus not availed of in plugging the shell though no bursting to blow out the plug was observed. It may not be unimportant to note, in view of the number of Bormann Fuze Wrenches issued for tightening that the model adopted in the Watervleit Fuze cannot be fitted by the Wrenches made and issued at this post and adapted to our own model. The sheet india rubber washers used between the fuze and inner plug are still of thin material reported upon in May — but two thicknesses are now used.[42]

The problems this lack of uniformity created for the units in the field were relatively limited as artillerymen seldom needed to unscrew a Bormann Fuze. However, the problems this would have created for ordnance officers who, upon occasion, had to disarm the projectiles, would have been significant. Lack of uniform, quality manufacturing was a significant problem, and although interchangeability had been achieved, it was far from a universal standard.

The paper fuze had a different set of problems from the Bormann Fuze. Brigadier General William Barry, Chief of Artillery, wrote to Brigadier General Ripley, Chief of Ordnance, in June 1862, "The fuses most complained of are the paper-case time fuse."[43] Paper fuzes were not as reliable as the Bormann Fuze since they were not weatherproof, had a tendency to be thrown out of spherical projectiles after they were fired, and did not burn consistently. This last problem was mainly due to the vertical layering of the powder by increments in contrast to the one-press horizontal powder train used in the Bormann Fuze. The Navy had the same problems, but they controlled the problem by manufacturing all of their Navy Watercap Fuzes at the Washington Navy Yard. The Army, in contrast to the Navy, manufactured paper time fuzes at a number of different arsenals. However, the increasing complaints about the quality of these fuzes led the Ordnance Department to issue a circular in 1862 that stated, "To secure uniformity in size and rate of burning, it is the intention of this Department, that all paper time fuzes shall hereafter be made at one place viz: Frankford Arsenal."[44] Consequently, as the war progressed, the number of complaints about the Army's paper timed fuzes decreased.

Ultimately, the paper timed fuze was never truly effective in rifled cannon. In April 1865, Captain Julius Hadley of the 25th Ohio Battery conducted a three-day field research test of various fuzes in Little Rock, Arkansas. When commenting on the paper time fuze he reported,

> I am of the opinion that the paper case fuze will never be reliable for a rifle projectile with so little windage as the Hotchkiss Patent for I cannot believe after my own experience and from observation of the firing of other batteries that there is an absolute certainty that the discharge of the piece will ignite the fuze.[45]

Hadley based his comments on the fact that during his test, 20 out of 37 case shot projectiles failed, for a 54 percent failure rate.[46] What makes Hadley's comments even more interesting is that by this time in the war, the Hotchkiss projectiles had three grooves cut in them to allow the flame from the propelling charge to reach the fuze. This was a feature other projectiles did not have, and if it was difficult to light the fuze with grooves cut into the projectile, it would have been even more difficult without them.

Beyond manufacturing and employment problems, the main problem the military experienced with time fuzes was how to create one that combined the reliability and ease of use of the Bormann with the longer burning time of the paper fuzes. An improved fuze was critical because artillery's range had increased beyond the five-second burning time of the Bormann Fuze. In addition, the expanding sabot used with rifled artillery did not allow the flame created by the propelling charge to reach the fuze for a long enough period of time to ensure ignition. Three different methods were tried by inventors: improvement of current fuze technology, creation of new fuzes, and modification of the projectiles.

Improving the current technology (Bormann Fuze) was limited due to its high level of technical sophistication. Still, inventors attempted to increase the amount of flame that would reach the fuze as well as the amount of time the Bormann Fuze would burn. The Patent Office issued two patents, 34,040 and 47,231, for "fuze hoods" that tried to increase the amount of flame that reached the fuze. The purpose of both inventions was to put a hood over the fuze to direct the flame to the fuze, in theory increasing the chances of ignition. While these hoods were manufactured, the military used neither type to any extent. The problems with such a hood were twofold. First, it had to be put on the projectile just prior to firing. If the hood was on the projectile during transport, it could become so damaged and tightly pressed against the projectile that flames would never reach the fuze. Or, when the projectile was rammed into the cannon, the ramrod could press the hood down upon the projectile, preventing flames from reaching the fuze. In the final analysis, the fuze hood was an impractical idea.

Inventors made at least two attempts to increase the burning time of the Bormann Fuze. George Wright's Patent No. 45,381 increased the burning time to 12 seconds, and Benjamin Hotchkiss's Patent 72,494 included a 14-second Bormann Fuze as part of a combination fuze. These attempts ended in a number of shortcomings. Space was the primary problem, as the Bormann Fuze required a horizontal track. There was a limit to the length of a track that a certain diameter fuze could fit. Consequently, the smaller projectiles that used the larger Bormann Fuze had to have a flat nose, and thus lost aerodynamic efficiency. Even though these inventions gave the Bormann

Fuze a longer burn time, the dilemma of ensuring ignition of the fuze when used on a rifled projectile still existed.

The Navy developed a different system of dealing with long-range gunnery for its large 15-inch spherical projectiles and in the process gained the additional benefit of reducing the amount of time required to load the guns. Initially the Navy only used one fuze with its 15-inch projectiles but changed to three fuzes sometime during the war. The Navy's 1866 *Ordnance Instructions* stated:

> All XV-in. shell shall be fitted with three fuze-holes, and issued for service fuzed with 3½, 5, and 7 seconds fuzes. When the distance of the object is known to be less than the range of the shortest fuze, and time will admit of doing so, uncap all the fuzes. At other times uncap the fuze suited to the distance, and the one of the longest time of burning.[47]

By adopting this policy, the Navy ensured there would be at least two fuzes that could possibly ignite in all cases, except at a very long range of over 2,000 yards.[48] In addition, the projectiles would have their fuzes already in place and the gunner would not have to take time to put the fuzes into the projectile.

The development of new fuzes was another possible solution to the operational failure of the prewar time fuzes. Inventors developed two new types of time fuzes: concussion activated and combination. Concussion time fuzes were activated by the force created when the gun was fired. The most common design was for the setback forces to break something in the fuze, which in turn would ignite a powder train set to burn for a period of time. Combination fuzes used at least two different methods to help increase the chances of the fuze flashing. Concussion time fuzes were more difficult to design than combination fuzes, as evidenced by the fact that there were only seven concussion time fuzes patented. All of the 29 combination fuzes patented used some sort of timing mechanism as one means of igniting the fuze.

Although Benjamin Hotchkiss held two of the seven concussion fuze patents, the military did not use any of them. While no mention has been found for the reasons why the military did not make use of these fuzes, some suppositions can be made. The primary problem was that most of these patents do not mention a method of controlling the length of time that the fuze would burn. This fatal error eliminated these fuzes from any real consideration. In addition, based on the patents, these fuzes would have been much more complicated to manufacture than most other fuzes. It is doubtful if these fuzes could have been manufactured in large enough quantities and sufficient quality at a reasonable cost. Frederic Toggenburger's Patent No. 47,586, which employed a clock mechanism, is such an example — complex, costly, and difficult to manufacture. However, Toggenburger's design was one that the military would use in the future. It was just too advanced a concept for the Civil War time period.

Combination fuzes were more numerous than concussion time fuzes, and more successful. Table 6.2 breaks combination fuzes into five different categories based on how they operated. The first three categories — Flame/Percussion, Flame/Concussion Impact, and Concussion Time/Percussion — were the most popular. However, the only three that are known to have been used by the military are the Schenkl Combination Fuze, Sawyer Combination Fuze, and Hotchkiss Combination Fuze. Both the Schenkl Combination Fuze (Patent Nos. 35,897 and 39,682) and the Sawyer Combination Fuze (Patent No. 38,699) worked in a similar fashion.[49] When the cannon was fired, setback forces would break a safety device and allow a striker to hit an explosive fulminate composition which in turn would ignite the powder train. The length of time the powder train would burn had been previously set by the gunner either mechanically for the Schenkl or by piercing a hole for the Sawyer.

If the time fuze did not work on the Sawyer Fuze before impact, a direct impact would crush a fulminate ring, which would ignite the main charge. If the time function of the Schenkl Fuze did not work before impact, a direct impact would drive the interior of the fuze forward exposing the main charge to the flame. In either case, there was an increased chance of an explosion. Although the explosion of a case shot projectile caused by an impact would not create any casualties it would, at least, keep the enemy from reusing the projectile.

Both the Schenkl and Sawyer combination fuzes had a long range. The Schenkl combination fuze could burn for 10 seconds, and the Sawyer combination fuze could burn for seven-and-a-half seconds. Abbot's field research tests at Petersburg gave the Sawyer Combination Fuze an 85 percent success rate but only gave the Schenkl Combination Fuze a 55 percent success rate.[50] Abbot complained that Schenkl's fuze was made out of a soft metal which was "liable to melt in about seven or eight seconds, and hasten the time of explosion accordingly."[51] Inasmuch as these flat-faced fuzes protruded in front

Table 6.2 — Combination Fuze Related Patents, 1855–1872

	Flame/ Percussion	*Flame/ Concussion Impact*	*Concussion Time/ Percussion*	*Flame/Percussion/Concussion Impact*	*Concussion Time/ Concussion Impact*
Number of Patents	8	7	9	2	3
Percent	27.6%	24.1%	31.0%	6.9%	10.3%

of the projectile by a number of inches, they were subject to a buildup of heat generated by the friction of flying through the air. The difference between the two fuzes in regard to this problem was that Sawyer's fuze was brass while Schenkl's fuze was zinc, which had a lower melting point. It also needs to be noted that both fuzes required extensive preparation compared to other fuzes. Consequently, gun crews needed to be well trained in the operation of these fuzes if there was to be any hope of either fuze operating properly.

The Hotchkiss Combination Fuze worked differently from either the Schenkl or the Sawyer Combination Fuze. The Hotchkiss fuze was a combination of a 14-second Bormann Fuze and a Hotchkiss Percussion Fuze. Consequently, it was dependent upon the flames from the propelling charge to ignite the timed fuze. However, if the time fuze failed, the percussion fuze would explode the projectile if the nose of the projectile made a direct impact. Abbot did not test this fuze, and there is no data on its effectiveness. It was developed later in the war than either the Sawyer or Schenkl fuzes and not used as much. One drawback with this fuze, as was common with many of the fuzes, was that it was not aerodynamically efficient. This inefficiency was due to the size of the flat Bormann Fuze that protruded from the nose of the projectile.

The last method of improving the performance of time fuzes was modifying the projectiles. Inventors utilized a variety of different techniques but the military never employed most of them. The Patent Office issued a

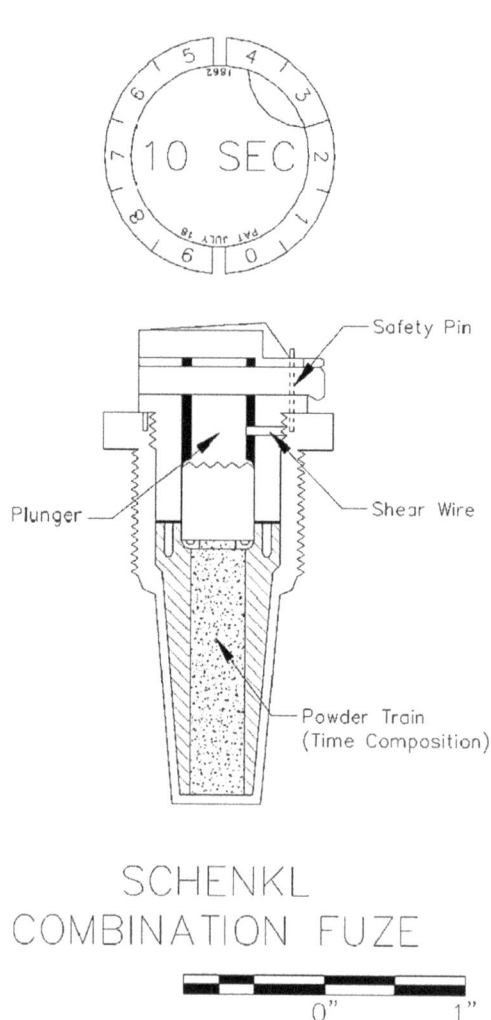

Schenkl Combination Fuze, a complex fuze that all too often prematurely detonated.

number of patents that created different methods of getting the flame to the fuze. Some, such as Patent Nos. 36,468, 43,922, and 46,965, extended a tube from base to front main fuze in the front of the projectile. Patent No. 43,801 added a primer to the fuze, while Patent No. 49,326 put the fuze hole on the side of the projectile and Patent No. 34,602 put the fuze in the base of the projectile. Benjamin Hotchkiss's modified projectile was the most common solution as his projectile and fuze were widely used by the military. Hotchkiss cut grooves in the expanding lead sabot that would allow easier passage of the flame. However, Parrott's projectiles were not modified and when armed with the Parrott Percussion Fuze had a 75 percent success rate based on Abbot's tests.[52] Thus, most of these projectile modifying patents were not needed as the widely used Hotchkiss projectile was easily modified, and a modification did not appear to be necessary on Parrott projectiles.

In the final analysis, the wartime changes developed by inventors to overcome time fuzes' operational failures did not work. The ideas existed, but manufacturing was not yet capable of producing the quality of work needed to transform these concepts into reality. Time fuzes, along with case shot projectiles, continued a slow but steady decline, and were not revived by the military until the advent of the airplane and the need for timed antiaircraft projectiles. Even then, the military only revived the fuze, but not case shot. In retrospect, it is safe to say the effectiveness of antiaircraft fire was limited until the invention of the variable time fuze during World War II. The variable time fuze also revived the case shot projectile, although under a different name, as it allowed a projectile to explode a set distance from the target even when the gunner could not see the target.

Impact Fuzes

Impact fuzes were used with shells, hollow projectiles filled with gunpowder. These fuzes gave artillerymen the ability to explode a shell on the ground at the point of impact. In addition, if the projectile did not hit the desired location, it was easier to determine where the round impacted and adjust the artillery fire than to adjust for a projectile that exploded in the air. However, these fuzes were untested in combat, and numerous flaws that negatively affected their operation soon appeared. One problem faced by artillerymen was that a rifled projectile armed with a percussion fuze had to hit a solid object nose first if it was to properly operate. Thus, if a rifled projectile tumbled, the chances of an impact fuze working decreased tremendously. Consequently, a feedback loop was critical in the continued development of these fuzes and their projectiles.

Although the military used percussion, combination, and concussion fuzes as impact fuzes, the operation of a Schenkl Percussion Fuze is the best example of how an impact fuze operated. The Schenkl Percussion Fuze was chosen because it had the best safety features of all the percussion fuzes, and the military used this fuze throughout the war. In addition, its original design was so superior that very few changes were made in the fuze during the war. The Schenkl Percussion Fuze had two safety features rather than the one that most fuzes had. The first safety device, similar to those on other percussion fuzes, was a threaded screw that fixed the slider in place until setback forces broke it free. One advantage the Schenkl Percussion Fuze had with its version of this safety device was that Schenkl designed it to break off smoothly. A smooth break was critical because a rough break could leave debris which could interfere with the movement of the slider. The second safety device was the anvil. The anvil had a concave side and a flat side. In the fuze's factory

1. Before placing the projectile into the cannon, the anvil is reversed—arming the fuse.
2. The shock of the cannon's firing causes the slider to move to the rear, breaking the safety screw.
3. Upon impact, the slider moves forward, allowing the percussion cap to strike the anvil. This creates a flash, igniting the powder train which in turn ignites the powder in the bursting chamber.

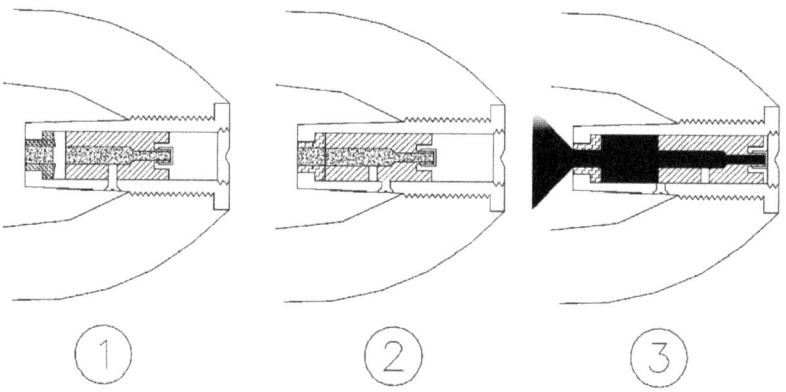

HOW A SCHENKL PERCUSSION FUZE WORKS

NOT TO SCALE

How a Schenkl Percussion Fuze works (drawing was inspired by one at the National Park Museum at Gettysburg).

configuration the concave side faced the slider. Thus, if the primary safety device, the screw, broke in transit the now free-moving slider and its percussion cap could not hit the anvil and detonate the fuze. This also gave the Schenkl Percussion Fuze another advantage over other percussion fuzes. If the battery commander ordered a gun crew to use solid shot, all the gunner had to do was to make sure that the anvil remained in the safe position.

The Parrott Percussion Fuze went through a number of modifications during the war. Initially, Parrott's percussion fuze used the West Point style without a safety device. This type of fuze was too dangerous, and Parrott added various safety devices. However, none of them seemed to have worked as well as Schenkl's. Brigadier General John Turner, Chief of Artillery for Major General Gillmore in South Carolina, reported in November 1863:

> Two kinds of percussion fuses were used, both of Parrott's invention. In the one, to the plunger is attached two metallic prongs for retaining it in a fixed position for transportation, and which are designed to be wrenched off by the rifle motion of the projectile in the first moments of flight, before the inertia of the plunger is overcome; in the other, the plunger is kept in position by a wooden washer over the nipple, and which is broken by the concussion when the projectile strikes. The metallic prongs in the former were found to be too stiff to be always wrenched off, as it is expected they will be, or, when broken off, they caught the plunger and retarded its motion sufficiently to prevent its striking with a force necessary to explode the cap. It therefore became necessary to take off these prongs before inserting the fuse in the shell. In this shape, this kind of fuse was used exclusively.[53]

Turner's report is important for three reasons. Foremost, users wrote extensive reports that emphasized the problems they were having and solutions they were attempting. Based on changes that the inventors and manufacturers made, the information contained in the reports must have reached them, and they, in turn, responded and corrected the deficiencies. Also, the units in the field were willing to modify equipment that was not functioning as expected. Last, artillery units could have a number of variations of the same type of fuze at any one time. This had an advantage in that it allowed the user to actively compare variations.

The Hotchkiss Percussion Fuze was also one of the most common percussion fuzes used during the war. Like the others there were a number of variations. The first Hotchkiss Percussion Fuze had the same basic West Point design as the Parrott Percussion Fuze. However, when it became obvious that a safety mechanism was necessary, Hotchkiss used a different safety system from either Schenkl or Parrott. Hotchkiss's safety system consisted of a safety wire connected to the slider. Hotchkiss had two versions of his safety system with the difference being how the safety wire was connected to the slider.

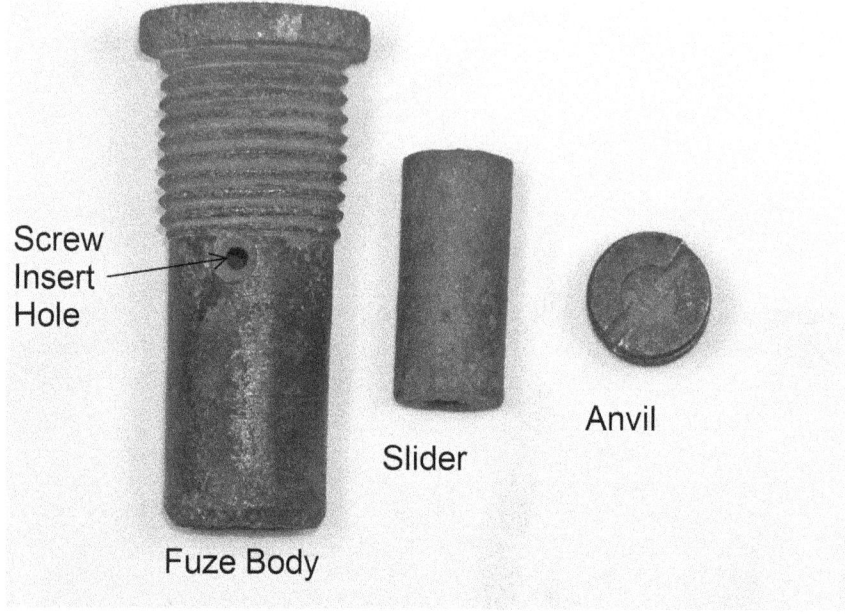

A Schenkl Percussion Fuze found on a battlefield (author's collection).

Hotchkiss also added an anti-bounce mechanism in his later designs. The Hotchkiss Percussion Fuze operated in the following manner. When the cannon was fired, setback forces moved the slider to the rear of the fuze which forced the safety plug out of the fuze body and released the safety wire. This opened up the base of the fuze so that the flame from the percussion cap could reach the main powder charge. When the projectile hit something hard enough to force the slider to move forward, the percussion cap would strike the anvil and explode. Based on the fuze's design, there were probably instances of the safety plug blocking the hole after it had been forced out as there was only a very limited amount of room for it in the cavity of the projectile. However, there are no reports about this problem.

Another type of impact fuze was the concussion impact fuze. Although invented prior to the war, the military only used a few during the war. The key advantage that concussion impact fuzes had over percussion impact fuzes was that a deflecting hit would still explode the projectile. Consequently, both rifled and smooth-bore projectiles could use these fuzes. Of the eight patented concussion time fuzes, the military only used the Tice Concussion Fuze. It was a good fuze as Abbot's field research tests gave it a 73 percent success rate. One problem with this fuze was that its operation and manufacture were more complex than the competing percussion fuzes. The fuze's arming stage

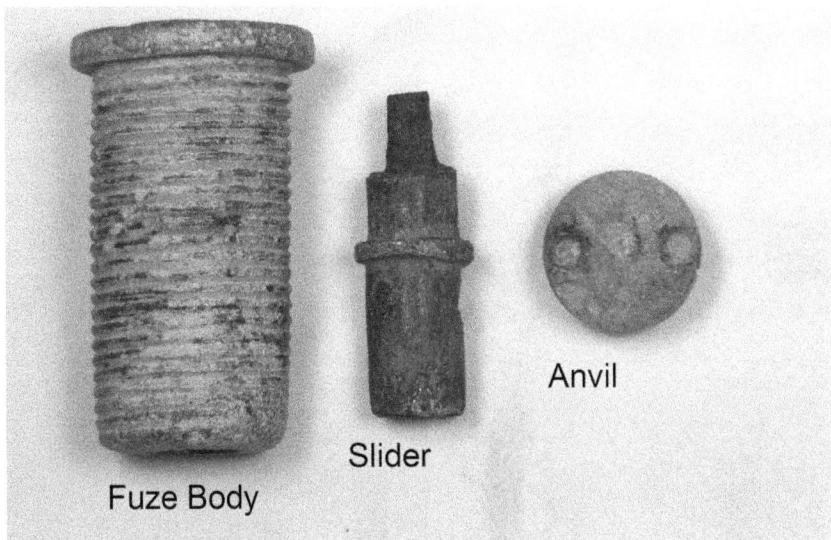

A Parrott Percussion Fuze found on a battlefield (author's collection).

was the same as other impact fuzes — when the cannon fired, setback forces broke the supports holding the spring in place. The similarity ended there as the movement of the spring uncovered the fulminate-filled glass vial, exposing it to the loose shot contained within the fuze. Once the vial broke, the fulminate flashed, igniting the powder in the fuze which in turn blew out the diaphragm. Assembling and manufacturing this fuze would have been more costly than a percussion fuze due to the additional parts and the quality machining they required. In addition, with only one safety device of cotton surrounding the vial to prevent accidental breakage, transporting this fuze would have been hazardous.

All of this does not mean that Southern inventors were not equally busy inventing new mechanical fuzes and rifled projectiles. Junius Archer, owner of the Bellona Foundry, and John Reed, two of the more famous southern ordnance inventors, were just as competent as their northern counterparts. However, the efforts of the southern inventors did not have the same impact for the Confederate cause as the northern inventors did for theirs. The reason was, again, the lack of an industrial base capable of producing high-quality machined parts.

The fuzes, especially the mechanical fuzes, used at the end of the war were superior to those fuzes used at the beginning of the war. Inventors listened to and responded to complaints from the field. Fortunately for the Union, its industrial base was able to make quality fuzes and modify them as

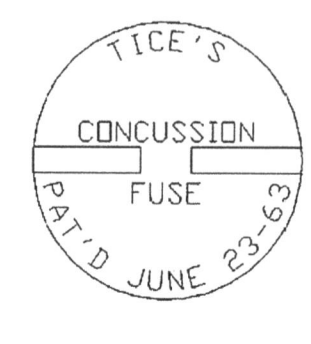

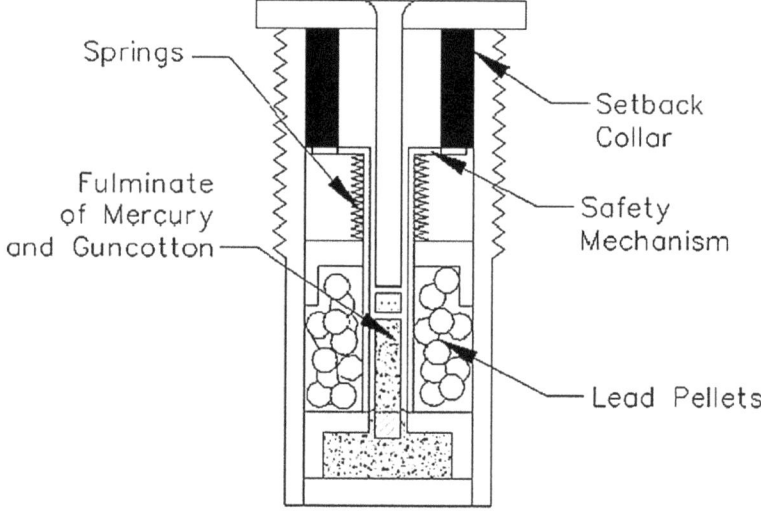

TICE CONCUSSION FUZE

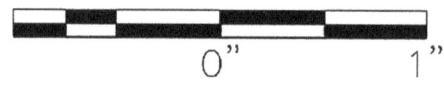

Tice Concussion Fuze. The only concussion fuze used by the Union during the Civil War.

needed. Although the modified fuzes used at the end of the war did not meet all of the criteria the military desired, they were far superior to anything that existed when the war began. The range and accuracy of rifled artillery combined with the deadliness of the new fuzes made the Civil War the first war in which if a person could be seen, he could be killed. There were no safe places on the battlefield.

Seven

Hotchkiss, Parrott, and Schenkl

It is a fact well known to artillerists and those skilled in the use of ordnance that a good and reliable fuse for a projectile or shell, one which is safe for transportation and free from defect, is a desideratum which has long existed.[1]

—John P. Schenkl, 1861

The three principle Union fuze and projectile inventors during the Civil War were Benjamin B. Hotchkiss, John P. Schenkl, and Robert P. Parrott. These three men were well connected to the military and industry prior to the war in addition to being ordnance experts. The evolution of the fuze during the Civil War can be traced by closely studying the changes in their fuze designs as each man faced the same problems. The common problems that all three dealt with were designing a safety device, reducing rebound, keeping the orifice from the fuze to the main charge open, and ensuring that the slider would be free to move. They also faced other problems that did not deal with the design of their fuzes, including getting their projectile to take the rifling, ensuring that the percussion caps worked, and training artillerymen to properly use their fuzes. Unfortunately, it took the hard school of combat to reveal some of these problems.

Benjamin B. Hotchkiss was one of the younger brothers of Andrew Hotchkiss who, unfortunately, died when he was 35 in 1858 before he had an opportunity to demonstrate his full inventive ability with the opportunities the war presented. Andrew was probably more inventive than his brother but a physical disability limited his activities and shortened his life. Still, he patented the initial design for the famous Hotchkiss projectile. In all likelihood Benjamin benefited from his older brother's guidance and genius. However, Benjamin was quite brilliant in his own right and was responsible for making revisions to the Hotchkiss projectile as well as to the Hotchkiss fuze as wartime field experience revealed flaws in the designs.

Between 1862 and 1867 Benjamin Hotchkiss received seven fuze-related patents. Four were for percussion fuzes, one was for a flame-ignited fuze, two were for time fuzes that were not flame-ignited, and one was for a Bormann and percussion combination fuze. Table 7.1 shows a timeline of Hotchkiss's patents as well as whether the military used them. Hotchkiss's first patent was for a wire safety device and a method of keeping the main powder charge from plugging up the fuze. There must have been problems with this arrangement either in the field or in manufacturing, because about eight months later Hotchkiss received another patent changing the arrangement and adding an anti-rebound mechanism. However, this design must not have worked as well as his other percussion fuze designs,

Andrew Hotchkiss, an inventive genius and older brother of Benjamin Hotchkiss (courtesy of the Sharon Historical Society, Sharon, Connecticut).

since there have not been any known field recoveries of this fuze. Hotchkiss's 1863 percussion fuze patent must have solved his problems with this type of fuze as his next four patents mainly dealt with case shot projectiles. Hotchkiss's last patent was a combination flame-ignited and percussion fuze that could be used with case shot or shell. The military did use this fuze to a limited extent during the latter part of the war. One possible reason for this combination on a case shot projectile was that if the time fuze did not work, the percussion fuze would, and as a consequence make the projectile unusable by the enemy.

John P. Schenkl was another inventive genius who, like Andrew Hotchkiss, died relatively young, when he was 38, in March 1864 in Germany. His early death, combined with the extended illness that preceded it, limited his contributions and opportunity to perfect his fuzes and projectiles based on information gained from wartime usage. Still, he was a very prolific inventor and received five fuze-related patents as shown in Table 7.2. In addition, he had a number of other patents beyond his fuze patents, and it is difficult to say what else he would have invented if he had lived longer.

Schenkl did not own his own factory, as Hotchkiss and Parrott did, but he did have a close relationship with the South Boston Foundry, owned by the Algers, which manufactured all of his fuzes and projectiles. Schenkl started out with the best percussion fuze design and maintained this superiority with his solution to eliminate bounce back. As with Hotchkiss, Schenkl worked to perfect his percussion fuze while working on a fuze that could be used with a case shot projectile. Schenkl's projectile was also unique in that its sabot was made of papier-mâché which meant that if the sabot separated from the projectile it would not harm anyone.

Robert Parrott was probably not the genius that Schenkl or Hotchkiss were. However, he understood military needs as well as manufacturing and foundry capabilities. Parrott's fuzes, projectiles, and cannons were not the best but they were more than adequate and produced in massive quantities. His loyalty to the Union was unquestionable, and he was more than willing to listen to complaints from the field and try to determine what could be done to fix a problem.

Parrott received two fuze-related patents and, as with Hotchkiss and Schenkl, neither his personal nor business papers have been located. Parrott's first fuze-related patent, No. 33,662, was a flame-ignited fuze that ignited the main charge when the projectile impacted on its nose if it had not already exploded. However, it was never used by the military. Parrott's second fuze-related patent, No. 41,937, was a percussion fuze that used centrifugal force to break the safety prongs. As noted previously, this was the same fuze that General Turner reported breaking the safety prongs off so that the fuze would work. Unfortunately, with only two patents, it is not possible to determine how Parrott's fuzes evolved. Luckily, relic hunters have found a large number of Parrott's fuzes, and from their finds,

Benjamin Hotchkiss, inventor of the Hotchkiss, Percussion Fuze (courtesy of the Sharon Historical Society, Sharon, Connecticut).

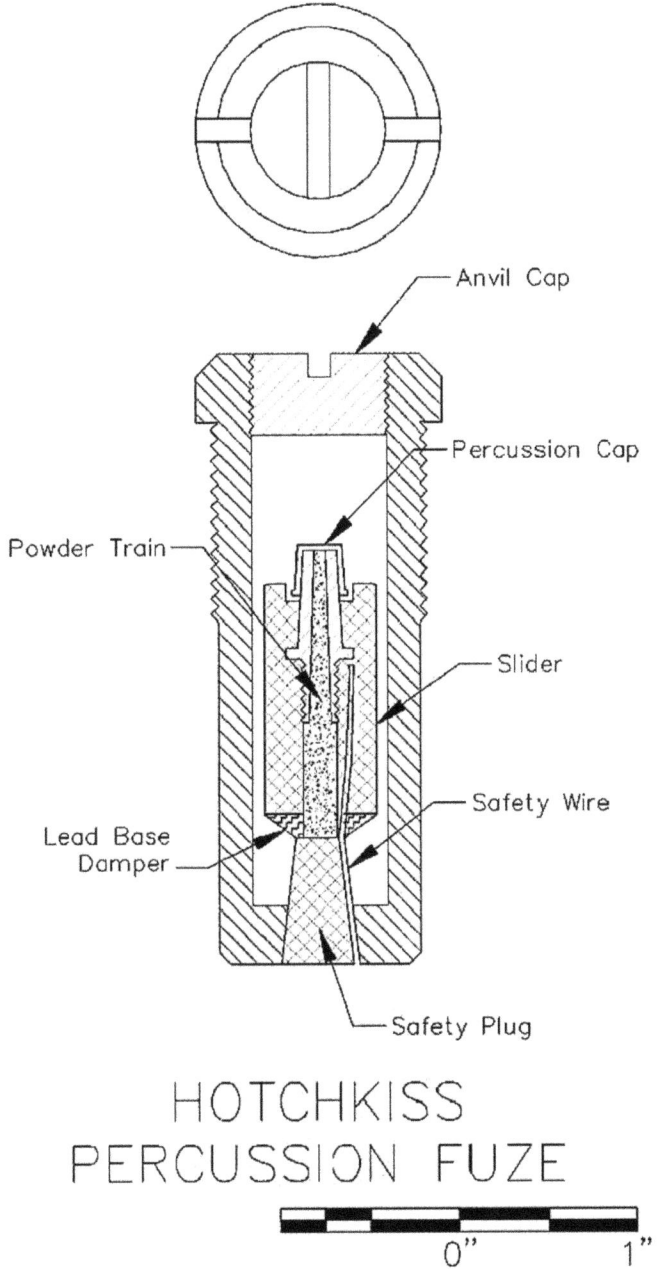

Hotchkiss Percussion Fuze. This design incorporates all of Hotchkiss's improvements.

Table 7.1—Hotchkiss Fuze Patents

Patent Number	Month & Year of Issue	Features	Status
35,611	Jun 1862	Percussion—used wire safety device and plug to keep the main powder charge from plugging the fuze	Used by the military.
36,465	Sep 1862	Percussion—used balls as the slider and safety device.	No known field recoveries.
37,756	Feb 1863	Percussion—improvement on 35,611, changed how safety wire is connected and added an anti-rebound mechanism.	Used by the military.
38,359	Apr 1863	Flame-ignited—bursting charge at rear of projectile.	Mainly dealt with the location of the bursting charge but key to success was the extended fuze train leading to the bursting charge. Used by the military
42,660	May 1864	Concussion time.	No known field recoveries.
43,993	Aug 1864	Concussion time.	No known field recoveries.
72,494	Dec 1867	Combination—flame-ignited and percussion	Used by the military.

it is possible to reconstruct how Parrott's fuzes changed. Charles H. Jones, in his book *Artillery Fuses of the Civil War*, has pictures of five Parrott percussion fuze types. The first is a West Point style, the second an improvement on that style, while the remaining three have various safety devices which keep the slider at the base of the fuze body, thus eliminating the need for an anti-rebound device. Parrott did not expand his fuze designs beyond the percussion fuze and a basic paper time fuze adapter. While it is unknown exactly why Parrott did not apply for more fuze-related patents, a comparison between his workload and those of Schenkl and Hotchkiss provides an answer. Schenkl had his manufacturing done by someone else; Hotchkiss manufactured 1,054,188 projectiles for $1,423,376.15 at his plant; while Parrott manufactured 1,315,790 projectiles for $3,166,144.57 at his plant, not including the thousands of cannons that were also cast there.[2] Parrott had much more to keep himself busy, and fuzes were only a minor part of his business.

It is interesting to note how all three men developed unique solutions to the common questions of safety devices and rebound. For safety devices, Schenkl used a concave anvil along with a screw, and Hotchkiss used a wire, while Parrott used interior metal braces. It appears from the records that Parrott's safety devices were the least successful. To solve the problem with

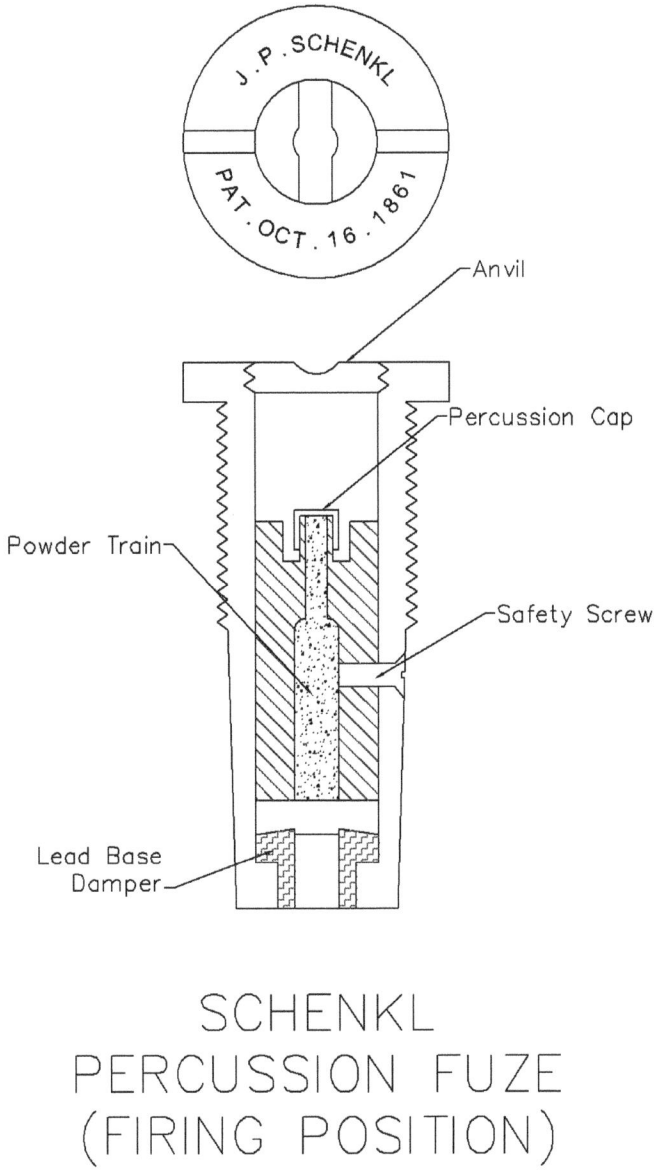

SCHENKL
PERCUSSION FUZE
(FIRING POSITION)

Schenkl Percussion Fuze in the firing position. The Schenkl Percussion Fuze was arguably the best percussion fuze used during the war.

Photograph of John Schenkl's gravesite in the Mount Auburn Cemetery, Cambridge, Massachusetts. No photograph of John Schenkl is known to exist even though there is an engineering scholarship in his name at the Massachusetts Institute of Technology (courtesy Mount Auburn Cemetery Historical Collections, Cambridge and Watertown, Massachusetts; photograph by Jennifer Johnston).

rebound, Schenkl put lead on the interior base of the body of his fuze, Hotchkiss put lead on the base of his slider, and Parrott kept his slider to the rear of the fuze body. As for keeping the base of the fuze unplugged with gunpowder from the main charge, both Parrott and Schenkl applied either a light metal or cardboard strip across the opening of the fuze which the explosion from the percussion cap destroyed. Hotchkiss took a different approach by making the plug part of his safety device. Making sure that the slider would move was solved by Schenkl by making his screw shear off smoothly. Hotchkiss' technique was to place the safety wire to the rear of the slider. Parrott never solved this problem as his safety device was in front of the slider, and could possibly stop the slider from moving by leaving metal remnants that would jam it.

One problem with the Schenkl fuze that neither the Hotchkiss nor Parrott fuzes experienced was that it could get stuck in the hollow of the rammer. However, this problem is only mentioned in one report even though it must have occurred throughout the war. Colonel Wainwright, Chief of First

Table 7.2 — Schenkl Fuze Patents

Patent Number	Month & Year of Issue	Features	Status
33,495	Oct 1861	Percussion — the standard percussion fuze.	Used by the military and received many positive comments during the Peninsula Campaign.
35,897	Jul 1862	Combination — flame-ignited and percussion	Used by the military but did not work very well.
36,236	Aug 1862	Percussion — improvement on 33,495, anti-rebound mechanism and different plug to keep the main powder charge from plugging the fuze.	Used by the military and was an improvement upon a successful design.
36,576	Sep 1862	Percussion — minor changes from Patent 36,236.	Used by the military with minor changes to a successful design.
39,682	Aug 1863	Combination — flame-ignited and percussion, an attempt to fix the problems with Patent 35,897.	Used by the military but, like its predecessor, did not work very well.

Corps Artillery, stated in his report to General Hunt, Chief of Artillery, on his unit's actions during the Chancellorsville Campaign that "the head of the fuse [sic] was found in some cases to stick in the hollow at the end of the rammer, and the shot displaced after being sent home, causing it to fail in taking the grooves."[3] How much of a problem this was is unknown, as no reports on tests concerning this problem have been found.

All three inventors faced common problems which were beyond the designs of their fuzes, such as projectiles not taking the rifling, bad percussion caps, compacted gunpowder, as well as poorly trained gun crews. As each of them designed their own projectiles they continuously worked on improving the sabots used on their projectiles so that they would take the rifling and be less likely to tumble. However, they were not completely successful in this regard. Percussion caps were also beyond their control and Captain Julius Hadley's report on his three-day test, which has been previously mentioned, included comments on percussion caps. During his test, 29 out of 41 percussion shells failed, with an additional two exploding in the gun. In his report, Hadley commented, "Of the failure of the percussion shell, there is no doubt as to the cause, it was simply the bad quality of the percussion caps used, for in shells examined after firing the caps was found to have received a blow severe enough to force the nipple entirely through the fulminate, and partly through the copper without exploding."[4]

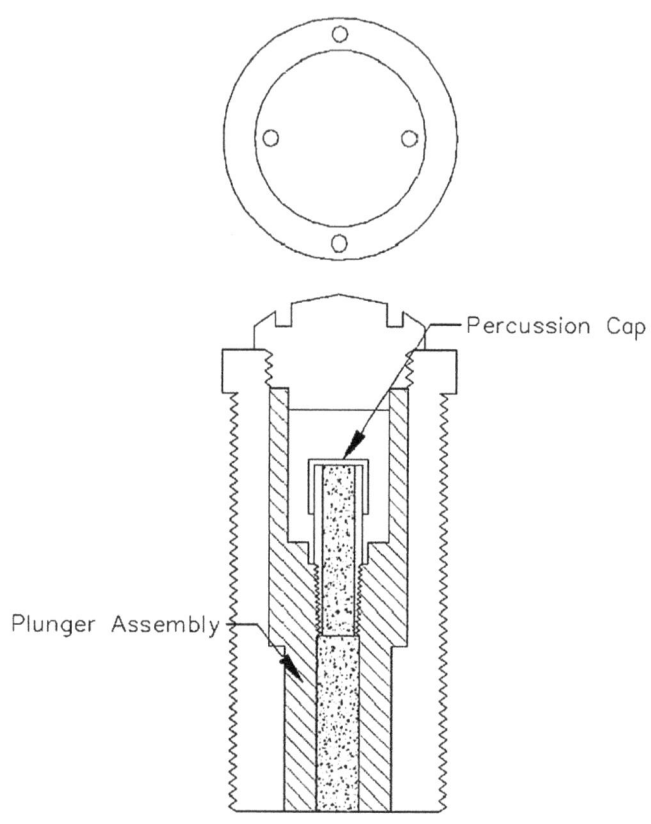

PARROTT PERCUSSION FUZE

Activated by centrifugal force, this version of Parrott's Percussion Fuze was not a good design because the prongs had to be broken before placing the fuze into a projectile. If the prongs were not broken, the fuze was not dependable.

Gunpowder, as with other loose powders, will compact if left undisturbed, decreasing its effectiveness. The military was aware of this problem, and regulations stated that artillery cartridge bags were to be regularly rotated. Loaded projectiles were a different problem. The Navy dealt with this problem by only loading projectiles as needed while the Army required that loaded projectiles carried in caissons or stored in magazines be placed fuze down. The Army placed the projectiles in this orientation so that if the gunpowder compacted, it would be compressed near the fuze where the flash from the fuze could still ignite it. However, these solutions did not help if the gunpowder was forced toward the rear of the projectile by setback forces. Schenkl tried to solve this problem with Patent No. 39,682 which included a powder chamber placed on either

Robert Parker Parrott (1804–1877, USMA Class of 1824), Thomas P. Rossiter, 1868, oil on canvas. Parrott was owner and operator of the West Point Foundry (West Point Museum Art Collection, United States Military Academy, West Point, New York).

side of the fuze case to "insure the firing of the shell charge even when more or less out of contact with or away from the fuse [sic]."[5] This problem was either not a serious one or one that the military did not spend the time investigating as it was not mentioned anywhere else.

The inventors also depended on artillery crews being properly trained in the use of their fuze. This was especially true for the Schenkl fuze, as the gunner had to unscrew the anvil from the fuze and then screw it back on with the flat part of the anvil facing inwards. High-ranking officers fully realized the necessity of training gunners to properly handle the fuzes and projectiles. General Hunt's Assistant Adjutant General, Jno. N. Craig, informed Lieutenant Colonel J.A. Monroe, Chief of Artillery, Second Corps:

> As both the Hotchkiss and Schenkl ammunition are provided, commanders of batteries can use either system, but in no case must two projectiles of the same kind be used in a battery. That is, no battery must have both Hotchkiss and Schenkl shell or both Hotchkiss and Schenkl shrapnel.

They may have Hotchkiss shell and Schenkl shrapnel, or vice versa, but he recommends strongly that, unless they have a marked preference for special projectiles, all should be of one system, either Hotchkiss or Schenkl.[6]

In the end, their fuzes were part of a larger system and were dependent upon the proper functioning of the larger system.

* * *

In 1861, Schenkl stated, "It is a fact well known to artillerists and those skilled in the use of ordnance that a good and reliable fuse for a projectile or shell, one which is safe for transportation and free from defect, is a desideratum which has long existed."[7] However, neither Schenkl nor any other inventor attained this lofty goal during the Civil War, for the Navy's 1866 *Ordnance Instructions* stated,

> Shells should be used against Ships at all distances where the penetration would be sufficient to lodge them. They are of no service in breaching solid stone walls, but are very effective against earthworks, ordinary buildings, and for bombarding. For these purposes a good percussion or concussion fuze is desirable, but no reliable fuzes of these kinds have as yet been devised.[8]

The Army agreed with this view as an 1868 Ordnance Board report stated, "The question of a good fuse [sic] for all conditions of service is still to be determined as not one of the many articles tried during the late war has given results sufficiently reliable to justify its exclusive adoption."[9] Nevertheless, fuzes improved and evolved during the war based on feedback received from the users. One problem was that the military did not have adequate specifications on what it needed because the technology was so new. For most equipment, the Ordnance Department had detailed manufacturing instructions, but to date no specifications have been found for the new mechanical fuzes either from the war years or for a number of years after the war. What makes this all the more interesting is that the British Army had detailed specifications for the testing of mechanical fuzes.[10]

Inventors responded to the failure of their fuzes and made improvements based on what the problems were. When the Ordnance Department tested their fuzes company representatives were regularly present. In addition, there was regular correspondence between the three principle fuze inventors (Hotchkiss, Parrott, and Schenkl) and various officers in the Ordnance Department. Fuze design was very competitive, and many inventors tried to get their fuzes adopted by the military. Any fuze, even if well established, that failed to meet the demands placed upon it during actual use quickly fell out of favor and was dropped from the inventory. Based on information from field research tests and reports provided by artillery commanders, feedback was given to fuze inventors and manufacturers. As a result, the military was continually evaluating the quality of the fuzes being sold to them. When quality became an issue, the military took steps to make certain that the problems were corrected, such as when the Army consolidated the production of paper fuzes at the Frankford Arsenal.

The fuzes invented during this short span of 17 years presaged all practical fuzes until the invention of the variable time fuze during World War II. Devices such as the use of springs, mechanically setting the time, delayed explosions, centrifugal force activation, chemical fuzes, multiple exploding devices inside of the projectile, and a clock mechanism were all patented during this time period. The technology existed, but in most cases industry was not capable of manufacturing the device or the technology was not fully understood. Fuze inventors of the mid–nineteenth century were imaginative and resourceful individuals who worked within constraints beyond their control. Technological ideas were advanced enough that in 1846, Navy Lieutenant Henry Moor wrote a confidential memorandum to President Polk suggesting that projectiles be exploded electronically by lengthy, small, attached wires; an idea far ahead of its time.[11] The inventive accomplishments of Benjamin Hotchkiss, Robert Parrott, and John Schenkl, along with other inventors and manufacturers, were crucial to the success of the Union cause. They are some of the lesser-known heroes of the Civil War for without their efforts it would have been, at best, a much longer and bloodier war before the country was reunited.

Eight

Postwar Developments

> *In 1856, Commander Dahlgren made the observation that without a good system of fuzes, artillery projectiles would be "bodies without souls." I would agree with that observation to a point, but would rephrase it as "bodies without minds."*[1]
>
> — Dr. Peter A. Bukowick, 1999

Although artillery and its associated fuzes played an important role during the Civil War, after the war, American artillery fuze innovation all but disappeared. The military continued using the pre–Civil War flame-ignited fuzes, and of the three principal mechanical fuzes used during the war, only the Hotchkiss continued in service. Robert Parrott lost interest in manufacturing fuzes, and without John Schenkl to provide the necessary innovation and drive, his fuze and projectile disappeared. However, the principal reason for the lack of innovation was a lack of interest on the part of Congress. Due to the end of the war and the absence of any real threats to the nation's security, Congress dramatically reduced military spending. The military knew how important it was to continue experiments with new inventions to determine if they were worth acquiring, and continually informed the politicians of this fact. Brigadier General Dyer, Chief of Ordnance, emphasized this desire in a report to Secretary of War Stanton in which he stated, "It will not do to stand still and rest content with what we have already attained. We must entertain and prove plans and devices for improving munitions of war if we are to keep pace in these with other nations, and in order to do so we must have the means of proving them."[2] However, Congress, faced with the enormous debt incurred by the Civil War, failed to act on these appeals and appropriate the needed money.

Even without the support of Congress the military tried to keep pace with other nations in regard to fuze technology. Between July 1877 and August

1878, an Ordnance Department Board tested eight percussion fuzes, three time fuzes, and nine combination fuzes. Unable to establish any one fuze as superior, the board reported in regard to the percussion and time fuzes "that no well established superiority exists in several of these fuzes, but the percentage of failures are so great in some cases that it would be useless to go to the expense of making further trials with them."[3] The report recommended that further tests be conducted on the German, Hotchkiss, English Royal Laboratory, and Schenkl percussion fuzes along with the German Time Fuze. As for the combination fuzes, the board's report stated that "no one of them may be said to have worked well."[4] The report further stated that "the Woodbridge and Gill No. 2, however, did considerably better than the other, and the board recommends that twenty-five more of each of these be made, with such improvements as Dr. Woodbridge and Mr. Gill may suggest, at Frankford arsenal, for further tests."[5] The board disliked the other seven combination fuzes, and wrote that "they are generally complicated and expensive, so that the board only recommends their further trials provided they are furnished without cost to the United States."[6] It is obvious that U.S. military fuze technology had not advanced in the 12 years following the Civil War.

The 1878 Ordnance Memoranda No. 21 illustrates the lack of technological progress on the part of the Army. This memoranda listed the flame-ignited wooden-case mortar fuze, the Bormann Fuze, and the paper fuze as the approved time fuzes, while the Hotchkiss Percussion Fuze was listed as the percussion fuze.[7] As for combination fuzes, the memoranda stated, "Many varieties of combination fuses [sic] have been proposed and tested, but without satisfactory results."[8] It also stated that "if a perfect combination fuse [sic] can be made, none other would be required, as it would have the properties of the other two, capable of use separately or combined."[9] However, by 1896 the Army had made some changes, although the wooden-case mortar fuze, Bormann Fuze, and paper fuze were still in the inventory. Now, the Army had two different Hotchkiss Percussion Fuzes, a Frankford Arsenal Combination Fuze, and a Merriam Delayed-action Fuze.

The 1896 Hotchkiss Fuzes included the Front Percussion Fuze and a Base Percussion Fuze. The former included the following parts: brass case (*a*); screw cap (*b*); projecting point (*c*); plunger (*d*) consisting of a brass case (*e*); a lead body (*f*) in which there is a double brass wire (*g*) and a priming charge of gunpowder (*h*); shoulder (*k*) upon which the plunger rests during flight; fulminate as the primer (*i*); and a lead plug (*j*) which was used to retain the safety wires and keep the fuze from getting plugged with gunpowder from the main charge. The only real differences between this fuze's operation and design and the Hotchkiss Percussion Fuze used during the Civil War was that this fuze had two safety wires, used explosive fulminate rather than a percussion cap containing fulminate, and had a projecting point to detonate the fulminate.

Hotchkiss designed his Base Percussion Fuze to pierce armor. Because of that it had a different means of operation from the Front Percussion Fuze. Setback forces activated the fuze causing the plunger (*e* in the large figure), consisting of a brass jacket and a lead body (*f* and *g* in the separate drawing

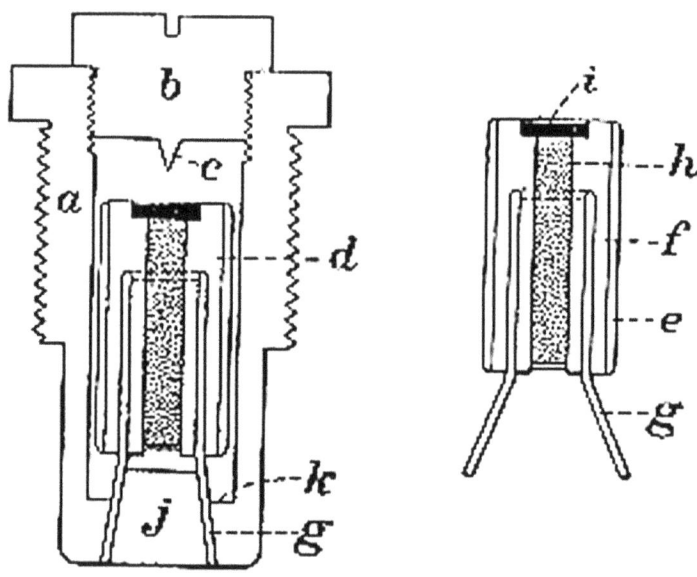

Above: 1896 Hotchkiss Percussion Fuze (Lawrence L. Bruff, *Ordnance and Gunnery*, page 335). *Below:* 1896 Hotchkiss Base Percussion Fuze (Bruff, page 336).

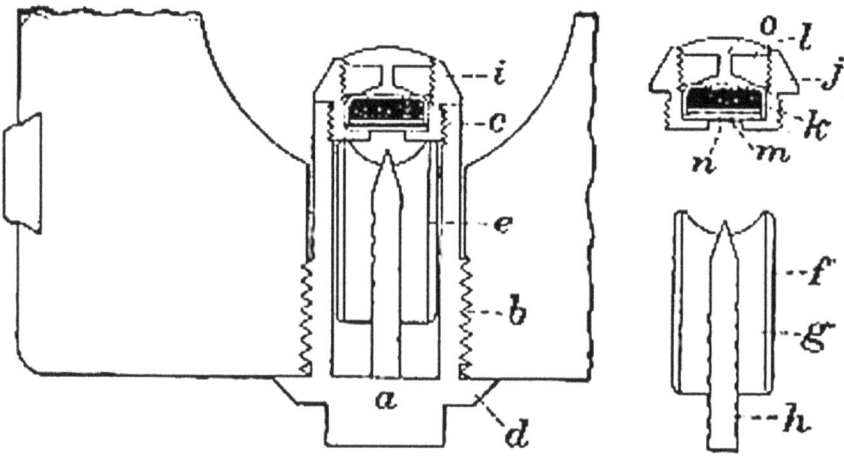

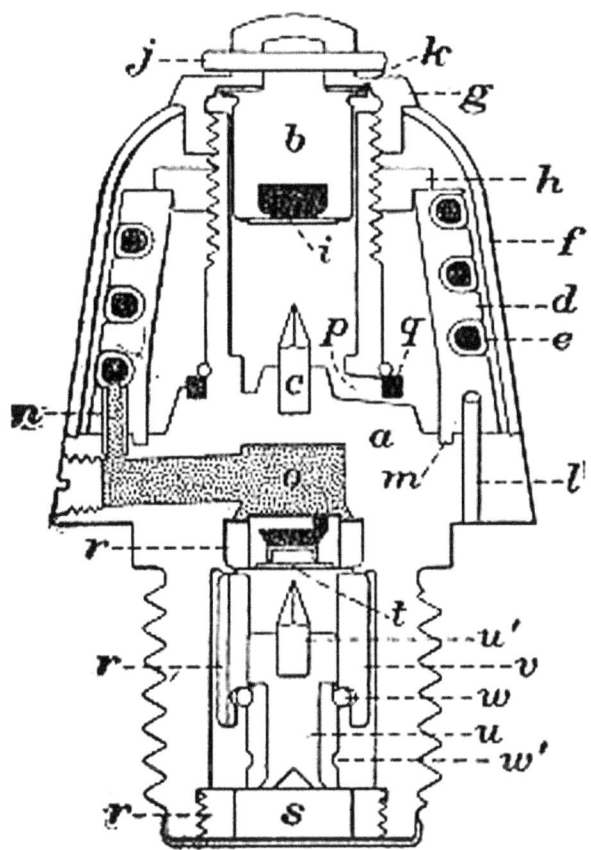

1896 Frankford Arsenal Combination Fuze (Bruff, page 338).

of the plunger), to move to the rear. When the projectile struck a solid object, the plunger and firing pin moved forward allowing the firing pin to strike and explode the fulminate, which in turn ignited the bursting charge. While this concept would not have seemed novel to Civil War era fuze inventors, better manufacturing processes had made this fuze possible.

The Frankford Arsenal Combination Fuze combined a time fuze with a percussion fuze. The nose of the fuze contained the time fuze while the rear contained the percussion fuze. Before firing, the gunner pierced the fuze for the appropriate number of seconds, which could vary from 1 to 15 seconds, and the safety pin (*j*) was removed. Setback forces broke the plunger (*b*) free, which then struck the firing pin (*c*) and exploded the fulminate. The flame from the fulminate ignited the timed powder train. If the main charge had not exploded by the time the projectile struck a solid object, the percussion

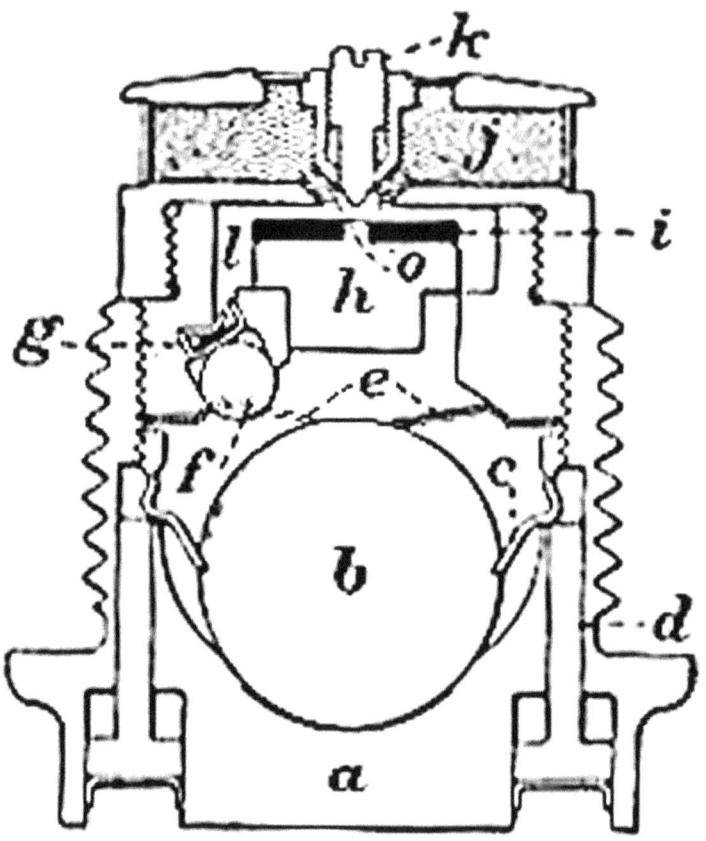

Merriam Delayed-action Fuze.

fuze would ignite it. The percussion fuze operated in the same manner as the previously discussed Hotchkiss Base Percussion Fuze. It is interesting to note that the powder train in this combination fuze was a horizontal train, the same design invented by Bormann before the Civil War. Bormann's horizontal powder train design was so superior to a vertical powder train that it is still in use today.

The Merriam Delayed-action Fuze was threaded into the base of the projectile. When the gun was fired, pressure from the propelling charge pushed two pistons (*d*) releasing the two clips (*c*) that held the ball (*b*) in place. Spring *e* kept ball *b* from moving forward until the projectile struck a solid object. Upon striking a solid object ball *b* would strike the smaller ball (*f*). In turn, ball *f* would strike the percussion cap (*g*), detonating it. Just before the percussion cap detonated, valve *h* closed the opening (*o*) which stopped the flame from igniting the main charge. The flame-ignited the compressed powder in ring *i*, which burnt until the projectile's forward movement stopped. When the projectile stopped valve *h* moved back and allowed the flame to ignite the main charge. If an instantaneous explosion was desired, screw *k* would be screwed down, which would keep valve *h* from blocking opening *o*. It is obvious that the Merriam Delayed-action Fuze was very complicated, and was only made possible by better manufacturing processes.

Changes in artillery technology prior to World War I affected artillery fuzes. Ranges reached the point where it was impossible for the gunner to accurately set a time fuze so that the projectile would explode the proper distance above the ground. While the time fuze found a new use in anti-aircraft gun projectiles, case shot began to lose its effectiveness. This trend continued into World War II, when a War Department technical manual stated, "shrapnel (case shot) are obsolete for future manufacture. The use is authorized for the present time while the stock on hand lasts."[10] The loss of case shot as an effective weapon meant that artillery projectiles only had percussion or delayed fuzes as choices. This resulted in a "cone of safety" in the immediate vicinity of an exploding projectile. The "cone of safety" was the area surrounding the point of impact where fragments from the projectile did not hit. In addition, anyone lying just below the surface would probably not get hit, as the explosion propelled fragments in an upward and horizontal direction.

However, the invention of the Variable Time (VT) Fuze during World War II changed the future of case shot. The VT Fuze was a product of the modern research lab, and was the first fuze technology that Civil War era fuze inventors would not have understood. The VT Fuze allowed projectiles to be fired at a target beyond the visual range of the gunner with the guarantee that the projectile would explode at a set distance above the ground. This ability made the case shot projectile an effective weapon again. The VT Fuze was also very deadly against aircraft. Without it American naval losses to Japanese Kamikazes would have been much higher during World War II. In addition, if Nazi Germany had developed a VT Fuze in all probability the Allied bomber offensive would have failed. The VT Fuze was the beginning of the era of the fuze becoming more than the soul of the projectile, it had become its mind as well.

Although the goal of the "perfect" fuze has not been fully achieved, its fruition is dependent upon the knowledge that can be gained by understanding how the Weapon System Pyramid Model works. The development and evolution of the artillery fuze during the Civil War is but one example of how this model demonstrates the interaction between the user's need, technical availability, and industrial capability. If need is not present, there will not be any advances in a weapon system, as demonstrated by the lack of an approved fuze for use in rifled artillery prior to the Civil War, as well as the lack of innovation immediately following the war. Bronislaw Malinowski stated in *A Scientific Theory of Culture* that "no invention, no revolution, no social or intellectual change, ever occurs except when new needs are created; and thus new devices in technique, in knowledge, or in belief are fitted into the cultural process of an institution."[11] However, Malinowski failed to recognize that for material items, both industrial capability and technological availability are also necessary.

Industrial capability plays an important role in the model. During the Civil War, both the Union and Confederacy had the same needs and the same technical availability. However, the South, due to its relative lack of industrial capability, could not produce the excellent Bormann Fuze. In addition, the mechanical fuzes invented by Confederate inventors, such as the Archer, Girardey, and Broun fuzes, were produced in such small quantities that their influence was negligible. While the technical prowess of the inventors in the Confederacy is not in question, the lack of an adequate industrial base crippled their development of the Fuze Weapon System Pyramid.

Even with its superior industrial base, northern inventors were not able to develop and manufacture a fuze that met all of the needs of the military

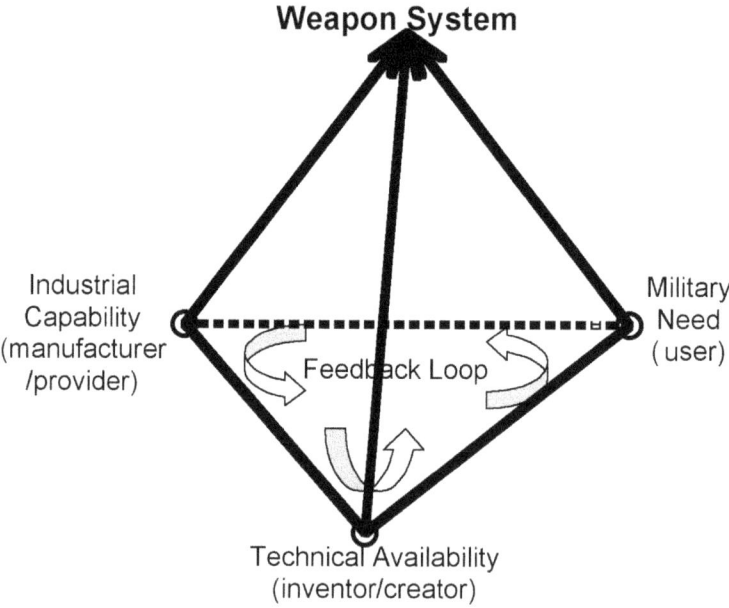

The Weapon System Pyramid. All three legs of the pyramid must work together if a weapon system is to achieve its greatest potential.

during the war. That was beyond the technological and industrial capability of the time period. A similar gap exists today in other weapon systems. The military would like to have an aircraft that does not need to land and refuel. The effort to develop a nuclear powered aircraft was one of the attempts to achieve this goal. Refueling techniques have extended the range of aircraft, but human limitations must still be taken into account. Someday, the military's desire to have an aircraft with unlimited range that is capable of carrying sufficient firepower will probably be achieved, but today's technology cannot provide it. In a like manner the creation of the "perfect" fuze has become a long and sometimes frustrating process.

Even if the technological capability is available, industrial capacity must also exist if an adequate and reliable number of the items needed are to be available for use. Today, countries purchase advanced weapon systems that they cannot maintain without outside support. While this may give them a short-term advantage over an enemy, it can lead to a long-term disadvantage. The problem is that they become dependent upon their supplier for parts to keep their equipment operational. This limits their long-term strategic options as they must keep the supplier (and in some cases the supplier's country) content. Nuclear weapons are another area in which manufacturing capacity plays a critical role. While there are literally thousands of individuals around the world who have the technical knowledge to create a nuclear weapon and a number of governments and individuals who would like to have a nuclear weapon, only a limited number of countries have the necessary industrial capability to make one. The desire and knowledge to own or create any weapon system is only part of the pyramid, and without the necessary industrial capability, it is a very weak and unstable structure.

Fuzes played an important role during the Civil War and in all conflicts since then. During the Civil War, the combination of reliable fuzes and long-range artillery fire increased the lethal zone of the battlefield far beyond what had been previously experienced. The development of these fuzes was dependent on the relationship between military need, technical availability, and industrial capability as modeled by the Weapon System Pyramid. All three legs of the pyramid, as well as the feedback loop, must be considered when any weapon system is under consideration. The height of the pyramid, or effectiveness of the weapon system, cannot be greater than the length of the shortest and weakest leg. All three legs must work in tandem with feedback between each of the parties. The evolution of the artillery fuze during the Civil War is but one example of an effective Weapon System Pyramid that was able to produce a better fuze and a more deadly battlefield in which if a man could be seen, he could be killed.

Appendix A

United States Fuze-Related Patents, 1855–1872

The choice of which patents to include had a degree of subjectivity on the part of the author including how to categorize them. Readers can decide for themselves whether or not they agree with the author on his choices as well as with his critique of each patent. The years 1855 and 1872 were chosen to be the beginning and ending years for this analysis as they are far enough away from the war's years to show the growth in fuze-related patents during the war. In addition, there were very few fuze-related patents issued in the years immediately preceding 1855 and following 1872.

Below are descriptions of specific patents which detail the date; title of patent; patentee; location; type of fuze, as well as claims and critiques.

13,138

June 26, 1855; Improved Fuse-Stock for Bomb-Shells; Abraham Powell Jr.; Mare Island, CA; Flame-ignited Fuze

Claims—A double-cylinder fuse-stock so graduated as to burst shell-shot at any required number of seconds.

Critique—A good idea similar to the British Boxer Fuze. However, it was in competition with the well-established and reliable Bormann Fuze.

13,469

August 21, 1855; Improvement in Percussion-Projectiles; Augustus McBurth; Elizabeth, NJ; Percussion Fuze

Claims—
1. The improvement in bomb-shells or missiles having four arms, b b' b" b'", and eight flutes with sharp edges, 1 2 3, Fig. 3, in the manner and for the purposes substantially as described.

2. A rod, h, Fig, 2, to pass through the shell in a longitudinal course, for the purpose as above set forth.

3. A hammer with a flat spring attached, together with a spiral spring, d, as substantially shown and described in the foregoing specification.

Critique— A shell which could be fired from a smooth-bore gun and in theory fly straight without tumbling due to the arms (wings). A rod passed through the projectile and when the nose of the projectile struck an object the rod would activate the fuze in the base of the projectile. An overly complicated system.

13,799

November 13, 1855; Improved Compound Projectile; Sylvanus Sawyer; Fitchburg, MA; Percussion Fuze

Claims—

1. Combining with the butt or flat rear end of the cylindro-conical iron shell a layer of lead or softer metal than that of which the body of the shell is composed, and united or not to a layer of such metal extended around the sides of the shell, as described, the same operating in manner as specified while the shell is being projected through the bore of a gun by a discharge of the powder therein.

2. Making the rear part of the shell tapering or conical, as seen at aa, combining therewith a ring or annulus, bb, of lead or its equivalent, the same being substantially in manner and for the purpose as herein before specified.

3. Confining the explosive screw-cap to the body of the shell by means of a softer or yielding metal or casing, which, when the cap or shell shall strike an object, shall give way under the force of the blow and let the cap down with force, so as to compress the percussion wafer or priming in it or on the main screw, stopper, or plug, and so as to create an explosion thereof, as stated.

Critique— More on shell design than fuze design. Weak fuze safety device but the concept was the most common percussion method. Sawyer's fuze designs would improve with time. Charles Jones (*Artillery Fuses of the Civil War*) stated that this fuze did not work very well when the projectile struck a glancing blow.

14,460

March 18, 1856; Improvement in Percussion Projectiles; John Lippincott; Pittsburg, PA; Percussion

Claims—The combination of the cylindrical chamber, piston, spiral spring, cap, and nose-piece, constructed and arranged as described, forming an improved percussion apparatus, to be inserted into the powder-chamber of bomb-shells, either in combination with or without a shallow sabot of lead of the shape described, the whole being constructed and arranged substantially in the manner and for the purposes hereinbefore set forth.

Critique—A very dangerous fuze as the piston used to activate the fuze projected beyond the front of the projectile. Thus, when being loaded pressure must be exerted on the piston, potentially forcing it onto the cap and causing a premature explosion.

17,312

May 19, 1857; Improvement in Projectiles; Christopher C. Brand; Norwich, CT; Flame-ignited Fuze

Claims—

1. The improved fuse tube or plug C, as constructed with two plug-chambers, k l, separated by a breech or partition, N, the same being for the purpose as specified.

2. The improvement of making said tube C with an encircling chamber or recess, o o, arranged therein, substantially in manner and for the purpose set forth.

Critique—An exploding harpoon that Brand said could be used for military purposes or for killing whales or other large animals. Never used by the military as it was in competition with the well-established and reliable Bormann Fuze.

18,866

December 15, 1857; Improvement in the Fuses of Shells and Other Projectiles; Nathan Scholfield; Norwich, CT; Flame-ignited Fuze

Claims—

1. The application of a perforated conical protecting plug, e, Fig 1, penetrating the end of the fuse cord, and the connecting it thereto by some plastic and adhesive substance, and also inserting this, with the fuse cord, in place in the conical cavity opening from the fuse to the vent chamber, for the purpose of securing more perfectly the ignition of the fuse, while the flame from the discharge of the gun is prevented from passing in outside of the fuse, or of forcing the fuse inward, substantially as described.

2. Opening and expanding the end of the fuse cord and applying it under the seat of a protecting plug, e, Fig 2, and causing the plug to be pressed firmly thereon, so as to secure it from being forced through the aperture by the discharge.

Critique—A winged projectile that would have been expensive to manufacture in addition to having an overly complicated method of manufacturing the fuze.

28,084

May 1, 1860; Improvement in Projectiles for Breech Loading Ordnance; William Wheeler Hubbell; Philadelphia, PA; Percussion Fuze

Claims—

1. The combination, of the recess x, shoulders r and w, with the band b and the wire coil o secured in the band, as described.

2. The beveled cylindrical lead band b, in combination with the flutes c c c, and the wire coil o in the recess x, so as to easily enter, compensated, and indent the band into the rifled bore and give it great comparative strength to retain its proper form and position under this action, and with certainty rotate the shell or shot in the breech loading rifled gun.

3. The beveled cylindrical canvas covering extending around and in front of the lead band, and secured by the groove and wire u to the body of the projectile,

in combination with the flutes c c c and the wire coil o, so that its beveled front may easily enter and indent in the rifled bore without stripping, and the flutes allow the lead to compensate under it to the lands and grooves, and the wire strengthen and hold the lead firm that the canvas may be enabled to assume a form and firmness of bearing to co–operate with the lead band in rotating the projectile in the breech loading rifled cannon.

4. The firing holes j' j' in front of the striker, in combination with the striker and the magazine m, to facilitate the explosion in shells adapted to long ranged rifled cannon.

5. The circular ribs y and z inside of and uniform around the axis of the shell, in combination with and at each end of the circular recess x and band b, so as to strengthen and support both the front and rear ends of the projectile, and the base of the circular recess resist the shock of discharge, the compression into the grooves, and the shock of penetration by restoring the strength lost in the application of the lead band.

Critique— Fuze was at the rear of the projectile so that it would explode after penetrating the hull of a ship. Sound idea except that Hubbell does not say how much time was added by putting the fuze in the back of the projectile. Also, Hubbell did not address the difficulty of penetrating an armored ship.

30,123

September 25, 1860; Improvement in Projectiles; John W. Cochran; New York, NY; Percussion Fuze

Claims—

1. The construction of projectiles with corrugations of hollow beads aa bb, made and applied, substantially as herein set forth and described, so that the force of the explosion of the charge will cause said corrugations to be expanded laterally, as and for the purposes herein set forth and described.

2. The mode of providing for the lubrication of the gun by perforations n n in the beads, fillets, or corrugations of the cap or other portion of the projectile.

3. Placing the missiles or substance to be scattered by the explosion of a hollow projectile within a cylindrical casing, D, fitted to the interior of the projectile, substantially as and for the purpose herein described.

4. The employment of the cup C of its equivalent with the cylinder A, as and for the purposes herein set forth and described.

5. The arrangement of the tube F, nipple g, plunger G, and spring H, in combination with the powder cylinder E, substantially as herein described.

Critique— Used a spring as a safety device. Strength of the spring would be key for if it was too strong the fuze would not work.

31,099

January 15, 1861; Improvement in Projectiles for Ordnance; S.C. Abbot; Zanesville, OH; Percussion Fuze

Claims—

1. So constructing the shell that it charges itself, or the interstices between

the grains of powder, with which it is loaded, with atmosphere under pressure, as it flies through the air, and at the moment of contact with a resisting object confines said compacted or compressed air, substantially as and for the purposes set forth.

2. The spiral planes C on the conical front portion of the shot or shell, in the described combination with the cylindrical rear portion, for the purposes explained.

3. Constructing the screw plug, which conducts the fire of the cap to the interior of the shell, in two parts, and fitting one part over the air nipple of the other part, substantially as and for the purposes set forth.

4. The employment, between the shell and the inner circumference of the gun, of a self detaching wedge shaped spring packing strip bent into the form of a ring, said strip being formed of leather, gutta percha, or other similar flexible substance which is softer than the metal of the gun, and rendered solid by means of soft metal plugs or rivets driven through its thickest edge, substantially as and for the purposes set forth.

Critique— Fuze was activated by the air that was compressed within the projectile as it flew through the air. Idea was too advanced for the time.

33,378

October 1, 1861; Improvement in Projectiles for Ordnance; Charles F. Brown; Warren, RI; Percussion Fuze

Claims—

1. A projectile constructed and operating substantially as herein specified.

Critique— It is a surprise that the patent was issued as no specific claims were made. A dangerous projectile as it had a rod that was used to active the fuze that could protrude from either end of the projectile.

33,495

October 15, 1861; Improvement in Safety Concussion-Fuse for Explosive Projectiles; John P. Schenkl; Boston, MA; Impact Concussion Fuze

Claims—

1. Securing the nipple carrier to one side of the inner wall of the case by means of a screw, and so countersinking the hole made through the case for the reception of such screw, as to form a sharp cutting edge, whereby the said screw shall be cut off smooth with the inner surface of the case and the outer surface of the nipple carrier, in manner and under circumstances as set forth.

Critique— The basic concussion fuze design used throughout the war.

33,662

November 5, 1861; Improvement in Applying Fuses to Shells; Robert P. Parrott; Cold Spring, NY; Combination — Flame-Ignited and Percussion Fuze

Claims—

1. The combination, with an aperture leading to the interior of the shell, of a transverse hole or passage, D, for the reception of the fuse, substantially as herein described.

2. The combination, with the transversely inserted fuse, of a plunger, C, applied and operating substantially as and for the purpose herein specified.

Critique— Combination fuze but a complex design that would be improved upon as the war continued.

33,835

December 3, 1861; Improvement in Percussion Shells; G. W. Gardner; Troy, NY; Percussion Fuze

Claims—

1. So constructing percussion shells that the hammer or its equivalent may be held by the side of the cap, or inoperative, until discharged from the gun, and then be placed upon the cap by the use of the fuse plug or its equivalent, and the combination of the cylinders and springs, substantially as herein set forth.

Critique— Purpose of the patent was to prevent premature explosions by the use of a spring.

34,040

December 24, 1861; Improved Fuse-Hood for Shells; Sylvanus Sawyer; Fitchburg, MA; Accessory — Fuze Hood for flame-ignited fuzes

Claims—The employment of a hood or other equivalent device, in combination with a fuse, substantially in the manner and for the purpose described.

Critique— Method of directing the flames to the fuze. Its usefulness is dubious.

34,059

January 7, 1862; Improvement in Explosive Shells for Ordnance; William W. Hubbell; Philadelphia, PA; Combination — Flame-ignited using concussion to allow the flame to reach the powder charge of the fuze and Percussion Fuze

Claims—

1. The vent 15 opposite and nearly or quite at right angles to the base of the chamber 4, to receive and discharge the fire as quick as possible, and deliver the water direct on the base of the chamber to diffuse it in the best manner, as described.

2. Expanding the fire in an enlarged chamber around the mouth of the burning column, so as to secure a large body of fire to insure the explosion of the shell, as described.

3. Combining the percussion exploder with the burning fuse by securing the cylinder F to the inner end of the fuse stock, and providing it with a head for the striker inside of the cylinder, so as to unite the percussion and the fuse principles for explosion, as described.

4. The lead stopper r, inserted in and secured to the inner end of the fuse stock, by screw threads or similar means, as and for the purpose described, and also forming the chamber or space t, between this topper and the burning column, as described.

5. The chamber q and its opening p, between the head M and the fuse column, as described.

6. The lead or metallic stopper Z Z, in the metal base or groove, covering the holes x, and releasing on concussion to explode the projectile, as described.

7. The fire chambered water capping, combined with the cylindrical fuse opening or stock carrying the burning column, with cylinder opening at the inner end, to hold the fire and explode the shell on impact, as described.

8. The adjustable metallic timing rod W, in the burning column or near its side, to adjust the fuse to explode the projectile at any instant of time, as described, also the strand of quick match u, in its lower end, to raise and lead the fire down on time, as described.

9. The fire chamber 4, in the capping between the water table or plate 2 and the capping vent formed by combining them, to prevent extinguishment of the fuse, as described, also the raised vent 3 of the water table into the chamber, as described, to increase its capacity to exclude water, also the chamber 1, between the vent 3 and the orifice of the column v, as described.

10. Forming an enlarged or priming chamber, 7, around or by the side of the timing rod, to insure an ignition of the fuse by presenting a large priming surface for the smaller vent, and allow the timing rod to extend through the capping and be adjusted without interfering with the priming, as described.

11. The file cuts or fracturing points on the side of the timing rod, so as to break it off without the use of an instrument, in adjusting the time in action, as described, also the quick or double three or four threaded screw on the timing rod, to adjust it quickly as described.

Critique—A long patent with lots of claims. Fuze tried to do everything but was far too complex.

34,233

January 28, 1862; Improved Composition for Fuse of Slow-Match for Igniting Powder Under Water; Thomas K. Anderson; Hornellsville, NY; Flame ignited Fuze

Claims—

1. A compound consisting of the four titled ingredients, in or about the same proportions specified, prepared and used in the manner as and for the purposes herein set forth.

Critique—Patent was to make a compound that would burn in a tube even if underwater using niter, charcoal, sulphur and muriate of soda. Anderson stated his fuze was "a superior fuze for shell and shrapnel to any before discovered or now in use." However, the military never adopted it.

34,242

January 28, 1862; Improvement in Shells for Rifled Ordnance; James M. Connel and John S. Hall; Newark, OH, and Columbus, OH; Percussion Fuze

Claims—

1. The explosive projectile made of two hollow parts, A A' B B', which are fitted together so that a space, C, exists between their facing ends a b and the part

A A', having circumferentially segmental cavities D, and the part B B', having angular cavities E, beveled projections F, and a beveled continuous circumferential edge, G, and the whole being encircled and held together by a lead packing ring, H, in the manner and for the purposes herein described.

2. Constructing the interior of one portion of the projectile with a front and rear rest or shoulder, c d, and arranging in or against the same an open ended hollow tube, K, for the purpose of separating the contents of the chamber J from the igniting magazine K', substantially as and for the purposes set forth.

3. In combination with the shoulders c d and tube K, providing a central opening, f, in the end a of the part A A', and a similar hole, g, in the end b of part B B', and arranging an igniting magazine, K' K^2, within the hollow tube K and in the openings f g, in the manner and for the purpose herein described.

4. The combination of a sliding igniting magazine with the hollow explosive projectile, substantially as and for the purposes herein described.

Critique— No sane artillery man would use this fuze/projectile. It was activated by a rod that protruded from the front of the projectile.

34,268

January 28, 1862; Improvement in Shells for Rifled Ordnance; John P. Rollins; Cedar Rapids, IA; Percussion Fuze

Claims—

The combination of a sliding spring rod, F, projecting in front of the shell, with a discharge nipple, c, formed upon a screw, D, inserted from the rear, all substantially as and for the purposes set forth.

Critique— No sane artillery man would use this fuze/projectile. It was activated by a rod that protruded from the front of the projectile similar to Patent No. 34,242.

34,602

March 4, 1862; Improvement in Canister or Case Shot for Ordnance; Elmer Townsend; Boston, MA; Flame-ignited Fuze

Claims—

1. The arrangement and combination of the wings h with the head H, the case A, and the charge of balls thereof, the whole being to operate together substantially as and for the purpose or purposes as specified.

2. The combination and arrangement of the part C with the shell case A, the sabot D, and the packing d.

3. The combination and arrangement of the cap G and one or more lateral orifices, f, with the fuse tube and a chamber, u, formed in the rear end of the sabot, as specified.

4. The combination of one or more flanges, k k, or the equivalent therefore with the loading chamber and the winged head applied thereto.

5. The construction of the cap l and the wings h — viz. in two separate parts — substantially in manner and so as to be combined together as described.

Critique—Fuze was lit from the rear as the gun was fired. There was no mention of timing for the fuze. It appears to be an idea that had not been tried before being patented.

34,685

March 18, 1862; Improvement in Explosive Shells for Ordnance; John M. Hathaway; New York, NY; Combination — Flame-ignited and Percussion Fuze
Claims—
1. The arrangement of the diverging barrels g g, connected together at their base by the circular groove S, surrounding the chamber h, and fired in the manner specified.
2. The lead ring c, provided with a corrugated sheet metal band, in combination with the circular and longitudinal grooves 4 at the tapering end of the bomb, as and for the purposes set forth.
3. The elastic base b, in combination with the tapering corrugated metal d, in the manner and for the purposes specified.
4. The disk c, through which the fuse I passes, when fitted as set forth, to regulate the length of said fuse, as specified.
5. In combination with the base b and disk e, the pin f, divided washer 6, and conical ring 7, for the purposes set forth.
6. The tapering sheet metal spring l, constructed as specified, and applied to sustain the detonating plug k, as set forth.
7. The rollers 2 2, arranged and applied as shown, to take the rifling grooves, for the purposes specified.

Critique—Too complex to easily manufacture and operate. Part of the projectile was supposed to be timed to explode just prior to impact with the main part of the projectile exploding upon impact. There were also rollers in the projectile to help it spin in the bore of the gun.

34,788

March 25, 1862; Improvement in the Plungers of Concussion Shells; Charles W. Smith and Thomas D. Stetson; New York, NY; Percussion Fuze
Claims—
1. The use of soft material — such as lead or its equivalent — in the percussion mechanism of shells, substantially in the manner, and so as to produce the effect herein set forth.

Critique—The first known patented attempt to help avert premature explosions by preventing bounce-back. The idea was to use a soft material in the slider to absorb the setback force when the slider hit the base of the fuze well. The question remains as to why in the title of their patent they say "concussion" but in the body of the patent they refer to percussion?

35,277

May 13, 1862; Improvement in Explosive Projectiles; Charles W. Isbell; New York, NY; Percussion Fuze

Claims—

1. The attachment of the hammer of the percussion apparatus to the rear portion or breech of the projectile, substantially as and for the purpose herein specified.

2. So constructing and applying the device for attaching and holding back the hammer within the projectile that it is caused to liberate the hammer by the driving forward of the rear portion of the projectile relatively to the front portion thereof y the act of discharging the projectile from the gun, substantially as herein specified.

Critique— Fuze was in the rear of the projectile.

35,503

June 10, 1862; Improvement in Explosive Projectiles for Ordnance; William E. Browne; Valley Falls, RI; Percussion Fuze

Claims—

The arrangement of the expanding wings D D to swing from recesses in the sides of the body of the projectile upon pins c c, arranged obliquely to planes passing through the axis of the projectile, substantially as and for the purpose herein set forth.

The combination of one or more expanding wings, D D, attached to the body of the projectile, and one or more nipples of their equivalents provided on the said body for the reception of percussion caps or other percussion priming, whereby the said wings are made to constitute hammers for the explosion of the percussion priming, substantially as herein specified.

Critique— Used wings so that it could be fired from a smooth-bore gun. The percussion caps were attached to the wings and upon impact the wings moved forward detonating the caps. Browne did not explain what would keep the wings from expanding in the gun as the safety device that kept the wings folded was removed before the projectile was placed in the gun. A dubious invention.

35,520

June 10, 1862; Improvement in Shells for Rifled Ordnance; H.N. Houghton and C.H. Denison; Halifax, VT, and Brattleborough, VT; Flame-ignited Fuze

Claims—

The employment of the screw bolt F, applied, as and for the purpose herein specified, as a fuse tube, substantially as herein described.

Critique— Used the bolt that held the two parts of the projectile together as the fuze tube. Good idea except for the fact that the projectile must be assembled in the field.

35,593

June 17, 1862; Improvement in the Exploding Device of Shells; John J. Dresbach; Circleville, OH; Percussion Fuze

Claims—

In combination with an exploding projectile, a plunger tube, E, having a tapered portion, E', and a conical spring plunger, H, working therein, substantially in the manner and for the purpose set forth.

Critique—An attempt to prevent premature explosions by using a spring to prevent bounce-back.

35,611

June 17, 1862; Improvement in Concussion Fuse for Explosive Shells; B.B. Hotchkiss; Sharon, CT; Percussion

Claims—The plug E and wire J, or their respective equivalents, arranged to operate in the percussion mechanism of explosive projectiles, substantially as herein set forth.

Critique—Fuze was activated by the setback forces created when the gun was fired. A wire was used as the safety device. A good, reliable fuze used throughout the war. Hotchkiss did improve upon it later in the war—see Patent Number 37,756.

35,824

July 8, 1862; Improvement in Projectiles for Rifled Ordnance; J.L. Henry; District of Columbia; Percussion Fuze

Claims—

1. Combining one or more flexible bands with a projectile for rifled ordnance in any manner, substantially as described and shown, for the purposes set forth.

2. Two or more separate sets of gas channels c, leading from the cavity d in the base of the projectile to the under surface of two or more bands, combined with the projectile, substantially as and for the purposes set forth.

3. Causing a portion of the bands, as set forth, or the metal which secures them to the shot, to neatly fit the bore, for the purposes set forth.

4. The combination of an inflexible stop or rest with a concussion piston, arranged substantially as set forth, for the purpose described.

5. The use of gas chambers beneath a band or bands, so proportioned as to contain just sufficient gas to cause the band or bands to effect the end desired, for the reasons set forth.

6. Combining a percussion piston with a shell, substantially as described and shown, so as to render unnecessary a spring or other equivalent heretofore used to prevent accidental explosion.

7. Combining an anvil screw or its equivalent with a shell in the manner substantially as shown, and for the purposes set forth.

8. The combination of the percussion piston and anvil screw with each other and with the shell, substantially as and for the purposes set forth and shown.

9. Combining a screw or its equivalent with a shell, so as to admit of being adjusted from the outside of the shell to explode the cap within, substantially as set forth.

Critique—A variation of the standard percussion fuze using a spring as a safety device if fuze was loaded well before the projectile was fired. Otherwise the exploding cap was placed in the fuze just prior to firing using a small wire to prevent a premature explosion. Too complicated an arrangement.

35,897

July 15, 1862; Improvement in Time and Concussion Fuses for Shells; John P. Schenkl; Boston, MA; Combination — concussion timed and percussion Fuze

Claims —

1. A rotary fuse having its covering or case, whether made of paper or other suitable material, provided with a series of holes so arranged that each, by a suitable movement of the fuse-case, may be brought into conjunction with some on of another series of holes made in the fuse-plug, the requisite motion of the fuse within its plug being effected by a fuse-rotator, and the fuse being provided with an igniting apparatus, all substantially as specified.

2. The combination of the wrench-pin E with the percussion striker, the rotator, and its latch-spring.

3. The combination of one or more ventholes, o o, and a closing annulus, a, or its equivalent, with the rotary fuse holder and fuse, when combined with the rotator and a percussion apparatus, substantially as described.

4. The arrangement of the perforations in the rotary fuse and its holder viz., in two semi-helices or parts of helices pitched in opposite directions in the fuse and its holder substantially as explained.

5. A rotary fuse and its holder, made with perforations r s, arranged as described, and also with a scale and index so applied as to enable the fuse to be adjusted so as to bring any one of its holes of its range s to open into a hole of the range r of the fuse-holder.

6. The combination of the latching apparatus n and the series of recesses t t with the scale of the holder B, when said holder is combined with a rotary fuse and both are provided with ranges of holes, as specified

Critique — Potentially a good design but with one major engineering flaw. The material chosen for the fuse had too low of a melting temperature and had a tendency to melt after seven or eight seconds of flight, causing a premature explosion.

36,037

July 29, 1862; Improvement in Fuses for Explosive Shells; Benjamin F. Sturtevant; Boston, MA; Combination — Concussion timed and Percussion impact Fuze

Claims —

1. In combination with the fuse plug A, a device which shall enter the same, and so extend beyond or out of its mouth that on impact against an object during flight of a shell in which the plug may be such device may be driven into the plug and caused to so cut or break it as to enable the flame proceeding from the upper or burning end of the fuse to enter the charge chamber of the shell, as specified.

Critique — Used multiple openings from the cap to the chamber. Sturtevant did not mention how long the timed fuze would burn. I would worry about premature explosion with this fuze.

36,038

July 29, 1862; Improvement in Fuses for Explosive Shells; Benjamin F. Sturtevant; Boston, MA; Combination — Concussion timed and Percussion impact Fuze

Claims —

1. An explosive friction apparatus or a plunger, a friction composition chamber, a plunger case, and a friction tongue, combined and arranged so as to be applied to a fuse plug and its fuse and operate therewith in manner and under circumstances substantially as hereinbefore set forth.

2. The plunger as made with an open bottom and a thin flexible edge or lower part capable of being upset or bent, so as not to cut through the shoulder or walls of the fuse plug under the blow of the shoulder imparted to the lower end of the plunger at the period of the discharge of a shell from a gun, as specified.

3. The extension of the chamber g into the chamber d' by means of a flexible annular flange, f, capable of being upset, so as to close the mouth of the chamber g, as above explained.

4. The friction tongue as made with two or more rasping prongs, arranged substantially as described.

5. The arrangement of the walls of the plunger with respect to the shoulder e and the fuse socket a, substantially as described, in order that the plunger or any portion thereof may not, at the period of the discharge of a shell from a gun, cause the fuse to be disarranged or driven backward in or through its socket.

Critique — A more detailed explanation of Patent No. 36,037.

36,039

July 29, 1862; Improvement in Fuses for Explosive Shells; Benjamin F. Sturtevant; Boston, MA; Concussion timed Fuze

Claims —

1. In combining with the channeled head of the fuse case and the part B therefore, one of more eduction passages, e e e, so arranged and formed in the part B as to discharge the flame of the priming either directly upon the entire surface of the cap of the fuse composition or so that it may be forced thereupon by the resistance of the atmosphere under circumstances substantially as set forth.

Critique — Sturtevant said that his invention was an improvement upon the Bormann fuze without the problems associated with the Armstrong concussion fuze. While the Bormann fuze was flame-ignited Sturtevant's was ignited by the concussion created when the gun was fired. In addition, he used multiple exits/entrances for the flame from the cap to the fuze. While the idea had merit it was very complicated.

36,172

August 12, 1862; Improvement in Combined Time and Percussion Fuses for Explosive Shells; Sylvanus Sawyer and Addison M. Sawyer; Fitchburg, MA; Combination — concussion timed and percussion

Claims — The combination, in one fuse stock, of a percussion fuse with a time fuse, substantially as described.

Critique — Used the percussion fuse from S. Sawyer's Patent Number 13,799 combined with a Bormann style flame-ignited fuse. General Abbot's research showed that this fuze had an 85 percent reliability. However, he only tested, 88 of the fuzes. In contrast 5,946 Parrott percussion fuzes were tested, with an 85 percent reliability. This fuze was later modified in Patent Number 38,699.

36,236

August 19, 1862; Improvement in Concussion Fuse for Explosive Shells; John P. Schenkl; Boston, MA; Percussion Fuze

Claims —

1. The arrangement and combination of the holding annulus h' and the percussion cap chamber f with the plunger B and its nipple e.

2. The construction of the inelastic abutment in such manner as to extend through the metallic bottom or breech of the case A and project over opposite sides or surfaces thereof, substantially as explained.

3. The formation of the inelastic abutment with a plug hole or passage for receiving a plug, to operate in manner and for purpose substantially as set forth.

Critique — An improvement on Patent 33,495. Schenk called it a concussion fuze but in reality it was a percussion fuze since it was dependent upon the fuze making a direct impact. A good, reliable fuze.

36,295

August 26, 1862; Improvement in Explosive Projectiles for Ordnance; William W. Hanes; Covington, KY; Percussion Fuze

Claims —

1. Constructing projectiles for ordnance with an outside shell, consisting of two parts screwed together, for the purpose and in the manner set forth.

2. An independent inside shell or charge chamber, with two or more nipples and percussion caps attached, for the purpose of securing greater safety in charging and certainty of fire when in use, substantially as described.

3. The cushion C, for the purpose and in the manner specified.

4. The projections or ribs E E, with their corresponding grooves, for the purpose herein set forth.

5. The combination of an outside shell, made in two parts, A A, with an independent charge chamber, B, containing two or more nipples and percussion caps, with the projections or ribs E E and cushion C, substantially as described.

Critique — Used a cushion to keep the caps from hitting the interior of the projectile. As the projectile would be made in multiple parts and would need to be loaded in the field it was too complicated for effective military use.

36,329

September 2, 1862; Improvement in Fuses for Explosive Shells; Francis Alger; Boston, MA; Combination — concussion timed and percussion Fuze

Claims —

1. The construction and arrangement of a sliding time fuse within a fuse case, so that the shell will be exploded by striking, substantially in the manner described.
2. The elastic packing ring h, applied and operating substantially as described.
3. The washer g. applied and operating substantially as described.
4. The arrangement of a hammer, fulminate, and time fuse substantially in the manner and for the purposes specified.

Critique— Could be considered a combination fuze for if it failed to explode before contact, upon contact inertia would allow an opening to occur between the fire and the main charge. As only one of my references lists this fuze it must have seen only limited field use.

36,465

September 16, 1862; Improvement in Percussion Fuses for Explosive Shells; B.B. Hotchkiss; Sharon, CT; Percussion Fuze

Claims —
1. The weakly connected plunger G and a weight, H, so arranged as to stop the orifice in the back of the case C until the discharge of the cannon, and so as to open the orifice certainly at the instant of said discharge, and no longer maintain any connection between the plunger and the weight, all substantially as and for the purpose herein set forth.

Critique— Lots of good ideas, such as using a ball as a hammer as it will not get cocked and stuck in the fuze, using a lead washer to absorb the initial force so that there would not be any bounce-back, but there were some problems. Hotchkiss did not mention if the second ball on the inside of the exploding chamber would block the flame from entering it and while he said that the flame from the cap will get around the ball hammer the space was so small that it would be difficult for that to occur.

36,468

September 16, 1862; Improvement in Igniting Explosive Shells; William Kingsley; New York, NY; Flame-ignited Fuze

Claims —
1. Making fuse shells with a tube or passage from the rear end to the fuse in front, substantially as and for the purpose specified.

Critique— Used a tube traveling the entire length of the projectile in which the flame from the gunpowder could travel and ignite the fuze. Potential problems are that the fuze would probably be blown out of the projectile when the gun was fired and the danger of igniting the main charge in the projectile as the flame moved down the tube. A very dangerous design.

36,553

September 30, 1862; Improvement in Combined Time and Percussion Fuses for Shells; Francis Alger; Boston, MA; Combination — concussion timed and percussion Fuze

Claims—

1. The combination, in one fuse case or stock, of a charged plunger and a time percussion fuse.

2. The apertures v v substantially as and for the purpose specified.

3. The plugged holes m m through the sides of the fuse case, for the purpose of transmitting fire to the interior of the shell, substantially as described.

Critique—A complex fuse whose secondary ignition was dependent upon a direct impact.

36,566

September 30, 1862; Improvement in Concussion Fuses for Shells; William Wheeler Hubbell; Philadelphia, PA; Combination—Flame-ignited using concussion to allow the flame to reach the powder charge of the fuze and Percussion Fuze

Claims—

1. The central metallic stem or fracturing tube surrounded by the burning composition, so that it shall withstand the heat and part at the fracturing point on concussion.

2. The head p, set in the top or front of the metallic stem or tube, so as to fly out of it and expose the central hole in the stem on concussion to explode the shell.

3. The plaster of paris lining inside of the metallic stem, for the purpose described.

4. The combined horizontal and vertical vents in the capping, and these also in combination with the conical or accelerating chamber.

5. Securing the capping by screwing it or otherwise to the front end of the paper case fuse, so as to set the fuse readily into any stock already capped for service when in action.

6. The paper facing surrounding the metallic fracturing stem, to support it and burn away and release it, substantially as described.

7. The fracturing stem, when constructed of sections of metal put together and operating in the manner and for the purpose substantially as described.

8. The conical or accelerating chamber l in side of the water capping, as described.

Critique—An even more complicated version of his fuze described in Patent No. 34,059.

36,576

September 30, 1862; Improvement in Percussion Fuse for Explosive Shells; John P. Schenkl; Boston, MA; Percussion Fuze

Claims—

1. The construction of the rear end of the plunger case A in such manner that the said rear end while the fuse may be fixed in a shell shall separate the plunger chamber e from the powder charge of the shell, and on explosion of the charge of the plunger be broken away thereby, so as to allow the flame of such explosion to communicate with the explosive charge of the shell.

2. The concussion fuse as made with an explosive charge arranged within its plunger, and to be fired by explosion of the cap or percussion powder of the nipple, such being for the purpose of setting fire to the bursting charge of the shell, as described.

Critique—A modification of Schenkl's basic fuze design which was one of the more successful of the Civil War percussion fuzes.

36,686

October 14, 1862; Improvement in Compound Explosive Projectiles; Mills L. Callender; New York, NY; Percussion Fuze

Claims—

1. A projectile having a steel bar or center inserted on a line with its axis, when said bar contains an independent exploding magazine.

2. The combination, in a projectile, of a discharging chamber and penetrating bar of steel or similar metal having an exploding magazine within it, and supplied with a percussion and fuse apparatus, for the purposes and in the manner as set forth.

Critique—Patent states that a rotary motion will be produced even in a smooth-bore gun and that it will penetrate hard and refractory substances before exploding. Does not consider bounce-back and uses the gases produced by the gunpowder to impart rotation. The use of the gases is before its time but it is very probable the projectile would prematurely explode due to bounce-back.

36,806

October 28, 1862; Improvement in Combined Time and Concussion Fuse for Shells; W.S. Smoot; District of Columbia; Combination—concussion time and concussion impact Fuze

Claims—

1. The improvement in the means of igniting time fuses by combining the windage and concussion principles, substantially as and for the purposes set forth.

2. The improvement, in time fuses, of providing them with a communication with the shell closed by a sliding valve or plunger just above the point at which the fuse ignited, substantially as and for the purposes set forth.

Critique—Too complex.

36,858

November 4, 1862; Improvement in Explosive Projectiles for Ordnance; William F. Rippon; Providence, RI; Concussion timed Fuze

Claims—

1. The combination of the mortar tube B, central tube, F, plate D, and the plug E with the shell A and the openings therein, a a, in the manner and for the purpose herein shown and described.

2. Having the tube F provided with a spiral fuse groove, e, so arranged as to conduct the fire from chambers between the tubes F B successively across the vents

b b b b of the mortars to the powder chamber G and the interior of the tube F, as and for the purpose herein shown and described.

The combination of the partition I with the mortar tube B and the shell A, thereby forming a ballast chamber, H, all as herein shown and described.

Critique— Projectile has multiple projectiles in it which were supposed to be launched at different times. An idea which would have to wait for the 20th century as technically infeasible in 1862.

37,200

December 16, 1862; Improvement in Concussion Fuses for Shells; Samuel R. Russell; Middletown, OH; Combination — flame-ignited but concussion impact activated Fuze

Claims—

1. The combination, with a projectile, of the perforated tube B, the plunger D, plug H, and fuse C, arranged and operated in the manner and for the purposes substantially as herein described.

Critique— Trusts a small metal cap to keep the fuse that is located in the rear of the projectile from being driven into the projectile. A potentially dangerous fuze and projectile.

37,275

January 6, 1863; Improvement in Percussion Fuses for Explosive Shells; John Webster Cochran; New York, NY; Percussion Fuze

Claims—

1. Weakly attaching the striker D to the cap C at the front end of the projectile, substantially in the manner and so as to secure the advantages herein set forth.

2. The construction and arrangement of the parts C, D, and F, so that the parts F F shall hook into the cavities C C, in the manner and for the purpose herein set forth.

3. Performing the triple function of, first, holding the striker directly connected to the front cap of the projectile until the discharge of the piece; second, partially overcoming the inertia of the striker before or in the act of their breakage; and third, absorbing the shock and inducing non–elasticity in the impact of the striker on the rear face of chamber B, all by the employment of the same wires, F F, or their equivalents, arranged and bent as herein shown.

Critique— A variation of the Parrott, Hotchkiss, and Schenkl percussion fuzes with the major difference being that Cochran's safety devices are vertical rather than horizontal. Problem is that if the safety devices are strong enough to prevent a premature explosion then, as they would be in the path of the hammer, they would also prevent the desired explosion. Charles Jones (*Artillery Fuses of the Civil War*) states that none of these fuzes have been found in Cochran projectiles so the fuze was probably never accepted for use by the military.

37,520

January 27, 1863; Improvement in Explosive Shells for Ordnance; Horace Resley; Cumberland, MD; Percussion Fuze

Claims—

1. The arrangement of the means or devices herein set forth for protecting the operating mechanism and providing for the discharge when desired.

Critique—Fuzes are placed on the sides of the projectile using hammers that extend out from the sides of the projectile that will allow the projectile to penetrate before exploding. This idea would make the projectile not very aerodynamic.

37,557

January 27, 1863; Improvement in Projectiles for Ordnance; Charles W. Stafford; Burlington, IA; Percussion Fuze

Claims—

1. A sub-caliber shot or shell formed with a cutting face of iron or steel, and surrounded with a cylindrical casing of wood or other light material, adapted to fit the bore of the gun, and formed, applied, and secured in any manner substantially as herein set forth.

2. The cap C, employed, in the manner described, to secure the rear end of the casing B, support and guide the rear end of the casting B, support and guide the rear end of the projectile within the bore, and afford means for the attachment of the packing ring D.

3. The cap G, employed, in the manner described, to secure and guide the front of the projectile within the bore, and effect the explosion of the charge by resistance against the surface of a body penetrated by the bolt A.

Critique—Projectile was designed to penetrate armor and then explode. Biggest problem is that there is no safety device on the fuze, which is located on the outer wall of the inner part of projectile and designed to strike the inner wall of the outer part of the projectile. Too much chance of a premature explosion.

37,566

February 3, 1863; Improvement in Percussion Exploders for Shells; J.M. Connel; Newark, OH; Concussion impact Fuze

Claims—

1. Suspending a plunger upon a projecting stem, b, of the screw plug A, in the manner and for the purpose set forth.

2. So applying a shell exploder to a shell that when the latter strikes obliquely or sidewise the said exploder shall be ignited by a leverage impact against the rear of the screw plug, in the manner substantially as described.

Critique—Fuze is designed to shift and explode when the projectile hits something. Problem is that Connel does not tell how the fuze is to shift when it is surrounded by case shot and its packing. It is doubtful if this fuze would work very well if at all.

37,675

February 17, 1863; Improvement in Percussion Fuses for Explosive Shells; John W. Cochran; New York, NY; Percussion Fuze

Claims —

1. The hollow tapering and contractible material G, arranged to operate, in connection with the striker of a percussion shell, substantially in the manner and so as to secure the advantages herein set forth.

2. The loaded cap or mass G, arranged to operate, in connection with the striker D and tapering contractible material F, in the manner set forth.

Critique — Called his fuze both a percussion and a concussion in different parts of the patent. Does not discuss the danger of a friction ignition of the powder in the projectile from the cone being driven into the powder when the gun is fired and the projectile is launched. Cochran does attempt to solve the problem of rebound by the slider.

37,756

February 24, 1863; Improvement in Percussion Fuses for Shells; B.B. Hotchkiss; Sharon, CT; Percussion

Claims — A percussion hammer or striker constructed substantially as herein described, having a hard exterior and a soft interior and base, for the purpose specified.

Critique — Changed the material the hammer was made of so that upon discharge of the gun it would not hit the rear of the fuze and bounce forward exploding the cap. Basically, Hotchkiss was making a fairly reliable fuze even more reliable.

37,830

March 3, 1863; Improvement in Percussion Apparatus for Explosive Shells; John J. Schillinger; District of Columbia; Percussion Fuze

Claims —

1. Dividing the interior space of a shell or the hollow part of a projectile into two separate chambers, one containing the charge of powder, the other containing a plunger, when the said plunger is secured to the shell, as herein before specified.

2. Fastening the said plunger to the end or rear part of the shell or projectile by means of a combustible cord, in the manner for the purpose substantially as herein described.

Critique — Fuze is in the center of the projectile and is struck by a plunger coming from the rear of the projectile. The idea has potential but, to the best of my knowledge, was never used by the military.

38,352

April 28, 1863; Improved Apparatus for Casting Fuses; George Wright; District of Columbia; For fuze manufacturing Fuze

Claims —

1. Removing the cope e and nowel f from the fuse while the latter is firmly held and supported by the cheeks KK or their equivalents, for the purpose herein set forth.

2. The arrangement of the cams G G, parts c and f and K K, and the means of guiding the same, substantially as and for the purpose herein set forth.

3. Molding and removing a secondary part in the same machine with the main part, substantially in the manner and with the advantage herein set forth.

Critique—An attempt to improve on the method of manufacturing Bormann Fuzes. Unluckily, the Bormann Fuze was shortly to become outdated.

38,359

April 28, 1863; Improvement in Explosive Projectiles for Rifled Ordnance; Charles W. Smith & G.H. Babcock and B.B. Hotchkiss & Charles A. Hotchkiss; New York, NY, and Sharon, CT; Flame-ignited Fuze

Claims—

1. In explosive projectiles for rifled ordnance, dividing the cavity into two parts by the plate B, or its equivalent, supported upon or by the body of the shell, so that it cannot be forced backward by the inertia of the balls C, but may be easily thrown forward by the explosion of the powder in D, substantially as and for the purpose herein set forth.

2. The combination of the tube E, plate B, and fuse plug K, so arranged that the bullets C may be inserted through the mouth of the shell after the tube E is in place, and the fuse plug caused to embrace the end thereof, substantially as herein shown.

3. An explosive projectile in which the point is cast in one piece with the body, with a weak line, G, and with the plate B inserted in the cavity thereof, in the manner herein specified.

Critique—A standard Hotchkiss projectile with a different interior arrangement. The new interior arrangement had a large bursting charge for a case shot projectile located in the rear of the projectile rather than the center. Consequently, a very long powder train was needed from the fuze to the charge. A good idea but it would have created a very focused pattern for the case shot. It is doubtful if it would have been a significant improvement over the standard case shot arrangement.

38,491

May 12, 1863; Improvement in Explosive Projectiles; Job Johnson; Brooklyn, NY; Concussion impact Fuze

Claims—

1. The cross bar g, screw spindle k, and internal flange, u, in combination with the cap f, nut l, and soft metal ring o, fitted and acting in the manner and for the purpose set forth.

2. The spring tube r, to hold on the detonating cap s, in combination with the rod q and screw t, that is driven in by the concussion, as set forth.

Critique—Cap is held in place by a spring and is on the end of a metal rod that goes from the front of the projectile to its rear. There is no mention of how to stop setback from causing the cap to prematurely detonate.

38,699

May 26, 1863; Improvement in Igniting Time-Fuses of Shells; Addison M. Sawyer; Fitchburg, MA; Combination — concussion timed and percussion

Claims—The employment, in combination with a time fuse, of an open socket and a detachable fulminating primer, or their equivalents, co-operating, as described, for the purpose of igniting the time fuse by the discharge of the gun, substantially as described.

Critique—A very successful fuze as it had an 85 percent serviceability rate in General Abbot's experiments. Had the disadvantage of the gunner needing to place the primer into the fuze after the projectile was placed in the muzzle of the gun.

38,797

June 2, 1863; Improvement in Concussion Fuse for Explosive Projectiles; J.L. Henry (Regular Army); Long Old Fields, MD; Combination — concussion timed and concussion impact Fuze

Claims—

1. The employment of a conical plunger, B, as described, in combination with an enlarged chamber, Q, and suitable concave seat, for the purpose of allowing a very wide lateral range of motion of the said plunger in case of an oblique impact of the shell.

2. The method of holding the plunger safely in its seat by means of the rotating rod u, with its catch or stop r and rear valve attachment, v, whereby it may be released only by the pressure of the discharge upon the said valve in the base of the shell, substantially as described.

3. The additional holding device of a hook or elbow stop, s, fixed in the cylindrical seat piece C, and a pin, I, in the plunger, or as an equivalent thereof, the use of the centrifugal balls q for the purpose of retaining the plunger securely until released by the rotation of the projectile due to the rifling of the gun, substantially as described.

4. The employment of a friction tap, o, in connection with the conical plunger, in the manner and for the purpose set forth.

5. The combination, with the conical plunger and friction tape, the twine or check string t, to prevent the released plunger from straining and igniting the primer before the shell impinges, substantially as described.

6. In concussion shells, a chamber for the plunger of such dimensions as that the plunger may move freely, not only directly forward, as usual, but also sidewise, and perform its function even before reaching the sides of its chamber, in case of side impact, substantially as described.

7. The use of two sets of "stops," the one rigid, the other to yield on impact, as and for the purposes set forth.

Critique—Uses the gas from the firing of the gun and the rotation of the projectile to deactivate the two safety devices. In addition, mentions other methods of releasing the safeties such as balls, plunger, and pistons. Too complicated.

38,994

June 23, 1863; Improvement in Concussion Fuse for Shells; Isaac P. Tice; New York, NY; Concussion impact Fuze

Claims—

1. The construction of the tube or plug of a percussion fuse, with two separate chambers or compartments, one for containing a fulminate and the other for containing sand or other hard granular substance, so arranged and combined by means of a lock that by the impact which is given to the projectile by the firing of the charge of the gun the said lock may be unlocked to permit communication between the said chambers to permit the admixture of their contents, substantially as and for the purpose herein specified.

2. So constructing and arranging the parts of the above mentioned lock that, though it shall be unlocked by the concussion produced by firing of the charge of the gun, the chambers containing the fulminate and hard granular substance shall not be allowed to communicate until after the projectile has left the gun, substantially as and for the purpose herein set forth.

3. The admixture of fulminates used in a percussion fuse with cotton, gun-cotton, wool, sawdust, or other soft material, substantially as and for the purpose herein described.

4. The lining of the sides of the chamber provided in a percussion fuse tube or plug for containing fulminate with flannel, cloth, or other soft material, and the placing of cushions of soft material at the ends of the said chamber, substantially as and for the purpose herein specified.

5. The employment, in the percussion fuse of an explosive projectile, of two fulminates, one of which is more sensitive and easily ignited, and the other of which burns more slowly or with a stronger flame, as fulminate of mercury, substantially as and for the purpose herein specified.

Critique— A very complicated fuse dependent upon many independent factors for it to work properly. General Abbot found it to have a 73 percent serviceability. The fuze was too complicated for the time period.

39,267

July 21, 1863; Improvement in Removable Charge Chambers for Explosive Shells; Francis Alger; Boston, MA; Accessory—Detonating charge connected to the fuze Fuze

Claims—

1. The use of a tube or pouch of India rubber cloth, or of other flexible material, containing gunpowder and attached to a fuse, one apparatus, which may be inserted into or removed from a projectile at a single operation

Critique— An excellent idea, which still needed some work, from an experienced fuze designer. Does not say how the pouch is to be connected to the fuze except that a groove would need to be cut in the fuze. Problem would be getting all of the fuze manufacturers to machine in the groove. He also does not mention the difficulty of loading a flexible tube when the gunner is in a hurry.

39,682

August 25, 1863; Improvement in Combined Time and Percussion Fuse for Shells; John P. Schenkl; Boston, MA; Combination — concussion timed and concussion impact Fuze

Claims—

1. The combination of the band or tape f^2 with the wrench pin E and the rotator C, and to operate in the manner therewith, and for the purpose or purposes substantially as hereinbefore described.

2. The combination and arrangement of the notch or recess t^2 with the rotator C, and the tape or band f^2, applied to it and the wrenchpin E, as specified.

3. The rotator as made, with the outlet m arranged so as to open out of its side or sides, in manner and for the purpose described.

4. The fuse-case, as not only constructed with a helical range of holes, but with a powder chamber arranged either on the outer surface of such fuse-case or in a groove thereof, and with respect to the range of holes, and for the purpose of igniting the main or bursting charge of a shell, as specified.

Critique— A follow-on of Patent Number 35,897. Its main improvement was the addition of a "reservoir or magazine of powder attached to the fuse holder." The purpose of the reservoir was to "insure the firing of the shell charge even when more or less out of contact with or away from the fuse." Schenkl was attempting to compensate for the problem caused when the main charge would be compacted toward the back of the projectile, due to setback, and thus not be close enough to the fuse to be ignited by it.

40,054

September 22, 1863; Improvement in Explosive Shells; William Maginn; New York, NY; Timed concussion Fuze

Claims—

1. The ring C and attached hammer b, applied to operate within a double groove, d d', in combination with a nipple, c, and fuse hole g, substantially as and for the purpose herein specified.

Critique— Uses centrifugal force to detonate the cap. A complex design that would have been difficult to manufacture.

40,350

October 20, 1863; Improvement in Fuses for Explosive Shells; James McIntyre; New York, NY; Combination — flamed-ignited, concussion impact

Claims— A ball or block cemented upon a tube or opening communicating with the interior of the projectile, and surrounded with fuse powder, as set forth, so that the explosion of the projectile will take place when the said ball or block is shaken off its seat by the projectile striking any object, as specified.

Critique— Almost a direct copy of the Belgium Splingard concussion fuse, which was 91 percent reliable, but it is doubtful that McIntyre's fuze was this reliable as he found it necessary to make improvements on it. Later improved in Patent Number 44,581.

40,396

October 27, 1863; Improvement in Explosive Projectiles; Thomas H. Burrowes; Chicopee, MA; Flame-ignited Fuze

Claims—

1. The arrangement within a projectile for ordnance of alternate layers of gunpowder, and of an inflammable material which is capable of setting fire to bodies on which it falls, substantially as herein specified.

2. The perforated fuse tube B, applied in combination with the two chambers a and b and the fuse shield C, substantially as and for the purpose herein specified.

Critique— Fuze is designed to detonate a series of explosions within the projectile to include a flammable mixture. A very dangerous arrangement.

40,538

November 3, 1863; Improvement in Explosive Shells; Halvor Halvorson; Cambridge, MA; Concussion, impact Fuze

Claims—

1. The exterior explosive chamber lying exterior and around the central passage, and in combination therewith and with the mouth, and air openings and passages for producing rotation of the shell, as herein set forth.

2. The cap h, in combination with the explosive chamber g, as and for the purposes herein described.

Critique— Uses the air produced by the flight of the projectile to create rotation but the projectile itself is blunt nosed and not very aerodynamic. There is no safety mechanism on the fuze and it just consists of caps on a ring surrounding the explosive chamber. A very dangerous design.

40,828

December 8, 1863; Improvement in Percussion Fuses for Shells; A.H. Emery; New York, NY; Percussion Fuze

Claims—

1. The combination and use of the flange D and thread F with the plunger C, substantially as and for the purposes herein described and set forth.

2. The combination and use of the washer E, when combined with the shell A, flange D, and screw thread F, substantially as and for the purposes herein described and set forth.

Critique— Uses threads to secure the plunger with the idea that the threads will be stripped by the initial force of the projectile being fired. Patent also claims a means of waterproofing the fuze by using a packing ring. It is hard to believe that the threads would easily be stripped by the firing. In addition, the patent is not a real improvement over the standard pin used to secure the plunger.

40,856

December 8, 1863; Improvement in Compound Projectiles for Ordnance; Lucius E. Reynolds; Mendon, IL; Percussion Fuze

Claims—

1. The combination of the major and minor projectiles, the interposed charge, and the fulminate priming, substantially as herein described, the whole forming a compound projectile operating as herein set forth.

2. The protecting ring e, applied substantially as and for the purpose set forth.

Critique— Has the plunger sticking out in front of the main projectile so that when it hits something it is forced into the main projectile and explodes the percussion cap. No artilleryman in his right mind would ever consider using this projectile.

40,885

December 8, 1863; Improvement in Percussion Fuses for Shells; William F. Patterson; Somerset, KY (now in U.S. Army); Percussion Fuze

Claims—

1. The holding of the inner tube, C, which is the hammer or plunger, in its place and to the outer tube, B, by means of a wooden pin, D, applied and acting as herein described and represented.

Critique— Uses a metal that can be cast versus the brass that has to be machined and uses a wooden pin rather than a metal one as the safety device. Entire purpose is to lessen the cost of making the fuzes. Problem is that a metal that melts at low temperatures would probably also melt from the friction temperature created by the fuze flying through the air. This was the same problem faced by Schenkl with his combination fuze.

40,888

December 8, 1863; Improvement in Explosive Projectiles; Joseph Nottingham Smith; Jersey City, NJ; Percussion Fuze

Claims—

1. The arrangement of the bent levers H H in pivot sockets in the wall of the missile, as also in relation to the front and rear shells, so as to simultaneously fulfill the two functions of direct hammers, and, through connecting wires, of operating other hammers in a distinct part of the missile, substantially as herein specified.

2. The protecting cap G, with its hollow cap arms g g, constructed, arranged, and operating substantially as herein set forth.

3. The arrangement of the spiral wings M M, in combination with the arms g g of the cap G, as herein set forth.

4. Locating separate shells in the extreme ends of the projectile, and exploding them simultaneously by the connecting wires l l, or their equivalent, substantially as herein described.

5. The separate inclosed hammer chambers N N, as set forth.

6. The peculiar construction and combination of the rear multi chambered shell C and plug D, as set forth.

Critique— Projectile is designed so that part of it remains outside of the gun. Uses four percussion caps — two on the front exploding chamber and two on the rear exploding chamber. Too complicated and obviously designed by someone who knows nothing about aerodynamics or artillery.

41,220

January 12, 1864; Improvement in Explosive Shells for Ordnance; Henry Helm; Salina, KS; Concussion impact Fuze

Claims —

1. The use in shells for ordnance of friction primers, the head of which projects from the surface of the shell so that on the impact of the shell the wire of the primer will be drawn sufficiently to explode it, substantially as described.

2. In combination therewith, the use of an adjustable time fuse for regulating the interval between the impact and explosion, substantially as described.

Critique — Uses a number of caps in different locations to ensure that one will take a direct hit and explode. He calls it a percussion fuze but in reality it is a concussion system. There were other less complicated concussion systems in place.

41,615

February 16, 1864; Improvement in Hand Grenades; George P. Ganster and Isaac S. Schuyler; New York, NY; Concussion impact, Chemical Fuze

Claims —

1. The combination of the chambers A B, cap C, plug b, frangible fuse D, and balls E, and constructed, arranged, and operating in manner as and for the purpose set forth.

Critique — Not an artillery fuze but the principles are the same and George Ganster was a known artillery projectile designer. Uses a ball to break a bulb filled with sulphuric acid which then will ignite the powder charge. The basic idea had been used before but had never caught on.

41,668

February 23, 1864; Improvement in Packing Projectiles for Rifled Ordnance; John Absterdam; New York, NY; Percussion Fuze

Claims —

1. Constructing a projectile for rifle cannon with one or more bands or bearings of an anti-friction metal that expands in cooling or that does not shrink in cooling, for the purpose herein described.

2. Sawing the end of the expanding cup in several cuts diagonally to the axis of the projectile, substantially as described.

Critique — Patent deals with a new method of allowing the projectiles to accept the rifling. It does tell how the fuze operated, which was the West Point method with a friction retainer.

41,882

March 8, 1864; Improvement in Canister Shells; William S. Williams; Canton, OH; Flame-ignited timed (two fuzes) Fuze

Claims —

1. The peculiarly formed hemispherical chamber C, in the described com-

bination with the shoulder h and final explosive chamber D, for the purposes specified.

2. The combination of the perforated plate H, resting upon a shoulder, h, the tapering tube I, permanently attached by its smaller end to the plate H around the aperture I, and the cap F, with a tampering neck, f, fitting within the large end of the tube I, all as herein shown and described, and for the purposes specified.

3. The fusible guard e, applied to the orifice of the fuse E in the manner and for the purposes explained.

Critique — Tries to combine an exploding projectile with a canister projectile. The canister portion of the projectile is expected to explode first and then the projectile will completely explode later. It is doubtful if the idea would work in reality. Two fuzes are involved. The first is ignited by the flame from the exploding gunpowder while the second is ignited from the explosion of the canister portion of the projectile.

41,937

March 15, 1864; Improvement in Percussion Fuse for Explosive Shells; Robert P. Parrott; Cold Spring, NY; Percussion

Claims — The construction and arrangement of the columns or arms f, substantially in the manner herein shown and described, so that said arms will be longitudinally strong, but laterally weak, and thus, when rapid rotation is imparted to the shell by discharge from the gun the arms will bend or break, but at all other times will remain firm and rigid, as set forth.

Critique — Dependent upon the centrifugal forces created when the projectile takes the rifling and spins to become armed. Based on a report in the Official Records the fuze had to be modified in the field by cutting the arms off for it to work.

42,082

March 29, 1864; Improvement in Concussion Bulbs for Fuses; George P. Ganster and Isaac S. Schuyler; New York, NY; Concussion impact (chemical) Fuze

Claims —

1. A percussion fuse consisting of a pear shaped bulb formed of glass containing sulphuric acid hermetically sealed, and having on its exterior a paste composed of chloride of potash and sulphur, all as herein described, and for the purpose specified.

Critique — Same basic fuze as used in Patent 41,615, a glass bulb filled with sulphuric acid that when broken will ignite the main powder charge. This patent only deals with the glass bulb. In the earlier patent it is stated that this fuze can be used with grenades or shells.

42,185

April 5, 1864; Improvement in Percussion Fuses for Shells; George P. Ganster; New York, NY; Concussion impact

Claims — A percussion fuse composed of a screw tube, A, closing-cap B, tube a, thin tube f, with attached annular plunger b, globule C, soft material j, and shot or grannular material g, the whole united in the manner herein shown and described.

Critique— Though Ganster called it a percussion fuze in reality it was a concussion fuze as it was not dependent upon a direct impact. The fuze probably saw limited use as only one of my references discusses it. It should have been a fairly reliable fuze.

42,363

April 19, 1864; Improvement in Hand Grenades; George P. Ganster; New York, NY; Concussion impact (chemical) Fuze

Claims—

1. The peculiar construction and arrangement of the compound chambers c d, in combination with the ball e, for separating the chambers c and d and their respective chemical contents, together with the detent f and its mechanical arrangements, substantially as described, and for the purposes set forth.

Critique— Patent deals with a new safety mechanism for Ganster's chemical concussion fuze.

42,660

May 10, 1864; Improvement in Time Fuses for Shells; B. B. Hotchkiss; Sharon, CT; Concussion timed Fuze

Claims—

1. In connection with the fuses of time shells, the time composition C, fulminate F, striker G, interior communicating passages, G', and exterior lateral discharge passages, I, combined and arranged substantially as and for the purpose herein set forth.

Critique— A new idea that should work. The hammer is released when the gun is fired and strikes the cap igniting the timed powder train. One problem is that the fuze is not very aerodynamic and susceptible to increased heat.

43,029

June 7, 1864; Improvement in Explosive Projectiles for Ordnance; Job Johnson; Brooklyn, NY; Percussion Fuze

Claims—

1. The screw plug f, formed with the cavity at the front and receiving the detonating cap on the end of the rod q, for the purposes and as specified.

2. A plug or plate of steel, forming a facing or surface to the softer metal of the plug f, for the purposes and as specified.

Critique— Refers to his previous Patent, 38,491, and makes changes to that patent so that the rod that holds the percussion cap will move straight back and not swerve. Obviously, there were problems with his original idea.

43,801

August 9, 1864; Improvement in Igniting Fuses for Shells; Charles W. Smith; Evans, NY; Flame-ignited Fuze

Claims—

1. A portable fuse primer adapted to be transported separately and to be attached at the end of a time fuse just previous to the insertion of the shell in the gun, for the purpose of igniting the fuse at the moment of discharge.

Critique— An invention that was attempting to keep a dying technology, flame-ignited fuzes, alive by adding a primer to the fuze in hopes of giving it a better chance of igniting.

43,922

August 23, 1864; Improvement in Time Fuses for Explosive Shells; Martin McDevitt; Beloit, WI; Flame-ignited Fuze

Claims—

1. The T shaped fuse A B, the central stem being introduced into the axis of the projectile at the front, while the arms are bent to correspond to the shape of the projectile, held in longitudinal channels in the same, and filled with composition, and graduated so as to be cut to suit the time of flight, substantially as and for the purpose set forth.

Critique— A hollow tubing system which fits over the projectile and has holes in its bottom where the flame from the discharge of the gun can enter. Lots of problems with this design besides that it is trying to extend the life of a soon-to-be-obsolete technology, flame-ignited fuzes. First, the projectile must be made smaller in diameter so that the fuze can fit over it. Second, the hollow tubes must be cut to length for the burn time desired. Too complicated to be useful.

43,993

August 30, 1864; Improvement in Percussion Ignitors of Time Fuses for Explosive Shells; B.B. Hotchkiss; Sharon, CT; Concussion timed Fuze

Claims—

1. Inclosing the striker D within a thin protecting case, B, and securing the parts B and D together, as herein shown, so that the striker and its case may be transported and handled, with the fulminate between them protected from friction or abrasion, substantially as and for the purposes herein set forth.

2. Constructing the case of a fuse ignitor in two parts, A and B, with the base and sides of each part formed in one piece, and one part fitted within the other nearly the whole length of each, substantially as and for the purpose above described.

3. In connection with the above, providing both ends of the device with fulminate C, so as to adapt it to operate equally well with either end forward, substantially in the manner herein set forth.

Critique— A well thought out idea by an experienced designer that used as much current military equipment as possible — fuze is designed to fit in the current Army and Navy paper case time fuzes. It is a small fitting that fits in the end of the time fuze and when the gun is fired the hammer inside of the fitting strikes a percussion cap which then ignites the timed powder train.

44,023

August 30, 1864; Improvement in Combined Time and Percussion Fuses for Shells; Charles W. Stafford; New York, NY; Combination — Flame-ignited and percussion Fuze

Claims —

1. The combination, in one fuse, of the following elements, to wit: first, the annular chamber E, extending from front to rear of the fuse, to contain a time composition; second, the apertures e', affording communication between the said chamber and the interior of the shell; and, third, the nipple plunger B, surrounded by and adapted to slide within the chamber E, the said parts being arranged to operate herein specified.

2. The cap b, provided with the apertures b', which operate in connection with the apertures a^3, in the manner described, so as to adapt the time fuse E to be ignited by the windage, or to be closed from communication therewith, as and for the purposes specified.

Critique — Stafford has a high opinion of his invention as he states in the patent, "This fuse is designed to be employed in connection with shells of any suitable construction, and constitutes an unfailing medium for producing the explosion thereof." Somewhat complicated but workable.

44,061

September 6, 1864; Improvement in Combined Time and Concussion Fuse; Clifford Arick; St. Clairsville, OH; Combination — flame-ignited and percussion Fuze

Claims —

1. Constructing a Bormann fuse case with its magazine on its index side and with an independent concentric fire chamber between its fuse chamber and magazine, substantially as described.

2. Combining with the magazine of a Bormann fuse case, and acting as a bottom to it, a hollow pin to serve as a means of fastening it in a shell or as a conductor of its flame through an intervening space or obstacle to the bursting charge thereof, substantially as set forth.

3. Combining with a Bormann fuse case thus constructed, with or without its independent fire chamber, by means of a central hollow pin, a concussion or percussion fuse, either or both, and whether ignitable by or independent of the windage flame, substantially as described.

4. So combining in a Bormann fuse case a fuse and concentric fire chamber that when the fuse is cut at the desired point the partition wall between the two chambers may be conveniently included in the cut, and they be thereby united, substantially as described.

Critique — Combines the Bormann flame-ignited fuze with the Tice percussion fuze. Tries to do everything and consequently is too complicated besides being more difficult to manufacture.

44,353

September 20, 1864; Improvement in Explosive Shells; B.H. Tripp; Culpeper, VA; Combination — Flame-ignited and percussion Fuze

Claims—

1. The central barrel, B, breech plug D, and time fuse b, in combination with an explosive projectile, constructed substantially as described.

2. The combination of percussion exploder g, time fuse b, and communication e with a central discharge projectile, which is constructed with a central barrel, B, chamber C, casing A, and breech plug D, substantially as described.

Critique— Two independent fuzes combined with a system in which the case shot portion of the projectile (timed) will explode prior to the remainder of the projectile exploding (percussion). Gunners would need to remember to loosen the safety device for the percussion fuze prior to loading the projectile. An idea which will not work as described as Tripp disregards some laws of physics.

44,546

October 4, 1864; Improvement in Combined Time, Percussion, and Concussion Fuse; Anson Merriman; New York, NY; Combination — concussion timed and percussion Fuze

Claims—

1. The combination and arrangement, in a fuse, of a friction primer (to fire the time fuse composition) located at the outer end of the fuse case, with a driver located at the inner end of said case, so that the former is outside of the time fuse (when it is in place) and the latter is inside of it, substantially as set forth.

2. The combination and arrangement of a friction primer located at the inner end of the fuse case (to fire the bursting charge of the projectile) with a driver located nearer the outer end of the fuse case, substantially as set forth.

3. The combination of the fuse tube with a driver so constructed and arranged that it can displace the time fuse when moved outward in the fuse tube or case.

4. The combination of the driver for operating a friction primer (or for displacing the time fuse) with a percussion primer so arranged relatively to the driver that said percussion primer may be exploded by the movement of the driver in performing its other function, substantially as set forth.

5. The combination of the driver with a friction casing or sleeve perforated and indented, substantially as set forth.

Critique— A very complicated fuze that was dependent upon one fuze to move out of the way of the other fuze so that the second one can function properly.

44,581

October 4, 1864; Improvement in Fuses for Explosive Shells; James McIntyre; New York, NY; Combination —flame-ignited and concussion impact

Claims— A tapering plug introduced into a tapering hole in, the powder of the fuse, with the larger end of the said plug toward the outer end of the fuse, for the purposes and as specified.

Critique—An improvement upon Patent Number 40,350. McIntyre must have had too many premature explosions in his original design for he found it necessary to taper the tube the stopper sat upon. Obviously, in the original design the stopper would fall off too early and allow the main charge to ignite.

44,588

October 11, 1864; Improvement in Fuses for Explosive Shells; Clifford Arick; St. Clairsville, OH; Combination—flame-ignited or percussion Fuze
Claims—
1. The formation of an annular fire chamber within the radius of a Bormann or curved fuse by combining a grooved head to its screw pin, or by combining the grooved head of a screw plug with the inner wall of its soft metal case, substantially as described.
2. A packing disk for an annular fuse, having on one side of it the necessary wedge or wedges for packing it, and on the other a magazine, as described.
3. The combination of an annular fire chamber situated within the radius of a Bormann fuse with an independent primer, so that the flame generated by the primer is instantly injected into such fire chamber, from whence, escaping at the cut, it will ignite the fuse, substantially as described.
4. So combining with a soft metal fuse case, a fuse plug, or a concussion or percussion fuse case as to securely hold the former in the projectile by the combined action of the screw thread and flanged head of the latter.
Critique—Some "improvements" in Arick's previous Patent, 44,061. Fuze is still too complicated.

44,861

November 1, 1864; Improvement in Combined Time and Concussion Fuse; William F. Goodwin; Powhatan, OH; Combination—flame-ignited timed and percussion impact Fuze
Claims—
1. The combination of the annular or Bormann time fuse B, the chambers C C', the solid sliding disk D, and the apertures a' a^2 a^3, all arranged and operating as and for the purposes specified.
2. In combination with the above, the friction primer b' b b^2 and apertures a, constituted and adapted to operate substantially as set forth.
Critique—Goodwin says that the fuze is a concussion but in reality it must hit directly on its nose if it is to work, so it is a percussion impact. Another attempt to improve upon the Bormann. This fuze would be complicated to manufacture.

45,024

November 15, 1864; Improvement in Fuse for Explosive Shells; John F. Cleu; New York, NY; Percussion Fuze
Claims—
1. The combination of the perforated tube B, extending through the charge

to be exploded, and the pin or rod E inserted into the said tube and cemented or held therein by the fulminate priming, substantially as herein specified.

Critique— Fuze was designed to ignite the main charge in a number of different locations simultaneously. In all probability, due to the burning rate of gunpowder, the idea would not work.

45,035

November 15, 1864; Improvement in Concussion Fuse for Shells; William F. Goodwin; New York, NY; Combination—flame-ignited and concussion impact Fuze

Claims—

1. A concussion fuse provided with a sectional tub, H H' H², constructed and adapted to operate in the manner and for the purposes herein described.

Critique— A fuze that was supposed to operate when the powder train is burned away enough so that a tube will fall away and expose the main charge to the flame. Goodwin does not mention how the powder will be packed firm enough around the tube to keep it from moving when the gun is fired. A dangerous design.

45,128

November 22, 1864; Improvement in Combined Time and Concussion Fuse for Shells; Clifford Arick; St. Clairsville, OH; Combination—flame-ignited and concussion impact Fuze

Claims—

1. The construction of a soft metal fuse case having an annular chamber or groove for the reception of an annular time fuse, and a vertical or other independent chamber or tube for the reception of a concussion or percussion fuse.

2. The union, in a single magazine, to an annular fuse, of the two ends of the fuse by independent vents, one operated in the usual way, on time, and the other by concussion or percussion.

Critique— An "improvement" on Arick's previous patents, 44,061 and 44,588. Too complicated.

45,381

December 6, 1864; Improvement in Time Fuses for Explosive Shells; George Wright; District of Columbia; Flame-ignited Fuze

Claims—

1. Making the fuse case annular and fitting or pressing it into a groove or channel around the charge hole, and connecting it with the cavity of the shell by an inlet distinct from that through which the bursting charge is introduced, substantially as and for the purpose specified.

2. Such a construction and arrangement of the fuse and shell as admits of the bursting charge being introduced or withdrawn from the shell either before or after and independently of the insertion of the fuse, substantially in the manner and for the purpose set forth.

Critique—Fuze is an attempt to improve the Bormann Fuze by increasing the amount of burn time (12 seconds versus five seconds) and making it safer to unload by creating a separate powder loading hole than that used by the fuze to ignite the main charge. Purpose was to allow the Bormann Fuze to be used in the longer-range guns. However, the idea came too late in the war to be of much use.

45,806

January 10, 1865; Improvement in Igniting Hand-Grenades; John S. Adams; Staunton, MA; Friction timed Fuze

Claims—
1. The combination of the recess E, the metallic disk G, the hook-slot F, the water-proof cap G, and the opening-tape H, all arranged substantially as and for the purposes set forth.

Critique—An improvement upon the standard friction primer fuze used to ignite hand grenades.

45,985

January 24, 1865; Improvement in Explosive Shells; Edwin Estabrook; Jersey City, NJ; Flame-ignited Fuze

Claims—
1. The plane or nearly plane faces B' B^2, &c., on the interior of an explosive shell, arranged relatively to each other in the manner and so as to produce the effect herein set forth.

Critique—Fuze ends in the middle of the main charge. Fuze is made of thin brass so that it collapses right after it ignites the main charge to keep the gases from escaping out the fuze hole. Projectile had a polyhedron shape but this would have been difficult to manufacture (though projectiles were made during the war with polyhedron shaped interiors) and fuze would have required more machining. Idea had potential.

45,986

January 24, 1865; Improvement in Fuses for Shells; Edwin Estabrook; Jersey City, NJ; Flame-ignited Fuze

Claims—
1. The employment, in explosive shells, of a fuse plug adapted to collapse and crush by the action of the exploding charge and to stop the escape of gas through the fuse plug, substantially as herein set forth

Critique—An addition to Estabrook's previous patent, 45,985, but no real change.

46,965

March 21, 1865; Improvement in Time Fuses for Explosive Shells; George Wright; District of Columbia; Flame-ignited Fuze

Claims—
1. The longitudinal time fuse B, constructed and located substantially as described, for the purpose set forth.

Critique— Cuts a groove in the projectile in which a length of fuze was put which would be lit by the exploding gunpowder. Would make the manufacture of the projectiles more difficult and expensive.

47,231

April 11, 1865; Improvement in Fuse Hoods for Explosive Shells; Thomas Taylor; District of Columbia; Accessory — Fuze Hood for flame-ignited fuzes Fuze

Claims—
1. The use of the flame hood E, located between the front end of the shell and the front of the fuse, held securely in place by the flange of the plug C, the same constructed and operated substantially as described.

Critique— An umbrella-shaped hood was placed over the flame-ignited fuze with the idea that it will help direct more flame to the fuze. The idea never caught hold and lessened the aerodynamics of the projectile.

47,586

May 2, 1865; Improvement in Timing Explosive Shells by Clock-Work; Frederic Toggenburger; Chicago, IL; Concussion Timed Fuze

Claims—
1. Exploding a bomb-shell by means of a clock-work applied within said shell, substantially in the manner described.

2. Providing the clock-work used within a bomb-shell for exploding the same with a regulating apparatus, by means of which said clock-work can be set to explode the shell at a given time.

3. Starting the clock-work within a shell, and by which it is to be exploded by the action of the powder-charge which is used in firing the shell from the gun.

4. The combination of the clock-work movement with the rod M and the fulminating capsule for exploding the shell, substantially in the manner described.

5. The combination, with the clock-work and the exploding device within the shell, of the yielding plug H, by means of which the clock-work is set in motion by the firing of the shell, substantially as herein described.

Critique— The first fuze using a clock mechanism. It was too advanced for the time.

47,803

May 23, 1865; Improved Percussion Fuse for Explosive Shells; John A. Curran (U.S. Army); U.S. Army; Percussion Fuze

Claims—
1. The combination of the plunger h, spring I, detent spring j, weight k, and

arm o, when constructed and arranged to operate as and for the purposes herein specified.

Critique— Fuze was located in the rear of the projectile. A complicated fuze and probably offered little advantage over the ones in common use.

48,167

June 13, 1865; Improvement in Concussion Fuses for Explosive Shells; George P. Ganster; New York, NY; Concussion impact Fuze

Claims—

The use of two cones, C and D, operating in a double coned chamber, substantially as shown and described.

Critique— Uses matches rather than percussion caps to create the fire which will go to the main powder charge. Uses a spring to keep the anvil and plunger apart and has another safety device, a wire. Ganster does not mention how waterproof the fuze was and if the matches could get wet and still operate.

48,642

July 11, 1865; Improvement in Compound Explosive Shells; Henry Barton; Baltimore, MD; Percussion impact Fuze

Claims—

1. The construction and arrangement of the independent chambers J within an external shell, A, so as to form a central chamber or magazine, K, communicating with each fuse-pipe L, as herein described, and for the purposes set forth.

Critique— Had eight separate exploding chambers within the projectile, each one having its own fuze. All of the fuzes were to be lit by the main fuze at the same time with each chamber exploding at the same time. It is doubtful if the timing would work. In addition, other inventors had already addressed this issue by creating projectiles with predetermined interior fracture lines.

49,326

August 8, 1865; Improvement in Explosive Shells for Ordnance; Lemuel Wells; New York, NY; Flame-ignited Fuze

Claims—

1. The fuse hole formed in the tapering portion of the shell, in combination with the projection k on the latter.

Critique— Moves the fuze hole to the side of the front sloping portion of the projectile. Another attempt to extend an obsolete technology.

54,027

April 17, 1866; Improvement in Percussion Fuse for Explosive Shells; John F. Shearman; Brooklyn, NY; Percussion Fuze

Claims—

1. The mode herein specified of allowing the projectile to rotate without at

first revolving the percussion hammer for preventing injury to the screw or its equivalent that holds said percussion hammer when the shell is projected as set forth.

2. In combination with the plunger g, fitted as that it can rotate as set forth, two or more nipples fitted to said plunger, as and for the purposes specified.

Critique— Uses multiple percussion caps and a different safety mechanism to stop premature explosions. Blames premature explosions on the rotating projectile causing the fuze to rotate, which is highly unlikely.

63,834

April 16, 1867; Improvement in Concussion Fuse for Explosive Shells; William S. Beebe; Philadelphia, PA; Concussion impact Fuze

Claims—

1. So attaching an inertia fuse to the interior of a hollow projectile that, while it is secure against any ordinary shock, it will be broken loose by the discharge of the cannon or mortar from which it is fired when such fuse is so constructed and arranged that, lying loosely in the powder during the flight of the projectile, it will turn its loaded end against the wall of the cavity in the projectile and explode when the flight of such projectile is suddenly arrested or checked, substantially as above described.

2. A percussion or frictional fuse which is constructed with a loaded head, A, terminating in a feathered tail, a, and adapted for use in spherical and other tumbling shells, substantially as described.

Critique— The key to the patent is that the fuze floating freely in the main charge will hit the interior of the projectile with its cap and explode, which was highly unlikely.

66,644

July 9, 1867; Improvement in Concussion Fuse for Explosive Shells; Andrew J. Simpson and John J. Janezeck; Philadelphia, PA, and District of Columbia; Percussion Fuze

Claims—

1. In combination with the tapering closed case A we claim the plunger D fitting snugly therein, the fulminate chamber B, fulminate tube C, friction wire b, washer c, pin d, and powder chamber e, all arranged therein and constructed as herein described for the purpose specified.

Critique— They called it a concussion fuze but based on their description the projectile must hit directly if the fuze was to work. Biggest problem is that the fulminate must be loaded into the fuze rather than already being contained in a percussion cap.

72,494

December 24, 1867; Improvement in Combined Time and Percussion Fuse for Explosive Shells; B.B. Hotchkiss; New York, NY; Combination —flame-ignited, percussion Fuze

Claims—

1. I claim the employment, in an explosive projectile, of a quantity of quick burning material, L, permanently attached and protruded beyond the front, and directly exposed to the contact of flame on all sides, in combination with the surrounding Borman C, substantially as and for the purpose herein described.

2. I claim the magazine G of quick powder, arranged in direct contact with the Borman, and adapted to be ignited at the proper time thereby, and to increase the force with which flame is thrown into the shell, substantially in the manner herein described.

3. I claim, in the cavity magazine G, arranged as represented, the use of powder in one or more large grains, in combination with the contraction g, smaller than said grains, and arranged to operate therewith and retain the powder but discharge the flame therefrom, substantially in the manner and for the purpose herein set forth.

Critique— Increased the complexity of the fuze both in operation and manufacture without an equivalent increase in reliability.

78,322

May 26, 1868; Improvement in Igniting Explosive Projectiles; Eugene Pertuiset, Auguste Mundel, and Jean Etienne Armide De Fleron; Paris, France; Concussion impact Fuze

Claims—

1. An explosive projectile, composed of a tube or equivalent hollow metallic body, filled with a detonating or fulminating compound, which will be ignited or inflamed by the action of the heat developed by the impact or penetration of the projectile, substantially as herein shown and set forth.

2. The fulminating mixture or composition, substantially as herein specified.

3. The percussion fuse, for containing the fulminating compound, made substantially as and for the purposes herein shown and set forth.

Critique— Uses fulminate without a percussion cap. Was dependent upon the heat developed by the impact of the projectile. However, that heat may not be sufficient to ignite the fulminate and does not explain how the heat developed in the gun during firing would not prematurely ignite the fulminate.

82,714

October 6, 1868; Improvement in Explosive Projectiles; A.O.H. Hardestein; Clinton, MS; Concussion timed Fuze

Claims—

1. The combination of the disk N and rod M with a projectile, substantially as herein described, when these parts are constructed and operate substantially as and for the purpose set forth.

2. The wedge formed bars A, in combination with a projectile, substantially as herein described, when the same are constructed and operated substantially as herein described, for the purpose set forth

3. The bars A, in combination with the disk N, when these several parts are constructed and operate as herein described, in connection with a projectile, substantially as herein described, for the purpose set forth.

Critique — No real improvement over fuzes that had been in use for years.

89,204

April 20, 1869; Improvements in Concussion Fuse; Edward A. Dana; Brookline, MA; Combination — Flame-ignited to arm, concussion impact activated Fuze

Claims —

1. The combination of the plunger, or cylinder B with the walls H', when the former is coated with a composition inflammable by friction against the latter, prepared substantially in the manner specified.

2. The combination of the plunger B, the plug G, and the powder block E, arranged substantially as described.

Critique — Used sandpaper on the interior of the fuze as the friction device for the fulminate but needed the flame from the exploding powder to burn away the safety device. In all probability an unreliable fuze.

91,701

June 22, 1869; Improvement in Shell Fuses; James D. Bacon; New York, NY; Combination — Flame-ignited and concussion impact Fuze

Claims —

1. In combination with the central tube of a paper case fuse stock, that is covered or surrounded by plaster, or other non-conductor, an exterior paper covering for said tube, substantially as described.

Critique — An attempt to improve upon the flame-ignited paper fuze by using a ball surrounded by plaster that would drop when the projectile hit something and thus allowing the flame to reach the main powder chamber. It would be hard to manufacturer.

95,137

September 21, 1869; Improvement in Projectiles; Abiather F. Potter; San Francisco, CA; Percussion Fuze

Claims —

1. A projectile, provided with wings B B and an elastic cushion, E, between the head and the explosive charge, substantially as described.

2. Also, the sectional elastic packing E, arranged between the wings in front of the explosive charge, and behind the head of the projectile, substantially as described.

Critique — Idea was to enable a smooth-bore gun to fire a cylindrical projectile that would spin and be stable in flight. The fuze was activated when the nose of the projectile was crushed down upon it. An idea that had been proposed in previous patents in other variations.

103,599

May 31, 1870; Improvement in Percussion Fuse; William Gardner; San Francisco, CA; Percussion Fuze

Claims—

1. The percussion fuse described, consisting of the tube A, caps B and C, clamps D, sliding bolt E, nipple F, and cap G, when combined and arranged as described, and adapted to be placed independently in any proper projectile without special attachment thereto.

Critique— Gardner used a much longer tube for his fuze and a slightly different looking hammer, otherwise it was the same basic design as a West Point style fuze.

110,219

December 20, 1870; Improvement in Shell Fuses; James Eggo; Jersey City, NJ; Percussion Fuze

Claims—

1. The improved fuse for rifle shells herein described, composed of the screw stock A, closed at its outer end, the hollow screw plugs B and C, tubular bar D, short tube E, and wire F, all relatively constructed, arranged as shown and described.

2. The safety pin G, passing in through the closed outer end of the stock A, with its inner end resting against the end of the plunger C, substantially as herein shown and described, and for the purpose set forth.

Critique— A slight variation on well-known percussion fuzes.

111,823

February 14, 1871; Improvement in Shell Fuses; Ellis Drake; Stoughton, MA; Combination — percussion and concussion timed Fuze

Claims—

1. The combination and arrangement of parts, as herein shown and described, whereby a time regulator, a time, a percussion, and a concussion fuse are contained in the same fuse case, substantially as described.

2. A plunger, C, arranged loosely upon a square or angular shank, B, formed with a fuse case, in combination with a fulminate upon the shoulder of said fuse case, as and for the purpose set forth.

3. The grooves c c, formed upon the inner wall of the front end of a fuse case, substantially as and for the purpose set forth.

4. The plunger D, formed or provided with legs b, in combination with the groove or grooves upon the inner wall of the front end of a fuse case, when said plunger is connected with the cap, substantially as described.

5. The case A, formed with the slot a, shank B, and grooves c, in combination with the plungers C and D, and cap F, substantially as described.

Critique— A complicated fuze that tried to do everything. It used fulminate rather than a percussion cap. Good idea but too complicated.

129,929

July 30, 1872; Improvement in Shell Fuses; John G. Butler (U.S. Army); U.S. Army (Fortress Monroe, VA); Concussion impact Fuze

Claims—

1. The perforated plunger P P', solid or in parts, and the serrated friction wires C D and C' D', and primed channels, in combination with fuse stock B, when provided with the washer W W and inserted in the base of a projectile, substantially as and for the purpose herein before set forth.

Critique— The idea was that a ball would be thrown forward if the projectile hit on its nose or would fall to the side if the projectile landed on its side, pulling wires that would, by friction, ignite the main charge. One potential problem was the question of whether there would be room for the ball to move when the projectile was filled with gunpowder. Butler's fuze was never adopted by the army. However, his Patent No. 119,313, for a rotating band for muzzle-loading rifled projectiles, was. (Information provided in an e-mail message from Joe Vann, U.S. Army Corps of Engineers.)

129,930

July 30, 1872; Improvement in Shell Fuses; John G. Butler (U.S. Army); U.S. Army (Fortress Monroe, VA); Percussion Fuze

Claims—

1. In an ordinary fuse stock, a primed disk and firing pin, said firing pin being constructed and arranged to ignite both a friction fuse and primed disk when struck by the ordinary plunger, as herein set forth.

Critique— Contradicted himself from what he said in Patent No. 129,929. In 129,929 Butler said that one major problem with percussion fuzes was that too often the projectile landed on its side and the fuze does not operate. Other than that contradiction the idea was sound. Only real difference between it and a lot of the previous percussion fuzes was that he located his fuze in the rear of the projectile.

Appendix B

British Fuze-Related Patents, 1855–1876

Shown below is a list of British fuze patents from 1855 to 1876, with notes on those which have a moving part to initiate the explosion or are of special significance. *Italics* show communication from abroad. Communication from abroad indicates that the inventor (whose name is in *italics*) was not living in Britain at the time of the application. This list and many of the notes were provided courtesy of John Day of England (B., Sc., Eng. M.I. Mech E., Member Ordnance Society, Principal Examiner H.M. Patent Office Retd.).

While the United States has had two different patent numbering systems, the British have used three. From 1617 to 1852 the British numbered patents consecutively, from 1853 to the end of 1915 the patent numbers began with No. 1 at the start of each year, and then from the beginning of 1916 the patents numbers again became consecutive starting with 100,000. Due to this variation in the numbering, the table shows the year and month that each patent was issued in addition to the patent number.

Year	*Month*	*Number*	*Patentee*	*Notes*
1855	Mar.	487	*Brooman*	Perforated plate covered by detonating mixture struck by hammer normally retained by marginal flange.
	May	1214	Bellford	
	Aug.	1774	Macintosh	
	Oct.	2409	Temperton	Supporting hammer by a spring which gives way on percussion.
	Nov.	2630	*Herdman*	Cap with central rubber ring held hammer to strike primer.
	Dec.	2818	Skelton	Hammer held safe by screwing into fuze body and by removable pin.

Year	Month	Number	Patentee	Notes
	Dec.	2922	Sawyer	Plug carrying fulminate screwed to lead wall yielding on impact.
1856	Jun.	1430	*Lippincott*	The outer part of the hammer unscrews for transit and is held away from the igniting cap by a rubber tube connected to the fuze body.
1857	May	1402	Roys	
1858	Apr.	779	Armstrong	Time fuze initiated by hammer held safe by frangible pin which breaks on firing. Percussion fuze hammer armed by pin breaking on firing and hits detonating pellet on impact.
1859	Mar.	685	Armstrong	As 779/68 but striker fixed on bolt, freed on firing, which can move laterally to detonate when shell strikes sideways.
	Jul.	1727	Ambler	Fuze comprises slider containing detonating powder.
	Nov.	2517	*Cochran*	Fuze consists of glass capsule containing fulminating compound carried in rubber tube kept in place with springs. Also, hammer in tube held by spring.
1861	Mar.	585	Britten, B.	Percussion fuze consists of striker within a cylindrical piece carrying percussion cap that hits a cap at the end of the tube.
	Aug.	2128	Hadden	The passage in which the needle slides is conical or enlarged at one end.
	Nov.	2852	Armstrong	As 779/58 but shear pin replaced by ring engaging projections on the hammer. Ring shears projections.
	Dec.	3245	McIntyre	
	Dec.	3250	Warner	
1862	Feb.	488	Haddan	Fuze ignited by plunger sliding in a hole, coned to ensure ignition when the blow is not direct.
	Jun.	1798	B.B. Hotchkiss	Fuze body carries hammer with percussion cap at front and held by soft metal ring. Firing arms and impact moves hammer to ignite. Other fuzes comprise two metal balls, joined by bent wire and wrapped in cloth which ruptures on firing to free one ball then the other strikes percussion cap on impact. Same basic patent as U.S. Patent 36,994.
	Jun.	1898	Garnier	
	Sep.	2649	Johnson	
1863	Feb.	484	Wiard	Tube containing hollow plunger filled with powder with percussion cap at

Year	Month	Number	Patentee	Notes
				end. Plunger attached to rear of tube by lead washer.
	Apr.	881	J.P. Tice	Primer of silver fulminate mixed in wool, etc., at rear of tube pressed forward by spring against plunger. Plunger and tube retained by lugs broken on discharge. Tube and primer move forward on impact. Same basic patent as U.S. Patent 38,994.
	Jun.	1628	Richards	Transverse pins blown out by powder and quick fuze on firing to free long needle held by wax and thin plate (or lead) until impact.
	Dec.	3005	Boxer	Percussion time fuze has plug striking fulminate to ignite through passages varying in depth. Concussion fuze has hammer connected by wire to cylinder, armed by wire fracture, cylinder held by lip. Nose and hammer coated amorphous phosphorus and substance igniting when in contact.
	Dec.	3250	*Eckel*	
	Dec.	3258	Nobel A.	
1864	May	1278	*Voruz*	Detachable fuze hammer prevented from accidental sliding by disc.
	Dec.	3015	Lancaster	
1865	Jan.	136	Cotter	
	May	1211	*Taylor*	
	Jun.	1552	B.B. Hotchkiss	If time fuze fails, percussive plunger, having powder and cap, released on firing acts on impact. Hotchkiss's patent specifications are 11 pages long. He combines all of his U.S. Patents that are not already British Patents in this one patent.
	Jun.	1595	*Frederika Schenkl*	A combination of John P. Schenkl's (Fredericka Schenkl was the executor of his estate) U.S. Patents 35,897 and 39,682.
	Aug.	1989	Noble A.	Armstrong fuze used as percussion fuze by second hammer, released on firing acts on impact by striking fulminate primer.
	Dec.	3275	*McEvoy*	
1866	May	1411	Sharp & anr.	
	Jun.	1555	McEvoy	Ball, coated with fulminate, released by breaking wire to give percussion fuze.
1867	Jan.	213	Berney	

Year	Month	Number	Patentee	Notes
	Mar.	961	Hahn	
	Apr.	1050	*Beebe*	Friction fuze in projectile detached on firing, inertia causes point to strike shell. Case can have rough edged wings to ignite fulminate by friction. Fulminate in tube ignited by serrated wire with weight at one end.
	May	1345	*Nobel A.*	
	Jun.	1806	Cochran	Bursting charge for shell in cylinder, with detonating cap at end, held by spring until impact.
	Aug.	2421	Dana	Chamber containing friction match material lined with sandpaper. On impact, pin broken to liberate match carrier to ignite fuze composition.
	Oct.	2837	*Pertuiset*	
	Oct.	3039	Meade	
1868	Feb.	386	Pettman	On firing, piston, secured by metal pins released, crushes lead cup freeing ball thrown forward on impact to explode fulminate.
1870	Jul.	2066	*Pertuiset*	
	Sep.	2424	Noble A.	Modification of Armstrong fuze, allows percussion only, guard ring can be turned to safe position.
	Nov.	3130	Bessemer	
1871	Mar.	844	Sanders	
	Aug.	2296	*Hotchkiss*	
1872	Aug.	2298	James	
	Sep.	2860	*Bazzichelli*	Time fuze initiated by cap holding striker. Drawing.
1873	Feb.	740	McEvoy	
1875	May	1739	Spill	
1876	Mar.	1256	*Montmagnon*	
	Jul.	2808	Smith	
	Jul.	2816	*Cosson*	
	Aug.	3072	Hunter	Striker rod passes through shell to detonating chamber in base. Shield over front initiates secondary detonators on glancing blow.
	Dec.	5000	Hellhoff	Rocket has bolt passing through mantle having five percussion bolts held in spring steel safety piece. The bolt is retained by thread burnt through by propellant and then moved forward on impact.

Appendix C

Short Biographies

This appendix gives a short biography of many of the individuals mentioned in this book who directly influenced the American artillery weapon system used during the Civil War. Unfortunately, for some individuals little or no information was found. If the individual was in the military his highest military rank will be shown.

Abbot, Henry Larcom: 1831–1927. Brevet Major General, United States Army. An excellent engineer, experimenter, and researcher. Graduated from the United States Military Academy in 1854 second in his class and commissioned in the Topographical Engineers. His initial assignment was to survey a route for a Pacific Railroad with his cavalry escort being under the command of Lieutenant Philip Sheridan. Just prior to the war Abbot worked on a hydrographic survey of the Mississippi River delta. During the war he served in various engineering positions in the Army of the Potomac as well as the Chief Topographic Engineer for General Banks' Expedition to the Gulf of Mexico. After his service with Banks he returned to Washington and was given command of the 1st Connecticut Artillery Volunteers. From that point on until the end of the war he was the commander of various siege trains. His book, *Siege Artillery in the Campaigns against Richmond*, was written based on his experiences as Commander of the Army of the Potomac's artillery siege train at Petersburg. While in command of this siege train he conducted numerous field experiments on the effectiveness of various artillery projectiles and fuzes as well as collecting samples of Confederate ordnance. After the war he worked on a number of different military engineering projects, including experiments on torpedoes (mines). Retiring from the Army he continued working as an engineer and was on the Board of Consulting Engineers for the Panama Canal and advocated for a lock canal over a sea-level canal.

Absterdam, John: Dates unknown. Holder of one fuze-related patent, number 41,668. General Abbot tested some of Absterdam's fuzes at Petersburg and found them to be unsatisfactory.

Alexander, Edward Porter: 1835–1910. Brigadier General, Confederate States Army. One of the most outstanding artillery officers in the Confederate Army. Graduated from the United States Military Academy in 1857 third in his class and commissioned in the Corps of Engineers. Prior to the war he served as an instructor at the Military Academy, an engineer on the Utah Expedition, and worked on the defenses of Alcatraz Island. He resigned his commission in May 1861 and joined the Confederate Army. During the war he was the Chief Ordnance Officer for the Army of Northern Virginia and later Chief of Artillery for the 1st Corps under General Longstreet. After the war he became a university professor as well as president of a number of different companies. Many years after the war he wrote his much quoted and critically acclaimed *Military Memoirs of a Confederate*.

Alger, Cyrus: 1781–1856. Inventor and owner of an iron foundry which developed into the South Boston Iron Company. His foundry produced the first cast-iron rifled cannons in the United States in 1834. Developed a bronze flame-ignited fuze for the Navy that was the standard United States Navy flame-ignited fuze before, during, and after the American Civil War.

Alger, Francis: 1807–1863. Son of Cyrus Alger. Inventor and industrialist. Assumed control of the South Boston Iron Company upon his father's death and continued his father's work on exploding artillery projectiles. Holder of three fuze-related patents, numbers 36,329, 36,553, and 39,267. Best known for his work in mineralogy.

Barry, William Farquhar: 1818–1879. Brevet Major General, United States Army. Graduated from the United States Military Academy in 1838 17th in his class and was commissioned in the artillery. An excellent organizer and commander of artillery. Before the Mexican War he served on the Canada border during the Canadian Border Disturbances. During the Mexican War he served as a staff officer in Patterson's and Worth's divisions. After the Mexican War he served in Florida against the Seminole Indians and then in various staff and artillery positions. Shortly after the Civil War began he became the Chief of Artillery under General McDowell. When General McClellan took command of the Army of the Potomac he remained Chief of Artillery and served in that position throughout the Peninsula Campaign. He is credited with making the Army of the Potomac's artillery a highly organized and efficient organization. From October 1862 until early spring 1864 he served on various artillery boards and was the Chief of Artillery for the defense of Washington. In late spring 1864 he became the Chief of Artillery for General Sherman serving with Sherman until the end of the war. After the war he continued to serve in a variety of command and staff positions until his death at Fort McHenry.

Benton, James G.: 1820–1881. Colonel, United States Army. Graduated from the United States Military Academy in 1842 11th in his class and was commissioned in the Ordnance Corps. An outstanding Ordnance officer and author. Held a variety of positions in the Ordnance Corps before, during, and after the war which included being the commander of the Washington Arsenal and Springfield Armory. Served on a number of Ordnance Boards, including the selection of the new rifled musket (1853–1857). Died at Springfield Armory. Author of *A Course of Instruction in*

Ordnance and Gunnery; Prepared for the use of the Cadets of the United States Military Academy.

Bormann, Charles (Karl Friedrich): 1796–1874. Major General, Belgian Army. Started his military career in the Royal Saxonian Army. Joined the Belgian Army where he invented the flame-ignited fuze named after him in 1835. This fuze was adopted by a number of armies including the U.S. Army.

Cochran, John: Dates unknown. Holder of three fuze-related patents, numbers 30,123, 37,275, and 37,675.

Dahlgren, John Adolphus Bernard: 1809–1870. Rear Admiral, United States Navy. Considered to be the father of American naval ordnance and the author of numerous books on naval ordnance. After over 20 years in the Navy he was assigned to ordnance duty at the Washington Navy Yard. While in this assignment he designed a boat howitzer and then the Dahlgren shellgun. During the war he was given command of the Washington Navy Yard when its commander, Franklin Buchanan, resigned his commission and entered the Confederate service. In 1863 he assumed command of the South Atlantic Blockading Squadron. After the war he again became the Chief of Ordnance, dying while on active duty. His main rival in the field of ordnance was Thomas Rodman.

Dyer, Alexander Brydie: 1815–1874. Brevet Major General, United States Army. Graduated from the United States Military Academy in 1837 sixth in his class and commissioned in the artillery. Outstanding ordnance office and inventor of a three-inch artillery projectile. Transferred to the Ordnance Corps in 1838 and served at a variety of arsenals and depots. During the Mexican War served as the Chief of Ordnance for the Army that invaded New Mexico. When the war started his loyalties were questioned as he had been born in Virginia. However, he was put in command of the vital Springfield Armory. Appointed as Chief of Ordnance in 1864 and held the post until his death in 1874.

Ganster, George: Dates unknown. Holder of five fuze-related patents, numbers 41,615, 42,082, 42,185, 42,363, and 48,167. However, none of his fuzes were adopted by the military.

Gibbon, John: 1827–1896. Brevet Major General, United States Army. Graduated from the United States Military Academy in 1847 20th in his class and was commissioned in the artillery. Famous as a field commander and author of the 1860 *The Artillerist's Manual*. Prior to the war he served in a variety of command and staff positions, including being on the board that tested breech-loading rifles in 1857. When the war started he initially served as Chief of Artillery of General McDowell's division but received command of his own brigade in May 1862. Gained fame as the commander of the "Iron Brigade" in the Army of the Potomac and eventually commanded a Corps. After the war he was in a variety of command and staff positions. During the 1876 campaign against the Sioux, Gibbon commanded one of the three columns, and it was his column that relieved the Little Big Horn survivors. In 1877, as commander of the 7th Infantry, he fought the Nez Perce Indians and was wounded.

Hotchkiss, Andrew: 1823–1858. Older brother of Berkeley Hotchkiss. Crippled at birth. An inventive genius with six patents to his credit when he died. One of his patents was for the successful Hotchkiss artillery projectile. Invented a rifled artillery gun in 1854 but his failing health did not allow him to continue his work.

Hotchkiss, Benjamin Berkeley: 1826–1885. Younger brother of Andrew Hotchkiss. Salesman, manufacturer, and inventor. Founder of the Hotchkiss armaments works in Europe. Inventor of the Hotchkiss machine gun. Held 42 U.S. patents as well as patents in Britain and France at the time of his death. His mechanical fuzes, along with Parrott's and Schenkl's, were the most common mechanical fuzes used by the Union during the war.

Hubbell, William Wheeler: 1821–1902. Lawyer and inventor. Holder of three fuze-related patents, numbers 28,084, 34,059, and 36,566. Hubbell had a long-term disagreement with the Alger family regarding who should get credit and payment for the waterproof navy fuze invented by Cyrus Alger. A Congressional hearing was held in 1938 and private bills were introduced in 1939 to pay Hubbell's children but the bills never left the Appropriations Committee.

Huger, Benjamin: 1805–1877. Major General, Confederate States Army. Graduated from the United States Military Academy in 1825 eighth in his class and was commissioned in the artillery. An excellent ordnance officer. Transferred to the Ordnance Corps in 1832 when it became a separate branch. Before the Mexican War Huger held a variety of staff positions in the Ordnance Corps, including commander of the Fort Monroe Arsenal. During the Mexican War he was General Scott's Chief of Ordnance. After the Mexican War he served as commander of various arsenals as well as the Harpers Ferry Armory in addition to serving on Ordnance Boards. Resigned his commission when South Carolina seceeded. Unsuccessful as a field commander Huger became an inspector of artillery and ordnance. After the war he became a farmer. His obituary for the Military Academy's Alumni Association was written by Alfred Mordecai.

Hunt, Henry Jackson: 1819–1889. Brevet Major General, United States Army. Graduated from the United States Military Academy in 1839 19th in his class and was commissioned in the artillery. An outstanding artillery officer and a tireless advocate of the artillery branch. Prior to the Mexican War Hunt served in a variety of staff positions and artillery units. During the Mexican War he served as an artillery officer in General Scott's army becoming a brevet major for gallantry. Between the Mexican War and the Civil War he served in a number of artillery units and Artillery Boards. During the Civil War he commanded the Reserve Artillery during the Peninsula Campaign and was responsible for the placement of the "grand battery" at the Battle of Malvern Hill. In September 1862 he was appointed Chief of Artillery for the Army of the Potomac serving in that position until the end of the war. After the war he served in a variety of positions until his retirement due to age. After retiring he was appointed Governor of the Soldiers' Home in which position he served until his death. His obituary for the Military Academy's Alumni Association was written by Joseph E. Johnston.

James, Charles Tillinghast: 1805–1862. Major General, Rhode Island Militia. A manufacturer and politician who became interested in armament manufacturing with the coming of the American Civil War. Inventor of the James Rifled Gun process that was used to rebore smooth-bore guns into rifled guns. Also invented an artillery projectile. He was killed by the explosion of one of his projectiles. The explosion of this projectile was probably due to the fact that his fuze's only safety device was based on friction. His artillery pieces and projectiles were disliked by the military and fell into disfavor.

McIntyre, James: Dates unknown. Holder of two fuze-related patents, numbers 40,350 and 44,581. The second patent was only a slight modification of the first. McIntyre's fuze was tested by General Abbot at Petersburg and was reported to be successful, but it was not adopted by the army.

Mordecai, Alfred: 1804–1887. Major, United States Army. Graduated from the United States Military Academy in 1823 first in his class and was commissioned in the Corps of Engineers. One of the premier ordnance officers in the United States Army with a worldwide reputation. After graduation he remained at the academy as an instructor and then went on to a variety of engineering and ordnance assignments. Was one of the three members of the Military Commission to the Crimea and Theatre of War in Europe. He resigned his commission in 1861 as he could neither fight against his friends in North Carolina nor fight against the Federal government. During and after the war he worked in private industry. Author of the 1841 and 1850 *Ordnance Manual*, as well as the 1849 *Artillery for the United States Land Service* in addition to other books and numerous articles.

Parrott, Robert Parker: 1804–1877. Graduated from the United States Military Academy in 1824 third in his class and was commissioned in the artillery. An inventor and industrialist. After commissioning he stayed at the academy as an instructor for five years and then went on to a variety of artillery and ordnance assignments. Transferred to the Ordnance Corp and was assigned as an ordnance officer to the West Point Iron and Cannon Foundry located at Cold Spring, New York, in early 1836. Resigned his commission in October 1836 to become the superintendent of the foundry. Inventor of the Parrott rifled artillery gun, projectile, and fuze which were used extensively by the Union Army and Navy. The government had such trust in him that his foundry was the only one authorized to both produce and inspect the items it manufactured. Unfortunately, his cannons had a tendency to fail and have their muzzles blown off, especially the larger diameter ones, a problem Parrott was never able to solve. These problems led to a congressional investigation but Parrott was completely exonerated. His loyalty to the Union was never questioned, and his profits from making armaments for the government were minimal. His mechanical fuzes, along with Hotchkiss's and Schenkl's, were the most common mechanical fuzes used by the Union during the war.

Read, Dr. John Brahan: 1816–1899. A surgeon and inventor. Patented the idea of attaching a sabot to the bottom of a rifled projectile. Robert Parrott bought the rights to the patent for manufacturing the projectile for the United States Government. Later, Read accused Parrott of patent infringement after Parrott improved upon the idea and patented the changes. Read lived in Alabama and sided with the

Confederacy during the war. His projectile became a popular rifled projectile for Confederate artillerymen.

Rodman, Thomas J.: 1815–1871. Brigadier General, United States Army. Graduated from the United States Military Academy in 1841 seventh in his class and was commissioned in the Ordnance Corps. An outstanding ordnance officer, experimenter, and innovator with a worldwide reputation. Served in a variety of ordnance staff and command positions as well on a number of Ordnance Boards. Invented a new process that allowed large cannons to be manufactured by cooling the cannon from the inside making it possible to cast extremely large guns. In addition, he developed a new style of gunpowder that could be safely used in these large guns. He died while on active duty as commander of the Rock Island Arsenal. His main ordnance rival was John Dalhgren.

Sawyer, Addison: Dates unknown. Brother of Sylvanus Sawyer. Holder of two fuze-related patents, numbers 36,172 and 38,699. Patent 38,699 was an excellent combination fuze. Patent 36,172 was an improvement upon his previous design.

Sawyer, Sylvanus: 1822–1895. Inventor and engineer. Inventor of a prewar rifled artillery gun and projectile. Design was unsuccessful and only a few ever saw active service. Invented a fuze hood, patent number 34,040, that was designed to concentrate the flame created by the burning gunpowder onto the fuze. Holder of two other fuze-related patents, numbers 13,799 and 36,172.

Schenkl, John P: 1826–1864. The most common mechanical fuzes used by the Union during the Civil War were invented by Robert P. Parrott, Andrew & Benjamin Hotchkiss, and John P. Schenkl. A large amount of biographical information is available on Parrott and the Hotchkiss brothers but very little is available on Schenkl even though he is the only one with a scholarship in his name. The scholarship, the John P. Schenkl Scholarship at the Massachusetts Institute of Technology, gave out slightly over $50,000 in his name during the past few years. When contacted about the scholarship MIT informed me that they did not know anything about the man as the scholarship had been established in 1922 from a bequest in Johanna Schenkl's (his daughter) will and that the bequest had not provided any information about him.

John Schenkl was born in 1826 in Germany and immigrated to the United States, settling in Boston, sometime before 1853, for in August of that year, he received the first of his 11 United States patents. Two of these 11 patents, although issued in his name, were applied for by his wife, Frederika, as administratrix of his estate. Frederika also filed a patent in her husband's name in Great Britain. Schenkl was a prolific and versatile inventor for his patents included a breech-loading rifle, a breech-loading cannon, various artillery fuzes, packing for rifled artillery projectiles, a spring-loaded pop-up umbrella, and an adjustable tension device for sewing machine shuttles.

By 1857, Schenkl was well-established in Boston as he was partners in Schenkl & Wenzel, manufacturers of a breech-loading rifle that Schenkl invented. The Boston newspaper, the *Daily Traveller,* described him as "an ingenious German mechanic."[1] The start of the war brought recognition and wealth to Schenkl. His percussion fuze was probably the best percussion fuze used during the war. Schenkl's fuze was so good that Brigadier General James Ripley, Chief of Ordnance, wrote to Major General George McClellan in April 1862 during the Peninsula Campaign that "the fuses used are Schenkl's, the best of their kind."[2] In June 1862 Ripley wrote to Robert Parrott requesting 8,500 30-pound projectiles and stated, "One-half of the projectiles should be prepared with Schenkl's percussion fuzes, as these seem to be the only fuzes that give perfect satisfaction at this point."[3]

Schenkl's projectile was unique in its design. While it had a very different shape from any other projectile, its major advantage was that it used a papier-mâché sabot. Sabots, whether made of wood, metal or paper, all too often separated in flight from the projectile, putting friendly troops at risk. Obviously, a sabot made from papier-mâché did not present this danger. However, the papier-mâché sabot was very difficult to manufacture, but as General Henry Abbot, Commander of the Siege Artillery during the Petersburg Campaign, stated, "When the sabot is well made and in good order, this is excellent ammunition."[4] Unfortunately, Schenkl's projectiles were often found to be unserviceable due to the sabot being damaged either by the weather or by being torn. The problem with the sabots was never solved although Cyrus Alger & Company in Boston, who manufactured all of the Schenkl fuzes and projectiles, tried a number of methods.

Schenkl died before the war ended in Heidelberg, Germany, on March 31, 1864, where he had gone for his health. Without Schenkl's genius there was no guiding force behind his inventions and, therefore, the quality of the manufacturing of his projectiles and fuzes decreased. As a consequence, the military ceased procuring Schenkl's projectiles and fuzes once the war ended, using up those left in the inventory. Schenkl was only 38 years old when he died, and it is hard to say what this ingenious man would have invented and manufactured if he had lived longer.

Schenkl was survived by his wife, Frederika, and two daughters, Johanna and Josephine. Schenkl must have left his family financially well off for when Johanna, who never married, died in 1921 her estate was worth $344,026 (many millions today). The bulk of her estate went to charities, with $20,000 going to MIT to establish scholarships in their Department of Mechanical Engineering. The scholarships were to be called "John P. Schenkl Scholarships" in honor of her father. Josephine married but her only child died at the age of 11 months. She died in 1932 and, like her sister, she left the majority of her estate to charities and gave $10,000 to MIT to be placed in her father's scholarship fund. All of the Schenkls, including Josephine's husband and infant son, are buried in the Mount Auburn Cemetery in Boston.

Tice, Issac P.: Dates unknown. Holder of one fuze-related patent, number 38,994. Tice's fuze was very sensitive and had to be handled carefully. His fuze was tested by General Abbot at Petersburg and found to be very successful.

Sources

A number of sources were used to gather this information with the United States Military Academy library being the best as they have extensive biographical information on the vast majority of their graduates. John Dahlgren's life is well-documented; *A Quest for Glory*, by Robert J. Schneller, Jr., is a recent biography. Information on the

Hotchkiss brothers mainly came from the booklet *The Inventors*. A letter from Rolf Wirtgen, Chief Curator, Bundesant für Wehrtechnik und Beschaffung, provided important information about Charles Bormann. Information on John Schenkl came from a number of sources, including obituaries. In addition, the Research Office at the Mount Auburn Cemetery, where Schenkl is buried, was very helpful. Some of the other individuals are mentioned in a number of encyclopedias and other references. Many of the men have disappeared from the historical record.

APPENDIX D

Prewar Armories, Arsenals, Navy Yards, Foundries, and Small Arms Manufacturers

I was disappointed while conducting my research that I did not find a source that discussed all of the various military armories, arsenals, and navy yards in use during the Civil War. Consequently, I decided to include this appendix to give the reader a short biography of the armories, arsenals, navy yards, foundries, and small arms manufacturers listed in this book. By no means does this biography include every arsenal, navy yard, foundry, and small arms manufacturer used by the Union, much less the Confederacy, during the war.

Armories and Arsenals

It is important to realize that during the Civil War era, there was a different definition for armories and arsenals than what is used today. Armories were sites where arms were manufactured, as well as stored, while arsenals only repaired and stored arms. Since that time, the definitions have been reversed.

Armories

Used to manufacture small arms. They also performed the additional roles of a place of deposit and accumulation of military stores as well as of supply and issue.

Springfield Armory: Springfield, Massachusetts — Established in 1794 and closed in 1968. Reopened in 1978 as a National Historic Site under the National Park Service. Although Springfield Armory manufactured weapons during the American Revolution, its official date of establishment is 1794. It was the first and last national armory. At its height, Springfield Armory was one of the premier design and manufacturing sites of small arms in the world.

Harpers Ferry Armory: Harpers Ferry, Virginia (later West Virginia) — Established in 1794 and destroyed during the Civil War in 1861. Due to its location, Harpers Ferry Armory never developed to the extent it was hoped it would. Still, it was at the Harpers Ferry Armory that John Hall machine-produced interchangeable parts for small arms, a world first. The equipment located at the arsenal was captured by Virginia state troops at the start of the war and taken to Richmond for use by the Confederacy. Harpers Ferry Armory is currently part of the National Park system.

Arsenals

a. First Class Arsenal of Construction: Besides being a depository and issue point, arsenals of construction manufactured many different types of ordnance, supplies excluding small arms.

b. Second Class Arsenal of Repair: Used as a storage, repair, and issue site. In addition, they had a major role in experiments conducted by the Ordnance Department on proposed equipment. Many of the second class arsenals could be quickly converted into first class arsenals as the necessary buildings to conduct manufacturing already existed at the locations.

c. Third Class Arsenal of Deposit: Only used as places of storage and issue. In reality they were not much more than depots.

Allegheny Arsenal: Lawrenceville, Pennsylvania — A first class arsenal of construction. Opened in 1814 and closed in 1906. After the war the site was mainly used as a storage depot and it never regained its wartime prominence. Between 1919 and 1926 the grounds were sold off with part of the site now being used as a park and another part being a public school. During the war the arsenal was a major manufacturing center with its workforce increasing from 308 to over 1,100. In 1862 an explosion destroyed the arsenal's laboratory killing 78 people.

Augusta Arsenal: Augusta, Georgia — A third class arsenal of deposit. Originally located in 1819 on the Savannah River just upstream of Augusta but moved between 1827 and 1828 to a healthier location. During the Civil War the arsenal's capabilities were upgraded by the Confederacy and the Confederate Powder Works was located there. After the war it continued to function as an arsenal until it was closed in 1955. The arsenal's buildings are currently being used by the Augusta State University for administrative purposes.

Baton Rouge Arsenal: Baton Rouge, Louisiana — A second class arsenal of repair. Opened in 1819 and closed in 1884. Used as a major staging site during the Mexican War. Equipment stored there was seized by Louisiana state militia at the start of the Civil War. Shortly after the war the site was transferred from the Ordnance Department to the Quartermaster Department. In 1884 it was transferred to the Department of the Interior and in 1886 given to the Louisiana State University. Currently the arsenal is being used as a state museum.

Benicia Arsenal: Benicia, California — A first class arsenal of construction. Established in 1851 but in 1855 Benicia Arsenal was still under construction. The Army's Camel Corps, during its short existence, was stabled at the arsenal. During the Civil War, the arsenal was a major staging area for Union troops in the west.

Later, the arsenal became one of the major shipping points for the military in the Pacific during World War II and Korea. The arsenal was closed in 1964. Its buildings are being used by a number of private firms and individuals as well as the Benicia Historical Museum.

Champlain Arsenal: Vergennes, Vermont — A third class arsenal of deposit. Established in 1816 and closed in 1872. During most of its existence there were only about three to four military personnel stationed there — one junior officer and the remainder enlisted men. During the Civil War activity increased but after the war and the lessening of tensions with Canada the arsenal was no longer needed. When the arsenal was closed, it was purchased by the State of Vermont and first used as a reform school. It is currently being used by the Department of Labor as the Northlands Job Corps Center.

Charleston Arsenal: Charleston, South Carolina — A third class arsenal of deposit. Established in 1825. The arsenal was seized by South Carolina troops at the start of the Civil War and the equipment stored there was used to outfit a number of their units. After the war, it was used by Federal troops during the reconstruction. In 1879 it was leased to Reverend Anthony Porter to be used as an orphanage and school. It was later sold to him in 1888. The school became known as the Porter Military Academy. The Medical University of South Carolina purchased the school in 1964 and while many of the buildings were destroyed, two remain.

Detroit Arsenal: Dearborn, Michigan — A third class arsenal of deposit. Established in 1816 in Detroit but moved in 1833 due to pressure by the Detroit City Government who felt that it was a safety and health hazard. The arsenal was a major staging site for units moving through the Detroit area during the war. The arsenal was closed in 1875 and the site sold. Four of the 12 original buildings are still standing with the Commandant's Quarters and Powder Magazine currently under the care of the City of Dearborn.

Fayetteville Arsenal: Fayetteville, North Carolina — A second class arsenal of repair. Established in 1836. During the Civil War it was used extensively by the Confederacy to manufacture arms and ammunition. General Sherman had it burnt when he occupied Fayetteville in 1865 and it was never rebuilt. The Museum of the Cape Fear Historical Complex now occupies a portion of the site.

Fort Monroe Arsenal: Fort Monroe, Virginia — A second class arsenal of repair. The arsenal was established in 1824 as part of the Artillery School of Practice. In the 1850s the arsenal specialized in the manufacture of seacoast gun carriages as well as the testing of artillery pieces. The arsenal buildings are currently in use as office buildings at Fort Monroe.

Frankford Arsenal: Frankford, Pennsylvania — A second class arsenal of repair. Established in 1816 and closed in 1977. Frankford Arsenal became a major manufacturing site during the Civil War. In October 1864 there were over 1,200 men working at the arsenal. The quality of work done at the arsenal was so good that in October 1862 the Ordnance Department instructed that all paper time fuzes were to be made at the Frankford Arsenal. Part of the site is now being used by the State of Pennsylvania while the remainder is being used by private industry.

Kennebec Arsenal: Augusta, Maine — A third class arsenal of deposit. Established in 1827. The arsenal was established so that supplies could be readily available for the defense of the Maine border against any attack from Canada. During the Civil War, the arsenal was expanded due to the need to produce ammunition. After the war the importance of the arsenal slowly declined. The arsenal was closed in 1901 and the post was abandoned in 1903. In 1905 the grounds were transferred to the State of Maine. Today, it is the best preserved of the pre Civil War arsenals.

Little Rock Arsenal: Little Rock, Arkansas — A third class arsenal of deposit. Authorized by Congress in 1836 with a site being selected in 1837 and work beginning in 1840. By 1851 the arsenal consisted of a complex of over 30 buildings. The arsenal was surrendered to Arkansas state units at the start of war and served as a Confederate arsenal until Little Rock was occupied by Federal troops in 1863. After the war it was again used by the government as an arsenal, finally being closed in 1890. In 1892, the buildings and property were transferred to the State of Arkansas. One of the stipulations in the transfer was that the property was to be used as a public park. Only the Tower Building remains of the original structures and the park is now named the MacArthur Park in honor of General Douglas MacArthur as he was born at the arsenal in 1880.

Mount Vernon Arsenal: Mount Vernon, Alabama — A third class arsenal of deposit. Established in 1828. The arsenal was seized by Alabama state units in 1861. The capture of New Orleans by Federal forces threatened the arsenal so much of its equipment was transferred to Selma. After the war it was used as barracks and then as a detention center for Apache Indians. In 1895 the site was transferred to the State of Alabama and is currently being used as a state psychiatric facility.

New York Arsenal: Governors Island, New York — A third class arsenal of deposit. Established in 1833 and transferred to the Second Corps Area in 1920. The site was never fully developed as an arsenal since any extensive expansion would have interfered with the firing capabilities of Fort Columbus. Consequently, the Ordnance Department made little use of the facility and most of the site was used by the Quartermaster Corps. The majority of the island is currently owned by the State of New York with 22 acres being part of the National Park Service.

Saint Louis Arsenal: Saint Louis, Missouri — In 1855 it was a second class Arsenal of Repair that was being converted to a first class arsenal of construction. Established in 1827. It was used to equip many of the troops from the northern Mississippi River states that were going to Mexico during the Mexican War. After the Mexican War, the arsenal was mainly used to support the troops stationed west of the Mississippi. At the start of the Civil War, the arsenal was a major objective for both sides with Federal forces retaining control. In 1872 the Army converted the arsenal to a cavalry post and transferred its ordnance functions first to Jefferson Barracks and then to Rock Island Arsenal. Today, the arsenal site is currently being used by the National Imagery and Mapping Agency.

San Antonio Arsenal: San Antonio, Texas — a third class arsenal of deposit. Established in 1859. During the Civil War it was used by the Confederacy as an ordnance depot. During the two World Wars it was a major supply depot. The arsenal closed in 1949 but the site continued to be used by other federal agencies for a number of years. Part of the site is now a park but the majority is used by private industry.

Washington Arsenal: District of Columbia — A first class arsenal of construction. Established in 1791. The British Army burnt the arsenal when they occupied Washington in 1814. The arsenal was rebuilt and one of its uses was to conduct artillery firing experiments. In 1826 work was started on the first federal penitentiary on land adjacent and just north of the arsenal. It was there that the Lincoln assassination conspirators were hung. An explosion in the laboratory on June 17, 1864, killed 21 female workers who had been assembling cartridge cases. The arsenal was closed in 1881 and the post was transferred to the Quartermaster Corps. The site of the arsenal is now part of Fort McNair.

Watertown Arsenal: Watertown, Massachusetts — A second class arsenal of repair. Established in 1816. The arsenal was a major supplier of military equipment to regiments from the northeast during the war. The military closed the arsenal in 1967 and large amounts of the property were sold off. The Army Materials and Mechanical Research Center (the AMMRC's name was changed to the Materials Technology Laboratory in 1985) was established on the remaining land in 1968. In 1995 the military closed the entire site. The property is currently owned by Harvard University.

Watervliet Arsenal: Watervliet, New York — A first class arsenal of construction. Established in 1813. During the war it was a major production center. At its busiest, the arsenal employed about 2,000 workers, one-fourth of whom were children. The Watervliet Arsenal is still in use today and is the nation's oldest manufacturing arsenal.

Navy Yards

The navy yards included in this book were those in operation just prior to the war. One navy yard that was not included was the Memphis Navy Yard since it was closed in 1853. However, the Confederacy made good use of its facilities until Memphis was captured by the Union. After its capture the Union Navy used the facilities to support their Mississippi River Fleet. Most navy yards just manufactured naval stores and only the Washington Navy Yard manufactured ordnance. Still, they were important centers of manufacture and were the nucleus of industrial centers that grew around them.

Boston Navy Yard: Boston, Massachusetts — Also known as the Charlestown Navy Yard. Established in 1800 where the Mystic and Charles Rivers meet on the Charlestown Peninsula. It had three building slips and one dry dock. During the war 19 ships were built or started there. It was closed in 1974 and the site is now the Boston National Historical Park and is where the USS *Constitution* is berthed.

Mare Island Navy Yard: San Francisco, California — Established in 1853 in the San Francisco Bay. It was the base for the Navy's Pacific Squadron and mainly used as a depot. During the war it assembled the USS *Camanche*, a monitor. The yard was closed in 1996 and is being used by private industry, government agencies as well as other entities.

New York Navy Yard: Brooklyn, New York — Established in 1800 on the East River in Brooklyn. Also known as the Brooklyn Navy Yard. During the war 21 ships were built or started there. The yard was mainly used to convert merchant and captured ships for blockade duty. At various times during the war over 6,000 people worked there. The yard was closed in 1966 and sold to New York City. It is currently being used by private industry. The former commander's quarters are a National Historic Landmark.

Norfolk Navy Yard: Portsmith, Virginia — Established in 1800 although the yard had been used by the Navy prior to that date. Attempts to destroy the yard prior to its capture by the Confederates were limited at best and approximately 1,200 cannons, including many heavy ones, were lost. The yard was recaptured in 1862 but was so destroyed by the retreating Confederates that it never regained its prominence during the war. It is still an active Navy shipyard.

Pensacola Navy Yard: Pensacola, Florida — Established in 1825 but was never a major facility. Captured by the Confederates at the beginning of the war, but it was not as great a prize as the Norfolk Navy Yard. Recaptured in 1862 it was put back into use mainly as a depot. It is still an active duty Navy post and is better known today as Pensacola Naval Air Station.

Philadelphia Navy Yard: Philadelphia, Pennsylvania — Officially established in 1800 although the Navy had been leasing the yard prior to that date. The size of the yard was restricted by Philadelphia and it was moved after the war to League Island. During the war 15 ships were either built or started there. The yard was closed in 1995 and is currently being used by private industry.

Portsmouth Navy Yard: Portsmouth, New Hampshire — Established in 1800 near the mouth of the Piscataqua River. In April 1861, 85 people were employed at the yard but within one month the number had increased to 820. During the war it employed over 2,000 people. It had one of the Navy's four balance floating dry docks. A total of 23 ships were either completed or started here during the war. It is still an active duty navy yard.

Washington Navy Yard: District of Columbia — Established in 1800 on the Anacostia River. It was the center of the Navy's ordnance efforts. Over 600 people worked in the ordnance department during its busiest time during the war. No ships were built there during the war although a number were repaired there. The yard's main efforts were directed toward ordnance and machinery. Although no longer a working navy yard it serves as the headquarters for the Naval District Washington.

Foundries

The foundries chosen to be included in this book were ones that had contracts with the Ordnance Department just prior to the Civil War. The foundries mainly manufactured large ordnance such as artillery and artillery projectiles. However, some, such as the Chicopee Foundry, also manufactured other ordnance items such as swords. The foundries were important to the Army as Congress would not authorize a national foundry that would be under the control of the Army. Consequently, the Army was dependent upon these privately owned foundries for all of its artillery. When the Civil War started, a number of additional firms began casting artillery but they are not listed for the reason given in the introduction to this appendix. This includes the Phoenix Iron Company of Phoenixville, PA, manufacturer of the excellent three-inch wrought-iron Ordnance Gun. It was not included even though its gun had been tested and approved by the Army because none were ordered prior to the start of the war.

Bellona Foundry: Black Heath, Virginia — Established in 1816 on the James River about 13 miles upstream from Richmond. In 1859, like the Tredegar Foundry, the Federal Government stopped placing orders with it due to the fact that the foundry refused to use the Rodman method of casting. The foundry never recovered after being destroyed during the war and is in ruins today. Its owner, Junius Archer, designed the Archer projectile that was used by Confederate artillery.

Chicopee Foundry (James T. Ames): Chicopee, Massachusetts — Established in 1829. Also known as the Ames Foundry. A manufacturer of brass cannons prior to the start of the war but it was better known for its swords. When swords were phased out by the military, the company did not make a transition to other items. In 1929 the company went bankrupt and was purchased by M.C. Lilley Company. During the war, the Chicopee Foundry manufactured $971,089.06 worth of artillery projectiles, 4 percent of the total for the Union.

Fort Pitt Foundry: Pittsburgh, Pennsylvania — Established in 1804 but it did not start manufacturing artillery until after the War of 1812. Before the Civil War it was one of the three foundries capable of casting large artillery pieces. It was at this foundry that Lieutenant (later General) Thomas Jefferson Rodman first manufactured cannons using his new method of cooling the gun from the inside out. During the war numerous 15-inch guns and six 20-inch guns were manufactured there as well as $176,776.73 worth of projectiles, 2 percent of the total. The foundry no longer exists today.

South Boston Foundry (C. Alger & Co.): Boston, Massachusetts — Established in 1817. In 1834 it manufactured the first U.S. made rifled cannon. During the war it manufactured a considerable number of bronze and large caliber iron artillery pieces as well as projectiles. It was the only manufacturer of the Schenkl Projectile, producing over 300,000 of them. The foundry's total projectile production was worth $971,089.06, 10 percent of the total. The foundry was not able to make the transition to steel and closed in the late 1800s.

Tredegar Foundry: Richmond, Virginia — Founded in 1837. Also known as the Tredegar Iron Works. The firm never made the switch to steel and continued making iron products until it closed in 1987. Until 1859 it was one of the three foundries contracted to cast large artillery pieces. At that time, the Federal Government stopped placing additional orders with it since the foundry refused to adopt the Rodman method of casting cannons. During the war Tredegar Foundry was one of the major industrial sites in the Confederacy. Surviving the war, the foundry stayed in business until the early 1950s when it was destroyed by a fire. Currently, the American Civil War Center is located on its former site.

West Point Foundry: Cold Spring, New York — Built in the 1820s close to the Hudson River, about 50 miles north of New York City. Before the war it was one of the three foundries capable of casting large artillery pieces. During the war, under the leadership of Robert P. Parrott, the foundry became one of the major artillery ordnance manufacturing centers for the Union. It manufactured $3,166,144.57, 32 percent of the total, worth of projectiles in addition to a large number of cannon. After the war the foundry did not make the transition to steel and lost its technological edge. In 1878, the West Point Foundry along with the South Boston Iron Company petitioned the Secretary of War for a subsidy so that their ability to manufacture iron artillery could be preserved. The petition was denied and the foundry went into receivership in 1889. It is currently in ruins and has been the site of archeological digs.

Small Arms Manufacturers

The small arms manufacturing firms chosen to be included in this book were found in prewar ordnance reports. In addition, these prewar small arms manufacturers produced most of the small arms manufactured by private firms used by the military during the war. The locations of these firms show the clustering effect of the arms industry and why the south was at such a manufacturing disadvantage when compared to the north. The arms manufacturers were in competition, as well as cooperation, with the Federal armories. During the early and middle parts of the 19th century most of the information/expertise flowed from the armories to the manufacturers. One of the keys to the expansion of high skilled machining knowledge in the north was the transfer of this knowledge by skilled workmen. During the war, the arms manufacturers were critical to national defense as the armories were not capable of supplying all of the small arms required by the Federal armies.

Bristol Firearms Company: Bristol, RI — Founded in 1855 by Ambrose Burnsides (later Major General Ambrose Burnsides) to manufacture a breech-loading carbine he invented. Only a few carbines were sold to the government prior to the war. During the war the company sold 55,567 carbines to the government. However, the firm went bankrupt shortly after the war.

E. Remington & Sons: Utica, NY — A major manufacturer of small arms for the government established around 1814. During the war, they were one of the major small arms manufacturers, making well over 100,000 rifles and pistols. Its arms manufacturing division is now known as Remington Arms.

Samuel Colt: Hartford, CT — The success of the Colt Revolver during the Mexican War made the Colt revolver the pistol of choice for the military. Although Colt made rifles during the war, they were best known for their Navy and Army revolvers. Is still a supplier of small arms to the United States military.

North & Savage: Middletown, CT — Renamed in 1860 the Savage Revolving Firearms Company. During the war, their revolvers were not well-received and relatively few were delivered to the government. The company is known today as Savage Arms.

Sharps Rifle Manufacturing Company: Hartford, CT — Established in 1851, it based its future on a breech-loading rifle invented by Christian Sharps in 1848 although Sharps left the firm in 1853. Sharps learned his trade when he worked under John Hall at the Harpers Ferry Armory. During the war 80,512 Sharps carbines and 9,141 Sharps rifles were purchased by the government. The firm made an excellent weapon but went out of business not long after the end of the war.

Sources

Information on many of the locations listed in this appendix can be found in a number of books, Ordnance Department records, as well as on various Web sites. Some, such as Harpers Ferry and Springfield armories, have been extensively written about. Information on others, such as the various small arms manufacturers, can be found in encyclopedias as well as books written on small arms. Some of the sites have been designated and marked as historic locations with national, state, or local historical societies maintaining them.

Chapter Notes

Introduction

1. Charles Guillaume Bormann, *The Shrapnel Shell in England and in Belgium* (Brussels: Louis Truyts, 1862), 2d ed., 15–16.
2. The projectile and part of the sternpost that it hit can be seen at the Navy Memorial Museum, Building 76, Washington Navy Yard, Washington, D.C.
3. Raphael Semmes, *The Confederate Raider Alabama* (Bloomington: Indiana University Press, 1962), 378.
4. Edward Porter Alexander, "The Great Charge and Artillery Fighting at Gettysburg," in *Battles and Leaders of the Civil War*, Robert Underwood Johnson and Clarence Clough Buel (Secaucus, NJ: Castle, 1982), Vol. 3, 358.
5. "The word 'fuze' is often spelt 'fuse' by those unacquainted with artillery usage. This is incorrect. 'Fuse,' derived from *fusus*, the past participle of *fundo*, means 'to melt,' e.g., the term 'fuse-wire' used in electrical circuits. 'Fuze,' on the other hand, is the shortened or modern method of spelling 'fuzee,' meaning a tube filled with combustible material. It is a derivation from *fusus*, a spindle and from the French *fusée*, a spindle full of thread." O.F.G. Hogg, *Artillery: Its Origin, Heyday and Decline* (Hamden, CT: Archon Books, 1970), 183.
6. "Weapon system" is used throughout this work as a fuze is a single weapon system, not multiple weapon systems.
7. J. F. C. Fuller, *Armament and History* (London: Eyre & Spottiswoode, 1946), 86.
8. William James, *The Naval History of Great Britain* (London: Macmillan and Co., 1902), Vol. 4, 228–229.
9. William Ley, *Shells and Shooting* (New York: Modern Age Books, 1942), 72.
10. Hogg, *Artillery*, 185.
11. T. J. Rodman, *Reports of Experiments on the Properties of Metals for Cannon, and the Qualities of Cannon Powder; with an Account of the Fabrication and Trial of a 15-Inch Gun* (Boston: Charles H. Crosby, 1861), 180–181.
12. Bormann, *The Shrapnel Shell in England and in Belgium*, 14–15.
13. *Ibid.*, 15.
14. John Gibbon, *The Artillerist's Manual* (Westport, CT: Greenwood Press, 1971 reprint), 62–63.
15. bid., 65.
16. Record Group 156, Records of the Office of the Chief of Ordnance, National Archives, Washington D.C., "Opinions and Recommendations of the Ordnance Board, October 1856."
17. The information on Parrott's contract comes from "Executive Document 99, Ordnance Department," 364–374. The weight of a Parrott Percussion Fuze was determined by weighing one in the author's collection.

Chapter 1

1. Edward Simpson, *A Treatise on Ordnance and Naval Gunnery, Compiled and Arranged as a Text Book for the U.S. Naval*

Academy (New York: D. Van Nostrand, 1862), 2d ed., 148.

2. Hogg, *Artillery*, 185.

3. William H. French, et al., *Instruction for Field Artillery* (Philadelphia: J. B. Lippincott & Co., 1860), 9; and Simpson, *Treatise on Ordnance and Naval Gunnery*, 154.

4. The information on the manufacture of U.S. military gunpowder in this paragraph came from John Gibbon's *The Artillerist's Manual*, chap. 1, and from T. T. S. Laidley and the U.S. Army's *The Ordnance Manual for the Use of the Officers of the United States Army*, 3d edition (Philadelphia: J.B. Lippincott & Co., 1862), chap. 9.

5. The information on Lammot du Pont's mission in this paragraph came from Gerard Colby's *Du Pont Dynasty* (Secaucus, NJ: L. Stuart, 1984), 67–71.

6. Gibbon, *The Artillerist's Manual*, 24.

7. Colby, *Du Pont Dynasty*, 88.

8. *Ordnance Instructions for the United States Navy*, 3d edition (Washington, D.C.: Government Printing Office, 1864), 36.

9. Laidley and U.S. Army Ordnance Department, *The Ordnance Manual*, 316.

10. Rodman, *Reports of Experiments on the Properties of Metals for Cannon*, 292.

11. *Ibid.*, 295–296.

12. John Adolphus Bernard Dahlgren, and U.S. Navy Department Bureau of Ordnance, *Ordnance Instructions for the United States Navy*, 2d ed. (Washington: George W. Bowman, 1860), 140.

13. Laidley and U.S. Army Ordnance Department, *The Ordnance Manual*, 3d edition, 295.

14. *Ibid.*, 293–294.

Chapter 2

1. John Adolphus Bernard Dahlgren, *Shells and Shell-Guns* (Philadelphia: King & Baird, 1856), 156.

2. Bormann, *The Shrapnel Shell in England and in Belgium*, 15.

3. Laidley and U.S. Army Ordnance Department, *The Ordnance Manual*, 3d edition, 293.

4. James Ward, *An Elementary Course of Instruction on Ordnance and Gunnery* (Philadelphia: Carey and Hart, 1846), 88–89.

5. Dahlgren, *Shells and Shell-Guns*, 155.

6. The first mention of the use of this iron plate that has been found by the author is in Ward, *An Elementary Course of Instruction on Ordnance and Gunnery*, 89. It appears that Cyrus Alger was the inventor of this device.

7. A long and bitter fight between Francis Alger, the son of Cyrus Alger, and William Wheeler Hubbell was fought over who invented the Alger Fuze. The military sided with the Alger family but Hubbell received $100,000 based on a patent that he filed in 1860, well after the fuze had been adopted by the Navy.

8. Dahlgren, *Shells and Shell-Guns*, 142.

9. Francis Alger, *A Petition to the National Government Embodying Facts and Statements in Furtherance of the Claim of the late Cyrus Alger* (Washington, D.C.: Franck Taylor, 1862).

10. U.S. Navy Department, *Instructions in Relation to the Preparation of Vessels of War for Battle* (Washington, D.C.: C. Alexander, 1852), I, 123.

11. *Ibid.*, 3.

12. Alger, *A Petition to the National Government*, 33.

13. Ibid, 39.

14. *Ordnance Instructions*, 3d edition (1864), I, 93.

15. The disadvantages of solely relying on field finds can be demonstrated by the Navy Fuze. Some authors have only relied on field finds to make their drawings of the Navy Fuze. As a consequence, their drawings are missing the lead safety knob and show the paper fuze extending past the base of the fuze. If they had carefully considered their drawings, they would have realized how dangerous and impractical extending the paper fuze past the base of the fuze would have been. Written information on the lead safety knob can only be found in a few Navy ordnance documents. Consequently, the existence of the lead safety knob is not well known.

16. Alger, *A Petition to the National Government*, 36.

17. S.V. Benét, comp., *A Collection of Annual Reports and Other Important Papers Relating to the Ordnance Department*, Vol. 2, 1845 to 1860 (Washington, D.C.: Government Printing Office, 1880), 134–135.

18. Benét, *A Collection of Annual Reports*, Vol. 2, 135.

19. B. Huger, "Report of Experiments etc, as required by Circular from Ordnance Office dated February 7th 1845, made at Fort Monroe Arsenal during the year ended June 30th 1849," RG 156, National Archives.
20. *Ibid.*
21. C. P. Kingsbury, and Charles Victor Thiroux, *An Elementary Treatise on Artillery and Infantry* (New York: G. P. Putman, 1849), 82.
22. Benét, *A Collection of Annual Reports*, Vol. 2, 264.
23. Dahlgren, *Shells and Shell-Guns*, 146.
24. Laidley and U.S. Army Ordnance Department, *The Ordnance Manual*, 3d edition, 295.
25. Simpson, *Treatise on Ordnance and Naval Gunnery*, 260.
26. Gibbon, *The Artillerist's Manual*, 249.
27. Edmund Rice, "Repelling Lee's Last Blow at Gettysburg," in *Battles and Leaders of the Civil War*, Johnson and Buel, Vol. 3, 389.
28. Gunther E. Rothenberg, *The Art of Warfare in the Age of Napoleon* (Bloomington: Indiana University Press, 1980), 77.
29. B. P. Hughes, *Open Fire: Artillery Tactics from Marlborough to Wellington* (Chichester, Sussex: Antony Bird Publications, 1983), 15.
30. Bormann, *The Shrapnel Shell in England and in Belgium*, 66–67.
31. *Ibid.*, 136.
32. *The War of the Rebellion: A Compilation of the Official Records of the Union and Confederate Armies* (Washington, D.C.: Government Printing Office, 1880–1901), Series I, Vol. XLII, Part II, 576.
33. James G. Benton, *Course of Instruction in Ordnance and Gunnery: Prepared for the Use of the Cadets of the United State Military Academy* (New York: D. Van Nostrand, 1867), 518. For a short biography on James Benton see Appendix E.
34. Report of the Ordnance Board, April 6, 1854, RG 156, National Archives.
35. Gibbon, *The Artillerist's Manual*, 268.
36. *Ibid.*
37. *Ibid.*, Appendix, 35.
38. Benét, *A Collection of Annual Reports*, Vol. 2, 321.
39. Alfred Mordecai and George Ramsay, "Report of the Trial of New Metal Fuzes for Spherical Case and Field Shell, at Fort Monroe Arsenal," July 21, 1854, RG 156, National Archives.
40. Benét, *A Collection of Annual Reports*, Vol. 2, 500.
41. Mordecai and Ramsay, "Report of the Trial of New Metal Fuzes."
42. *Ibid.*
43. *Ibid.*
44. George Ramsay, "Firings Made at Fort Monroe Arsenal to Test Fuzes for Spherical Case Shot Spherical Shells," Sept. 6, 1854, RG 156, National Archives.
45. Alfred Mordecai, "Report of the Trial of Böttcher's Fuze at Washington Arsenal," August 2, 1852, RG 156, National Archives.
46. *The War of the Rebellion, O.R.A.*, Series I, Vol. XXV, Part II, 151.
47. More detailed information on how the Bormann Fuze was manufactured can be found in Laidley and U.S. Army Ordnance Department, *The Ordnance Manual*, 3d edition, 296–297.
48. Gibbon, *The Artillerist's Manual*, 284.
49. All ranges and times are from Laidley and U.S. Army Ordnance Department, *The Ordnance Manual*, 384–390.
50. Dahlgren, *Shells and Shell-Guns*, 148. John Biemeck measured the dimensions of a Bormann punch in his collection and came up with 0.07 inches by 0.20 inches, or 0.014 square inches.
51. The diameter of the paper fuze was obtained from John F. Biemeck in his unpublished work, *Identification, Deactivation and Preservation of Black Powder Artillery Projectiles: 1761–1865.*
52. Henry L. Abbot, *Siege Artillery in the Campaigns Against Richmond* (Washington, D.C.: Government Printing Office, 1867), 112.
53. Abbot, *Siege Artillery in the Campaigns Against Richmond*, 112.
54. *Ibid.*, 42.
55. Gibbon, *The Artillerist's Manual*, 285.
56. Abbot, *Siege Artillery in the Campaigns Against Richmond*, 112.
57. Gibbon, *The Artillerist's Manual*, 280.
58. O.F.G. Hogg, *The Royal Arsenal* (London: Oxford University Press, 1963), Vol. II, 1403.
59. Hogg, *Artillery*, 188.
60. Hogg, *The Royal Arsenal*, Vol. II, 1110.
61. Twelfth Congress, Session I, Chapter LXXXIII, May 14, 1812.

62. Alexander Dyer, "Rifled Cannon, Fort Monroe Arsenal, 1854" RG 156, National Archives.
63. *Ibid.*
64. John Gibbon discusses the experiment in *The Artillerist's Manual* on page 323 but does not go into great detail.
65. This statue was not part of a Southern conspiracy, as Representative Sherman of Ohio, brother of William T. Sherman, the future Union general, chaired the committee in which the bill originated.
66. Bénét, *A Collection of Annual Reports*, Vol. 2, 690–691.
67. *Ibid.*, Vol. 3, 206.
68. *Ibid.*, Vol. 2, 672.
69. Gibbon, *The Artillerist's Manual*, 295.
70. *Ibid.*, 292.

Chapter 3

1. Vivian Dering Majendie, *The Arms and Ammunition of the British Service* (London: Cassell, Peter, & Galpin, 1878), xi.
2. Ulysses S Grant, *Personal Memoirs of U.S. Grant*, Vol. I (New York: C. L. Webster & Co., 1885), 95.
3. Gibbon, *The Artillerist's Manual*, 267–268.
4. *Ibid.*, 268.
5. *Ibid.*
6. French, et al., *Instruction for Field Artillery*, 11.
7. Gibbon, *The Artillerist's Manual*, 269.
8. Laidley and U.S. Army Ordnance Department, *The Ordnance Manual*, 3d edition, 455.
9. Gibbon, *The Artillerist's Manual*, 271.
10. H.L. Scott, *Military Dictionary* (New York: Greenwood Press, 1968) lists the maximum strength of United States Army regiments and companies on page 50.
11. Philip St. George Cooke, *Cavalry Tactics, or Regulations for the Instruction, Formations, and Movements of the Cavalry of the Army and Volunteers of the United States*, Volume II (Washington: Government Printing Office, 1861), 62.
12. *Ibid.*, Vol. I, 42.
13. U.S. War Department, *Cavalry Tactics*, Part Two (Philadelphia: J. B. Lipincott & Co., 1862), 197.
14. H. L. Scott, *Military Dictionary*, 50.
15. Gibbon states in *The Artillerist's Manual* on page 248 that the height of a man standing is considered to be 5 feet 5 inches tall, while a man on a horse is considered to be 8 feet 4 inches.
16. Gibbon, *The Artillerist's Manual*, 249. The effective range for a rifle musket was determined during tests conducted by the army, which found that a bullet from a rifled musket passed completely through a three-inch solid white pine plank at a distance of 1,000 yards (Gibbon, Appendix, 51). However, the horizontal deviation was found to be three feet at that distance when a strong wind was blowing perpendicular to the direction of flight of the bullet (H. L. Scott, *Military Dictionary*, 30).
17. Alfred Mordecai, "Report of the Trial of Böttcher's Fuze."
18. The types of rings and the material they were made of varied greatly. These rings were called sabots, as a holdover from the wooden sabots that were used with spherical projectiles.
19. Benton, *Course of Instruction in Ordnance and Gunnery*, 525.
20. *Ibid.*, 518.
21. *Ibid.*, 525.
22. *Ibid.*, 486.
23. *Ibid.*
24. C.H. Owen, *An Essay on the Motion of Projectiles Fired from Rifled Arms* (London: W. Mitchell, 1862), 68.
25. This is a very simplistic view of air resistance as there are many more variables, but for Civil War artillery projectiles, it is a good approximation.
26. *The War of the Rebellion*, *O.R.A.*, Series I, Vol. V, 653.
27. Charles Shiels Wainwright, and Allen Nevins, ed., *A Diary of Battle: The Personal Journal of Colonel Charles S. Wainwright, 1861–1865* (New York: Harcourt, Brace & World, 1962), 145–146.
28. *The War of the Rebellion*, *O.R.A.*, Series I, Vol. XLII, Part II, 579.
29. *Ibid.*, Vol. I, 369–370.
30. Bormann, *The Shrapnel Shell in England and in Belgium*, viii.
31. "Summary Statement of Ordnance and Ordnance Stores on Hand in the Artillery Regiments in the Service of the United States, 1861–1865." Microfilm M1281, National Archives, District of Columbia.
32. *The War of the Rebellion*, *O.R.A.*, Series I, Vol. XXXVIII, Part I, 119–123.

33. *Ibid.*
34. Gibbon, *The Artillerist's Manual*, 269. Gibbon stated that the maximum effect for canister was from 400 to 450 yards. If enemy troops were too close, the balls did not have sufficient dispersion, and if too far away, the balls became too dispersed.
35. *The War of the Rebellion, O.R.A.*, Series I, Vol. XXXVIII, Part I, 401.
36. Laidley and U.S. Army Ordnance Department's *Ordnance Manual* states that a 12-pound light gun canister projectile had four tiers, with seven shot in the first three tiers and six in the fourth tier, for a total of 27 shot. A radiograph picture of a 3-inch canister round shown on page 120 of John D. Bartleson's *A Field Guide for Civil War Explosive Ordnance* (Washington, D.C.: Government Printing Office, 1973) shows seven tiers of shot. There is room for four shot of the same size as that used in a 12-pound light gun canister projectile in each tier. If the first six tiers hold four shot and the last tier holds three shot, the projectile would hold a total of 27 shot, the same as a 12-pound light gun canister projectile.
37. *The War of the Rebellion, O.R.A.*, Series I, Vol. XXVII, Part I, 754.
38. Bormann, *The Shrapnel Shell in England and in Belgium*, 15.

Chapter 4

1. Fuller, *Armament and History*, 140.
2. Merritt Roe Smith, *Harpers Ferry Armory and the New Technology* (Ithaca, NY: Cornell University Press, 1977), 28.
3. U.S. Department of State, *U.S. Statutes at Large*, 3rd Congress Session I, Chapter XIV, April 2, 1794, Vol. I, 352.
4. Benét, *A Collection of Annual Reports*, Vol. 2, 291.
5. *Ibid.*, Vol. 1, 420–425.
6. Most of the information in this paragraph was obtained from chapters four and five of James Farley, *Making Arms in the Machine Age: Philadelphia's Frankford Arsenal, 1816–1870* (University Park: Pennsylvania State University Press, 1994), 47–86.
7. *Ibid.*
8. Most of the information in this paragraph was obtained from Marius B. Peladeau, "The Champlain Arsenal: A Brief History," in *Military Collector & Historian* (Fall, 1965), 69–75.
9. Farley, *Making Arms in the Machine Age*, 78.
10. *The War of the Rebellion, O.R.A.*, Series III, Vol. I, 1.
11. Benét, *A Collection of Annual Reports*, Vol. 2, 85–86.
12. *Ibid.*, 86.
13. *Ibid.*, 647.
14. *Ibid.*, 678–679.
15. J. W. Mallet, "Work of the Ordnance Bureau," *Southern Historical Society Papers*, Vol. XXXVII, 10.
16. William Le Roy Broun, "The Red Artillery," *Southern Historical Society Papers*, Vol. XXVI, 372.
17. A check of the data from Jefferson County, Virginia, where the Harpers Ferry Arsenal was located, only showed one firearms manufacturer that employed two men and had an $800 value placed on its annual production. Obviously, the value of the production from the arsenal was not included. Based on this information I have assumed that the value of the production of all of the military controlled facilities were not included in the census data.
18. Wayne Stark, "U.S. Army Projectile Suppliers," *The Artilleryman*, spring 1993, 8–9.
19. E. P. Alexander, "Confederate Artillery Service," *Southern Historical Society Papers*, Vol. XI, 104–105.
20. Abbot, *Siege Artillery in the Campaigns Against Richmond*, 112.
21. Edward Porter Alexander, and Gary W. Gallagher, ed., *Fighting for the Confederacy: The Personal Recollections of General Edward Porter Alexander* (Chapel Hill: University of North Carolina Press, 1989), 304.
22. Warren Ripley, ed., *Siege Train: The Journal of a Confederate Artilleryman in the Defense of Charleston* (Columbia: University of South Carolina Press, 1986), 12.
23. Benét, *A Collection of Annual Reports*, Vol. 2, 443.
24. Alexander and Gallagher, *Fighting for the Confederacy*, 122.

Chapter 5

1. Bronislaw Malinowski, *A Scientific Theory of Culture* (New York: Oxford University Press, 1960), 41.
2. Philip Racine, ed., *Unspoiled Heart:*

The Journal of Charles Mattocks of the 17th Maine (Knoxville: University of Tennessee Press, 1994), 22.

3. *The War of the Rebellion, O.R.A.*, Series I, Vol. I, 24–25.

4. Starting in the 1840s and continuing up to the beginning of the war, the Army constructed a series of coastal masonry forts. The Corps of Engineers conducted extensive testing to ensure that the forts could resist fire from smooth-bore artillery as best as possible. These tests were conducted from 1852 to 1855 at West Point, and projectiles as large as 42 pounds were fired at casemate embrasures constructed out of various materials in a variety of ways. The results of these experiments can be found in Joseph Gilbert Totten and U.S. War Department Corps of Engineers, *Papers on Practical Engineering No. 6, Report Addressed to the Hon. Jefferson Davis, Secretary of War, on The Effects of Firing with Heavy Ordnance from Casemate Embrasures: and also The Effects of Firing Against the same Embrasures with Various Kinds of Missiles* (Washington, D.C.: Taylor and Maury, 1857).

5. *The War of the Rebellion, O.R.A.*, Series I, Vol. VI, 134.

6. Gibbon, *The Artillerist's Manual*, 454.

7. *The War of the Rebellion, O.R.A.*, Series I, Vol. VI, 161.

8. *Ibid.*, 163.

9. E.L. Gallwey, and H. J. Alderson, *Report upon the Military Affairs of the United States of America*, British National Archives: Record WO 33/14 (British War Office, 1864), 13.

10. As previously discussed, when the war started, a sabot was a piece of wood strapped to the base of a projectile. The purpose of the sabot was to ensure that the gunner correctly oriented the projectile in the cannon with the fuze facing out. The word sabot comes from French and originally referred to a wooden shoe. Its transfer to artillery is logical, as an artillery sabot is a wooden shoe for a projectile. With the advent of rifled artillery the form and function of the sabot changed. The sabots used with rifled artillery had the function of expanding to allow the projectile to catch the rifling. Most of the rifled sabots used during the war were made out of a relatively soft metal, with the exception of the Schenkl sabot, which was made out of paper.

11. *The War of the Rebellion, O.R.A.*, Series I, Vol. XLII, Part II, 577.

12. *Ibid.*

13. Theodore Lyman, "Letter from Theodore Lyman to Elizabeth Russell Lyman, August 1, 1864," in *Meade's Headquarters, 1863–1865: Letters of Colonel Theodore Lyman from the Wilderness to Appomattox*, George R. Agassiz, ed. (Boston: Atlantic Monthly Press, 1922), 370.

14. *The War of the Rebellion, O.R.A.*, Series I, Vol. XXXVII, Part I, 799–803.

15. *Ibid.*, Vol. LII, Part I, 52.

16. *Ibid.*, Vol. XXVII, 320.

17. Benton, *Course of Instruction in Ordnance and Gunnery*, 476.

18. Warren Grabau, *Ninety-Eight Days* (Knoxville: University of Tennessee Press, 2000), 408–409.

19. *The War of the Rebellion, O.R.A.*, Series I, Vol. XXVIII, Part II, 57.

20. *Ibid.*, Part I, 30.

21. *Ibid.*, 33–34

22. *Official Records of the Union and Confederate Navies in the War of the Rebellion*, Series I, Vol. XXII, 763.

23. *The War of the Rebellion, O.R.A.*, Series I, Vol. X, Part I, 622.

24. *Ibid.*, 166.

25. *Official Records of the Union and Confederate Navies in the War of the Rebellion*, Series I, Vol. XXV, 163.

26. *The War of the Rebellion, O.R.A.*, Series I, Vol. XI, Part I, 223.

27. Ripley, *Siege Train*, 13–14.

28. *The War of the Rebellion, O.R.A.*, Series I, Vol. XXXVII, Part I, 348.

29. *Ibid.*, Vol. XX, Part I, 456.

30. *Ibid.*, 786.

31. French, et al., *Instruction for Field Artillery*, Plate 29.

32. *The War of the Rebellion, O.R.A.*, Series I, Vol. XIX, Part I, 845.

33. Jennings Wise, *The Long Arm of Lee*, Vol. 1 (Lynchburg, VA: J.P. Bell, 1915), 299.

34. J. G. Barnard and William F. Barry, *Report of the Engineer and Artillery Operations of the Army of the Potomac, from its Organization to the Close of the Peninsular Campaign* (New York: D. Van Nostrand, 1863), 105.

35. Barnard and Barry, *Report of the Engineer*, 110.

36. Gallwey and Alderson, *Report upon the Military Affairs*, 32.

37. *Ibid.*, 75.
38. *Ibid.*, x.
39. Special Orders No. 124, Headquarters Army of the Potomac, Washington, D.C., October 31, 1861, National Archives RG 156.
40. *Ibid.*
41. Report of the Board of Officers assembled under Special Orders No. 124, Headquarters Army of the Potomac, Washington, D.C., October 31, 1861, National Archives RG 156.
42. *Ibid.*
43. *Ibid.*
44. *The War of the Rebellion, O.R.A.*, Series I, Vol. XI, Part III, 106.
45. Regretfully, no correspondence has been found that details the results of his visit.
46. James Ripley, Chief of Ordnance, letter to Robert Parrott, 26 June, 1862, 40th Congress, 2nd Session, Ex. Doc. No. 99, 339.
47. *Ibid.*, 352.
48. Captain Alfred Mordecai was the son of Major Alfred Mordecai, the individual who traveled to Europe to study their ordnance system.
49. *The War of the Rebellion, O.R.A.*, Series I, Vol. XXXVI, Part III, 720–721.
50. *Ibid.*, Vol. XIX, Part I, 956–957.
51. *Ibid.*, 33.
52. *Ibid.*, Vol. XXI, 579.
53. *Ibid.*, 200.
54. *Ibid.*
55. *Ibid.*, 634.
56. Alexander and Gallagher, *Fighting for the Confederacy*, 260.
57. Henry J. Hunt, "Artillery," Papers of the Military Historical Society of Massachusetts, Vol. XIII, Civil and Mexican Wars 1861, 1846 (Wilmington, NC: Broadfoot Publishing Company, 1990), 372.
58. Hunt, "Artillery," 375.
59. *The War of the Rebellion, O.R.A.*, Series I, Vol. XXVII, Part I, 881.
60. *Ibid.*, 750.
61. *Ibid.*, Part II, 651.
62. *Ibid.*, 321.
63. *Ibid.*, Vol. XLV, Part I, 431–432.
64. *Ibid.*, 737.
65. Abbot, *Siege Artillery in the Campaigns Against Richmond*, 90.
66. *The War of the Rebellion, O.R.A.*, Series I, Vol. XXXVIII, Part III, 61.
67. *Ibid.*
68. *Ibid.*, Vol. XV, 650–651.
69. *Ibid.*, Vol. XXIII, Part II, 967–968.
70. Alexander and Gallagher, *Fighting for the Confederacy*, 60–61.
71. *The War of the Rebellion, O.R.A.*, Series I, Vol. XXVII, Part II, 355–356.
72. Gallwey and Alderson, *Report upon the Military Affairs*, x.
73. *The War of the Rebellion, O.R.A.*, Series I, Vol. XXXVIII, Part I, 122
74. *Ordnance Instructions for the United States Navy* (1864), Part I, 107.
75. B. F. Wade, Daniel W. Gooch, and U.S. Congress Joint Committee on the Conduct of the War, "Heavy Ordnance," in *Report of the Joint Committee on the Conduct of the War, at the Second Session Thirty-Eighth Congress* (Washington, D.C.: Government Printing Office, 1865), 1.
76. E. Simpson, *Report on a Naval Mission to Europe, Especially Devoted to the Material and Construction of Artillery*, Vol. I (Washington, D.C.: Government Printing Office, 1873), 263.
77. *Ordnance Instructions for the United States Navy* (1864), Part I, 93.
78. *Official Records of the Union and Confederate Navies in the War of the Rebellion*, Series I, Vol. 25, 60.
79. *Ibid.*, 60.
80. U.S. Navy Department, *Instructions in Relation to the Preparation of Vessels of War for Battle: To the Duties of Officers and Others when at Quarters: and to Ordnance and Ordnance Stores* (Washington, D.C.: C. Alexander, 1852), Part I, 123.
81. Dahlgren, and U.S. Navy Department Bureau of Ordnance, *Ordnance Instructions for the United States Navy* (1860), Part I, 5.
82. U.S. Navy Department Bureau of Ordnance, *Ordnance Instructions for the United States Navy* (Washington, D.C.: Government Printing Office, 1866), Part 1, 91.
83. This information was provided by John Biemeck.
84. Bormann, *The Shrapnel Shell in England and in Belgium*, 15.

Chapter 6

1. Henry Petroski, *Design Paradigms* (Cambridge: Cambridge University Press, 1994), 1.

2. Hunt, "Artillery," 115.

3. Abbot, *Siege Artillery in the Campaigns Against Richmond*, 112.

4. *Ibid.*

5. One problem when dealing with the statistical aspects of the evolution of the fuze during the Civil War is that the data is very limited. Data for various fuze experiments can be found in Ordnance Department Reports but battlefield data is scarce. Luckily, Brigadier General Henry Abbot conducted a series of experiments while Commander of the Union Siege Artillery during the Petersburg Campaign. However, his data must be used with care as about one-third of the projectiles/fuzes he tested were listed as uncertain and are not included in his final results.

6. Nathan Rosenberg, George Wallis, and Joseph Whitworth, *The American System of Manufactures: The Report of the Committee on the Machinery of the United States, 1855* (Edinburgh: Edinburgh University Press, 1969), 29.

7. W. S. Smoot, United States Patent No. 36,806.

8. Samuel R. Russell, United States Patent No. 37,200.

9. *Ibid.*

10. J. D. Henry, United States Patent No. 35,821.

11. John P. Rollins, United States Patent No. 34,268.

12. *Ibid.*

13. Letter from Major Laidley, Frankford Arsenal, PA, to Char. Potts, April 1, 1862, National Archives, RG 156.

14. *Ibid.*

15. Letter from General Barry, Inspector of Artillery, to J. Wallace, October 26, 1863, National Archives, RG 156.

16. Both Bartleson and Jones included other inventors in their books but they were not included in the count. The inventors who were not included invented a wide range of adaptors for the paper fuze, the Naval Water Cap Fuze, the Bormann Fuze, and a few British fuzes.

17. Charles Jones, *Artillery Fuses of the Civil War* (Alexandria, VA: O'Donnell Publications, 2001), 32.

18. *Ibid.*

19. Even though a number of different sources were investigated and inquires made, the business papers of none of these individuals were found. Places searched or where inquires were made include The Sharon Historical Society, National Archives, Massachusetts Historical Society, The Boston Society, Hagley Museum & Library, The New-York Historical Society, Foundry School Museum and the Putnam County Historical Society, and The Historical Society of Pennsylvania.

20. Report on Abst017dam's Projectiles made by Lieutenant H. Stockton, Ordnance Dept. at Washington Arsenal, January 9, 1865, National Archives RG 156.

21. *Ibid.*

22. It is this author's opinion that Cyrus Alger invented the Naval Water Cap Fuze, contrary to the opinion of the Court of Claims. The reasons are that Hubbell's patent was filed well after the military adopted the Alger Fuze, Hubbell did not ask for compensation until after anyone who could effectively dispute his claim was dead, and Navy correspondence gives positive reports on Alger's fuze but mainly negative ones on Hubbell's inventions. In addition, Hubbell made 15 claims with patent number 26,904 and 11 claims with patent number 34,059. Hubbell's claims tried to cover every possibility. Also, Hubbell was a good lawyer and able to effectively argue his case in court.

23. John P. Schenkl, U.S. Patent 33,495.

24. Benjamin F. Sturtevant, U.S. Patent 36,039.

25. William Wheeler Hubbell, U.S. Patent 36,566.

26. John Cochran, U.S. Patent 37,675.

27. B. Hotchkiss, U.S. Patent 37,756.

28. It is interesting to note that 12 threads per inch remained a standard for the U.S. Military for a number of years. Today, while 12 threads per inch are still widely used, some of the newer fuzes have a different number of threads per inch. One reason for the different number of threads per inch is the desire not to have fuzes mixed up. This information was provided in an e-mail message from Patrick Owens, Historian, ARDEC Historical Office and Museum.

29. The information on the number of threads per inch comes from Jones, *Artillery Fuses of the Civil War*, 97–105.

30. *Ibid.*, 108–110.

31. Abbot, *Siege Artillery in the Campaigns Against Richmond*, 108.

32. Though no correspondence has been

found between any of these individuals, in all probability they at least knew of each other, especially when it is realized that they all lived and worked within the same geographic area.

33. The Bormann design was so reliable and preferred by the military that the number of seconds of delay was increased to 14 by the end of the war. This was done so that Bormann-type fuzes could be used with the longer-ranged rifled artillery. Patent Number 72,494 is one example.

34. Wainwright and Nevins, *A Diary of Battle*, 58.

35. *Ordnance Instructions for the United States Navy* (1864), Part I, 1.

36. *Official Records of the Union and Confederate Navies in the War of the Rebellion*, Series I, Vol. 25, 19.

37. *Ordnance Instructions for the United States Navy* (1864), Part 1, 94.

38. *The War of the Rebellion*, O.R.A., Series I, Vol. XXV, Part II, 151–152.

39. Lieutenant William Prince, "Report on 12 Pounder Ammunition from Watervleit Arsenal," Washington Arsenal, May 4, 1864, National Archives RG 156.

40. *Ibid.*

41. *Ibid.*

42. *Ibid.*

43. *The War of the Rebellion*, O.R.A., Series I, Vol. XI, Part III, 242.

44. Ordnance Office Circular dated October 23, 1862, signed by J. W. Ripley, Brigadier General, Chief of Ordnance, provided by Thomas Publications, Gettysburg, PA.

45. Report from Captain Julius Hadley, 25th Ohio Battery, Little Rock, Arkansas, April 18, 1865, to Brigadier General Dyer, Chief of Ordnance. National Archives, RG 156.

46. *Ibid.*

47. *Ordnance Instructions for the United States Navy* (1866), Part 1, 112.

48. The range of a 15-inch shell at 6.5 seconds was 1,900 yards, and at 7.7 seconds was 2,100 yards. *Ordnance Instructions for the United States Navy* (1866), Appendix B, No. I, xv.

49. Sawyer had a previous patented combination fuze, Patent Number 36,172, but it is not included here as it was a flame-ignited-percussion combination and there is not any evidence that the military ever used it. In contrast, Schenkl's second patent is an improvement on his first and is not a completely different design.

50. Abbot, *Siege Artillery in the Campaigns Against Richmond*, 112.

51. *Ibid.*, 111.

52. *Ibid.*, 112.

53. *The War of the Rebellion*, O.R.A., Series I, Vol. XXVIII, Part I, 221–222.

Chapter 7

1. Schenkl Patent No. 33,495.

2. James Ripley, Chief of Ordnance, letter to Robert Parrott, May 23, 1863, 40th Congress, 2nd Session, Ex. Doc. No. 99

3. *The War of the Rebellion*, O.R.A., Series I, Vol. XXV, Part I, 260.

4. Hadley report to Brigadier General Dyer.

5. Patent No. 39,682.

6. *The War of the Rebellion*, O.R.A., Series I, Vol. XXIX, Part II, 413–414.

7. Schenkl Patent No. 33,495.

8. *Ordnance Instructions for the United States Navy* (1866), Part I, 75.

9. Ordnance Board, 4 January, 1868, National Archives RG 156.

10. Vivian Dering Majendie, *Ammunition: A Descriptive Treatise on the Different Projectiles, Charges, Fuzes, Rockets, &c., at Present in Use for Land and Sea Service, and on Other War Stores Manufactured in the Royal Laboratory* (London: W. Mitchell & Co., 1867), 286.

11. Confidential Memorandum from Navy Lieutenant Henry Moor to President James Polk, May 10, 1846, National Archives RG 156.

Chapter 8

1. Peter A. Bukowick, Keynote Speech, 43rd Annual Fuze Conference, April 7, 1999.

2. *The War of the Rebellion*, O.R.A., Series III, Vol. IV, 803.

3. S.V. Benét, *Annual Report of the Chief of Ordnance to the Secretary of War for the Fiscal Year Ended June 30, 1878* (Washington, D.C.: Government Printing Office, 1878), 421.

4. *Ibid.*

5. *Ibid.*

6. *Ibid.*

7. S.V. Benét, *Ordnance Memoranda, No. 21, Ammunition, Fuses, Primers, Military Py-*

rotechny, etc. (Washington, D.C.: The Ordnance Board, 1878), 71.
 8. *Ibid.*
 9. *Ibid.*
 10. Ley, *Shells and Shooting*, 98.
 11. Malinowski, *A Scientific Theory of Culture*, 41.

Appendix C

 1. *Daily Traveller*, April 21, 1857, National Archives RG 156.

 2. *The War of the Rebellion, O.R.A.*, Series I, Vol. XI, Part III, 106.

 3. James Ripley, Chief of Ordnance, letter to Robert Parrott, June 26, 1862, 40th Congress, 2nd Session, Ex. Doc. No. 99, 339.

 4. Abbot, *Siege Artillery in the Campaigns Against Richmond*, 94.

Bibliography

Primary Sources — Fuzes and Artillery

Abbot, Henry L. *Siege Artillery in the Campaigns Against Richmond, with Notes on the 15-Inch Gun, Including an Algebraic Analysis of the Trajectory of a Shot in its Ricochets Upon Smooth Water.* Washington, D.C.: Government Printing Office, 1867.

Alexander, Edward Porter, and Gary W. Gallagher, ed. *Fighting for the Confederacy: The Personal Recollections of General Edward Porter Alexander.* Chapel Hill: University of North Carolina Press, 1989.

Alger, Francis. *A Petition to the National Government, Embodying Facts and Statements in Furtherance of the Claim of the Late Cyrus Alger for Remuneration for the Adoption and Use, by the United-States Army and Navy, of Certain Inventions of His Relating to Fuzes and Shells, as Herein Set Forth; With Corroborative Official Documents, Testifying to Their Introduction into the United-States Service, and Their Indispensable Value.* Washington, D.C.: Franck Taylor, 1862.

Barnard, J. G., and William F. Barry. *Report of the Engineer and Artillery Operations of the Army of the Potomac, from its Organization to the Close of the Peninsular Campaign.* New York: D. Van Nostrand, 1863.

Benét, S.V. *Annual Report of the Chief of Ordnance to the Secretary of War for the Fiscal Year Ended June 30, 1878.* Washington, D.C.: Government Printing Office, 1878.

_____, comp. *A Collection of Annual Reports and Other Important Papers, Relating to the Ordnance Department, Taken from the Records of the Office of the Chief of Ordnance, from Public Documents and from Other Sources.* Vol. 1, *1812 to 1844.* Vol. 2, *1845 to 1860.* Vol. 3, *1860 to 1889.* Washington, D.C.: Government Printing Office, 1878–1890.

_____. *Ordnance Memoranda, No. 21, Ammunition, Fuses, Military Pyrotechny, etc.* Washington, D.C.: The Ordnance Board, 1878.

Bormann, Charles Guillaume. *The Shrapnel Shell in England and in Belgium: With Some Reflections on the Use of this Projectile in the Late Crimean War: A Historico-Technical Sketch.* 2nd ed. Brussels: Louis Truyts, 1862.

British Patents (see "Appendix B" for a list of the patents).

Butler, John Gassam. *Projectiles and Rifled Cannon with Practical Suggestions for Their Improvement, as Embraced in a Report to the Chief of Ordnance, U.S.A.* New York: D. Van Nostrand, 1875.

Cochran, John Webster. *Improvements in Ordnance, Firearms, and Projectiles.* New York: J.W. Orr, 1860.

Dahlgren, Jozhn Adolphus Bernard. *Report on the Thirty-Two Pounder of Thirty-Two Cwt.* Washington, D.C.: C. Alexander, 1850.

———. *Shells and Shell-Guns.* Philadelphia: King & Baird, 1856.

"Executive Document No. 99, 40th Congress, 2nd Session, House of Representatives, Ordnance Department, Message from the President of the United States in answer to a resolution of the House of 15th March last, asking for information concerning the ordnance department and its transactions, January 14, 1868."

Farragut, David Glasgow, and U.S. Bureau of Ordnance and Hydrography. *Experiments to Ascertain the Strength and Endurance of Navy Guns.* Washington, D.C.: A.O.P. Nicholson, 1854.

Gallwey, E. L., and H. J. Alderson. *Report upon the Military Affairs of the United States of America.* British National Archives: Record WO 33/14. British War Office, 1864.

Gibbon, John. *Personal Recollections of the Civil War.* New York, London: G.P. Putnam's Sons, 1928.

Gillmore, Quincy Adams, Joseph Gilbert Totten, and U.S. Army Corps of Engineers. *Official Report to the United States Engineer Department, of the Siege and Reduction of Fort Pulaski, Georgia, February, March, and April, 1862.* New York: D. Van Nostrand, 1862.

Gorgas, Josiah. "Notes on the Ordnance Department of the Confederate States of America." Typescript carbon. U.S Army Military History Institute, 1911.

Hale, William. *Treatise on the Comparative Merits of a Rifle Gun and Rotary Rocket, Considered as a Mechanical Means of Ensuring a Correct Line of Flight to a Body Impelled Through Space.* London: W. Mitchell, 1863.

Hotchkiss & Sons. *Hotchkiss' Patent Projectiles for Rifled Ordnance.* New York: Torrey Brothers, 1861.

House of Commons. *Report from the Select Committee on Ordnance.* London: His Majesty's Stationery Office, 1862.

Hubbell, William Wheeler. *Remarks by William W. Hubbell on the Subject of his Patent Fire Arms: With Copy of Patent, and His Explosive Destructive Concussion Shell.* Philadelphia, 1844.

"Hubbell Patents." Hearings before the Committee on Patents Subcommittee on Hubbell Patents. House of Representatives, Seventy-Fifth Congress, Third Session, H.J. Res. 401, March 3, 1938. Washington, D.C.: U.S. Government Printing Office, 1938.

Hunt, Henry Jackson. "Artillery." Papers of the Military Historical Society of Massachusetts. Vol. XIII, Civil and Mexican Wars 1861, 1846. Wilmington, NC: Broadfoot Publishing Company, 1990.

Jeffers, William N. *A Concise Treatise on the Theory and Practice of Naval Gunnery.* New York: D. Appleton, 1850.

Kingsbury, C. P., and Charles Victor Thiroux. *An Elementary Treatise on Artillery and Infantry.* New York: G.P. Putnam, 1849.

Lyman, Theodore. "Letter from Theodore Lyman to Elizabeth Russell Lyman, August 1, 1864." In *Meade's Headquarters, 1863–1865: Letters of Colonel Theodore Lyman from the Wilderness to Appomattox,* edited by George R. Agassiz. Boston: Atlantic Monthly Press, 1922.

MacDonald, John. *A Circumstantial and Explanatory Account of Experiments.* London: T. Egerton, 1819.

Majendie, Vivian Dering. *Ammunition: A Descriptive Treatise on the Different Projectiles, Charges, Fuzes, Rockets, &c., at Present in Use for Land and Sea Service, and on Other War Stores Manufactured in the Royal Laboratory.* London: W. Mitchell & Co., 1867.

———. *The Arms and Ammunition of the British Service.* London: Cassell, Peter, & Galpin, 1878.

———. *English Guns and Foreign Critics.* Woolwich: Royal Artillery Institution, 1870.

Mallet, John W. *Rules to Be observed in the Laboratories of C.S. Arsenals and Ordnance

Depots. Gettysburg, PA: Thomas Publications, 2002.

_____. "C. S. Central Laboratory Additional Rules." Macon, GA: May 30, 1863.

_____. "C. S. Central Laboratory Circular." Macon, GA: August 17, 1863.

_____. "C. S. Central Laboratory Circular." Macon, GA: March 14, 1864.

_____. "C. S. Central Laboratory Circular." Macon, GA: April 30, 1864.

Mordecai, Alfred. "Report on Rifled Cannon, Fort Monroe Arsenal, 1854." July 21, 1854. National Archives, District of Columbia, RG156. Records of the Office of the Chief of Ordnance, Reports of Tests and Experiments on Various Types of Ordnance and Ordnance Stores, 1846–61.

_____, and U.S. Army Ordnance Department. *Artillery for the United States Land Service.* Washington, D.C.: J. and G.S. Gideon, 1849.

_____, Julius Schön, and Josiah Gorgas. *Military Commission to Europe in 1855 and 1856. Report of Major Alfred Mordecai, of the Ordnance Department.* Washington, D.C.: George W. Bowman, 1861.

Official Records of the Union and Confederate Navies in the War of the Rebellion. U.S. Naval War records. Washington, D.C.: Government Printing Office, 1894–1922.

Owen, C. H. *An Essay on the Motion of Projectiles Fired from Rifled Arms.* London: W. Mitchell, 1862.

Paixhans, Henri Joseph. *An Account of the Experiments Made in the French Navy for the Trial of Bomb Cannon, etc.* Philadelphia: Dorsey, 1838.

Regulations for the Proof and Inspection of Cannon, Shot, and Shells, Adopted by a Board of Officers and Approved by the Secretary of the Navy, June 1845, J. and G.S. Gideon, Washington, 1848.

Ripley, J. W. "Ordnance Department Circular, Oct. 23, 1862." Washington, D.C.: Ordnance Department, 1862.

Ripley, Warren, ed., *Siege Train, The Journal of a Confederate Artilleryman in the Defense of Charleston.* Columbia, SC: University of South Carolina Press, 1986.

Rodman, T. J., *Reports of Experiments on the Properties of Metals for Cannon, and the Qualities of Cannon Powder; with an Account of the Fabrication and Trial of a 15-inch Gun.* Boston: Charles H. Crosby, 1861.

Schenkl, J. P., *Description of the Combination and the Concussion Fuze.* Boston: John Wilson and Son, 1862.

Simpson, E. *Report on a Naval Mission to Europe, Especially Devoted to the Material and Construction of Artillery.* Vol. 1. Washington, D.C.: Government Printing Office, 1873.

Southern Historical Society Papers, Richmond, VA.

"Summary Statement of Ordnance and Ordnance Stores on Hand in the Artillery Regiments in the Service of the United States, 1861–1865." Microfilm M1281, National Archives, District of Columbia.

Tidball, John, and U.S. War Department. *Report of an Inspection of the Artillery School, Fort Monroe, VA, May 1882.* Washington, D.C.: Government Printing Office, 1882.

Tousard, Louis de. *American Artillerist's Companion.* Philadelphia: C. and A. Conrad, 1809.

U.S. Army Ordnance Department. *Proceedings of the Ordnance Board, September 12, 1863.* Washington, D.C.: Government Printing Office, 1864.

_____. *Proceedings of the Ordnance Board, December 17, 1867.* Washington, D.C.: Government Printing Office, 1868.

U.S. Navy Bureau of Ordnance and Hydrography. *Circular: Parrott's Rifled Cannon.* Washington, D.C.: September 1, 1861.

U.S. Patents. See "Appendix A" for a list of the patents.

Wade, B. F., Daniel W. Gooch, and U.S. Congress Joint Committee on the Conduct of the War. "Heavy Ordnance." In *Report of the Joint Committee on the Conduct of the War, at the Second Session Thirty-Eighth Congress.* Washington, D.C.: Government Printing Office, 1865.

_____. *Report of the Joint Committee on the Conduct of the War, Second Session, Thirty-Eighth Congress.* Washington, D.C.: Government Printing Office, 1865.

Wainwright, Charles Shiels, and Allan Nevins, ed. *A Diary of Battle, The Personal Journals of Colonel Charles S. Wainwright, 1861–1865.* New York: Harcourt, Brace & World, 1962.

The War of the Rebellion: A Compilation of the Official Records of the Union and Confederate Armies. Washington, D.C.: Government Printing Office, 1880–1901.

Wiard, Norman. "Communication of Norman Wiard." In *Supplemental Report of the Joint Committee on The Conduct of the War,* Sherman, et al. Supplemental to Senate Report No. 142, 38th Congress, 2D Session, Vol. 2. Washington, D.C.: Government Printing Office, 1866.

Primary Sources — Manuals and Textbooks

Benton, James G. *A Course of Instruction in Ordnance and Gunnery; Prepared for the Use of the Cadets of the United States Military Academy.* New York: D. Van Nostrand, 1867.

Bruff, Lawrence L. *Ordnance and Gunnery: A Text-Book Prepared for the Use of Cadets of the U.S. Military Academy.* New York: John Wiley & Sons, 1896.

Cooke, Philip St. George. *Cavalry Tactics, or Regulations for the Instruction, Formations, and Movements of the Cavalry of the Army and Volunteers of the United States.* Volumes I and II. Washington, D.C.: Government Printing Office, 1861.

Dahlgren, John Adolphus Bernard, and U.S. Navy Department Bureau of Ordnance. *Ordnance Instructions for the United States Navy.* Second Edition. Washington, D.C.: George W. Bowman, 1860.

French, William H., et al. *Instruction for Field Artillery.* Philadelphia: J. B. Lippincott, 1860.

_____. *Instruction for Field Artillery.* New York: D. Van Nostrand, 1864.

Gibbon, John. *The Artillerist's Manual.* Westport, CT: Greenwood Press, 1971 reprint.

Kingsbury, C. P., and Charles Victor Thiroux. *An Elementary Treatise on Artillery and Infantry, Adapted to the Service of the United States.* New York: G. P. Putnam, 1849.

Laidley, T. T. S., and U.S. Army Ordnance Department. *The Ordnance Manual for the Use of the Officers of the United States Army.* 3rd and 4th editions. Philadelphia: J. B. Lippincott & Co., 1862 & 1865.

Metcalfe, Henry, and U.S. Military Academy. *Ordnance and Gunnery, U.S.M.A., Part I: Explosives, Metallurgy and Projectiles.* West Point, NY: United States Military Academy Press, 1889.

Ordnance Instructions for the United States Navy. Third Edition. Washington, D.C.: Government Printing Office, 1864.

Ordnance Instructions for the United States Navy. Fourth Edition. Washington, D.C.: Government Printing Office, 1866.

Owen, Charles Henry, and T. L. Dames. *Elementary Lectures on Artillery, Prepared for the Use of the Gentlemen Cadets of the Royal Military Academy.* Woolwich, London: Royal Artillery Institution, 1860.

Picatinny Arsenal, U.S. Army Office of the Product Manager for Fuzes. *A Guide for Fuze Development Programs.* Dover, NJ: U.S. Army Office of the Product Manager for Fuzes, Picatinny Arsenal, 1990.

Roberts, Joseph, *The Hand-Book of Artillery for the Service of the United States.* New York: D. Van Nostrand, 1863.

Simpson, Edward. *A Treatise on Ordnance and Naval Gunnery, Compiled and Arranged as a Text Book for the U.S. Naval Academy.* 2nd Edition. New York: D. Van Nostrand, 1862.

Tidball, John C. *Manual of Heavy Artillery Service. Prepared for the Use of the Army and*

Militia of the United States. Washington, D.C.: J.J. Chapman, 1880.
Tschappat, William H. *Text-Book of Ordnance and Gunnery*. New York: John Wiley & Sons, 1917.
U.S. Army Ordnance Department. *The Ordnance Manual for the use of the Officers of the United States Army*. Washington, D.C.: J. and G.S. Gideon, 1841.
U.S. Military Academy. *Military Pyrotechny, for the Use of the Cadets of the U.S. Military Academy, West Point*. West Point, NY: U.S. Military Academy Press, 1839.
U.S. Military Academy Department of Ordnance. *Fuzes*. West Point, NY: Department of Ordnance, U.S. Military Academy, 1950.
U.S. Navy Department. *Instructions in Relation to the Preparation of Vessels of War for Battle: To the Duties of Officers and Others When at Quarters: and to Ordnance and Ordnance Stores*. Washington, D.C.: C. Alexander, 1852.
U.S. Navy Department Bureau of Ordnance. *Manual Exercise of Pivot Guns*. Washington, D.C.: Navy Department Bureau of Ordnance, 1869.
_____, *Manual Exercise of Pivot Guns*. Washington, D.C.: Navy Department Bureau of Ordnance, 1874.
U.S. War Department. *Cavalry Tactics*. Philadelphia: J. B. Lippincott & Co., 1862.
Ward, James Harmon. *An Elementary Course of Instruction on Ordnance and Gunnery*. Philadelphia: Carey and Hart, 1846.
Whittemore, James M., and F. Heath. *Ammunition, Fuses, Primers, Military Pyrotechny, Etc.* Ordnance Memoranda No. 21. Washington, D.C.: Government Printing Office, 1878.
Wilson, Arthur Riehl, and Robert M. Danford. *Field Artillery Manual*. Vol. II, Third Revised Edition. Menasha, WI: George Banta Publishing Company, 1928.

Primary Sources — Not Directly Related to Fuzes or Artillery

Grant, Ulysses S., *Personal Memoirs of U.S. Grant*. Vol. I. New York: C.L. Webster & Co., 1885–6.
Hardee, William Joseph. *Rifle and Light Infantry Tactics*. Philadelphia: J.B. Lippincott & Co., 1861.
Johnson, Robert Underwood, and Clarence Clough Buel. *Battles and Leaders of the Civil War*. Secaucus, NJ: Castle, 1982.
Mattocks, Charles, and Philip Racine, ed. *Unspoiled Heart: The Journal of Charles Mattocks of the 17th Maine*. Knoxville: University of Tennessee Press, 1994.
Record Group 156, Records of the Office of the Chief of Ordnance. National Archives, Washington D.C.
Record Group 404, Records of the United States Military Academy. National Archives, United States Military Academy.
Rosenberg, Nathan, George Wallis, and Joseph Whitworth. *The American System of Manufactures: The Report of the Committee on the Machinery of the United States, 1855*. Edinburgh: Edinburgh University Press, 1969.
Semmes, Raphael. *The Confederate Raider Alabama*. Bloomington: Indiana University Press, 1962.
Totten, Joseph Gilbert, and U.S. War Department Corps of Engineers. *Papers on Practical Engineering No. 6, Report Addressed to the Hon. Jefferson Davis, Secretary of War, on The Effects of Firing with Heavy Ordnance from Casemate Embrasures: and also The Effects of Firing Against the same Embrasures with Various Kinds of Missiles*. Washington, D.C.: Taylor and Maury, 1857.
U.S. Census Office. *Statistics of The United States in 1860: Compiled from the Original Returns of the Eighth Census*. [New York]: Arno Press, 1976.
U.S. Congress. *The Congressional Globe*. Washington, D.C.: Blair & Rives, 1859–1861.

U.S. Department of State. *United States Statutes at Large.* Washington, D.C.: Government Printing Office, 1937–.

Secondary Sources — American Civil War Fuzes and Artillery

Bartleson, John D., and U.S. Naval School Explosive Ordnance Disposal. *A Field Guide for Civil War Explosive Ordnance.* Washington, D.C.: Government Printing Office, 1973.

Canney, Donald L. *Lincoln's Navy.* London: Conway Maritime Press, 1998.

Cole, Philip M. *Civil War Artillery at Gettysburg.* Cambridge, MA: Da Capo Press, 2002.

Dickey, Thomas S., Peter C. George, and Floyd W. McRae. *Field Artillery Projectiles of the American Civil War.* Atlanta: Arsenal Press, 1980.

Evans, Ronald D. "Notes Concerning Wiard's System of Field Artillery." *Military Collector & Historian* (Winter 1968): 103–108.

Farrow, Edward S. *Farrow's Military Encyclopedia.* New York: The author, 1885.

Gibbons, Tony. *Warships and Naval Battles of the Civil War.* New York: Gallery Books, 1989.

Hackley, F. W. *A Report on Civil War Explosive Ordnance.* Indian Head, MD: U.S. Naval Propellant Plant, 1960.

Hagerman, Edward. *The American Civil War and the Origins of Modern Warfare, Ideas, Organization, and Field Command.* Bloomington: Indiana University Press, 1988.

Haskin, William L. "The Organization and Material of Field Artillery in the U.S. Army Before the Civil War." *Journal of the Military Service Institute of the United States,* Vol. III, No. XII (1882): 403–416.

Hazlett, James C. "Parrott Guns in the Civil War." *Civil War Times Illustrated* (November 1966): 27–33.

_____, Edwin Olmstead, M. Hume Parks. *Field Artillery Weapons of the Civil War.* Newark, NJ: University of Delaware Press, 1983.

Hogg, Ian V. *The Illustrated Encyclopedia of Ammunition.* Secaucus, NJ: Chartwell Books, 1985.

_____. *Weapons of the Civil War.* Greenwich, CT: Brompton Books, 1987.

Hogg, Ian V., and John H. Batchelor. *Artillery.* New York: Scribner, 1972.

Hunt, O. E. *The Photographic History of the Civil War 5. Forts and Artillery.* New York: Review of Reviews, 1911.

Isleib, Charles R. and Jack Chard. *The West Point Foundry & The Parrott Gun.* Fleischmanns, NY: Purple Mountain Press, 2000.

Johnson, Curt, Richard C. Anderson, and Joseph Mills Hanson. *Artillery Hell: The Employment of Artillery at Antietam.* College Station: Texas A&M University Press, 1995.

Jones, Charles H. *Artillery Fuses of the Civil War.* Alexandria, VA: O'Donnell Publications, 2001.

Lewis, B. B. *Review of Dr. J. B. Read's Improvements and Discoveries in the Material and Form of Projectiles for Rifled Ordnance.* Tuscaloosa, AL: W.H. Sugg, 1884.

Lewis, Berkeley R. *Notes on Ammunition of the American Civil War 1861–1865.* Washington, D.C.: The American Ordnance Association, 1959.

Longarce, Edward G. *The Man Behind the Guns: A Biography of General Henry Jackson Hunt, Chief of Artillery, Army of the Potomac.* Cranbury, NJ: A.S. Barnes, 1977.

Lord, Francis A. *Civil War Collector's Encyclopedia.* New York: Castle Books, 1965.

Manucy, Albert. *Artillery Through the Ages.* Washington, D.C.: United States Government Printing Office, 1949.

McCaul, Edward B. "Ordnance — Civil War Artillery Fuses." *America's Civil War* (March 1997): 8, 80–82.

Melton, Jack W., and Lawrence E. Pawl. *Guide to Civil War Artillery Projectiles.* Kennesaw, GA: Kennesaw Mountain Press, 1996.

Naisawald, L. Van Loan. *Cannon Blasts.* Shippensburg, PA: White Mane Books, 2004.

_____. *Grape and Canister*. New York: Oxford University Press, 1960.
Nash, Howard P. "The Princeton Explosion." *American History Illustrated* (August 1969): 4–12.
Nesmith, Vardell Edwards. "The Quiet Paradigm Change: The Evolution of the Field Artillery Doctrine of the United States Army, 1861–1905." Dissertation for Department of History. Durham, NC: Duke University, 1977.
Oliver, John Ryder. *Notes on Field Artillery Projectiles*. London: W. Mitchell & Co., 1873.
Paulding, J. N. *The Cannon and Projectiles Invented by Robert P. Parrott*. New York: Imprint, 1879.
Peterson, Harold L. *Round Shot and Rammers*. South Bend, IN: South Bend Replicas, 1964.
Ripley, Warren. *Artillery and Ammunition of the Civil War*. New York: Promontory Press, 1970.
Roberts, B. S. *Description of Newly Patented Solid Shot and Shells for Use in Rifled Ordnance*. Davenport, IA: Gazette Steam Book and Job Rooms, 1864.
Saint-Robert, Count Paul De. *The Movement of Projectiles from Rifled Cannon*. Paris, 1861.
Schneller, Robert J. *A Quest for Glory: A Biography of Rear Admiral John A. Dahlgren*. Annapolis, MD: Naval Institute Press, 1996.
Scoffern, J. *Projectile Weapons of War*. London: Longman, Brown, and Co., 1859.
Sifakis, Stewart. *Who Was Who in the Civil War*. New York: Facts on File Publications, 1988.
Wise, Jennings. *The Long Arm of Lee*. Vol. 1. Lynchburg, VA: J.P. Bell Company, 1915.
Wright, Mike. "The Infernal Machine." *American Heritage of Invention & Technology* (Summer 1999): 44–50.

Other Secondary Sources

Adelman, Arthur. "Artillery Ammunition Development." *Army Ordnance* (May–June 1922): 361–363.
Bacon, Benjamin W. *Sinews of War*. Novato, CA: Presidio Press, 1997.
Bailey, J. B. A. *Field Artillery and Firepower*. Annapolis, MD: Naval Institute Press, 2004.
Bishop, J. Leander. *A History of American Manufactures from 1608–1860*. Philadelphia: Edward Young & Co., 1868.
Booton, John G. "Mechanical Time Fuzes." *Army Ordnance* (March–April 1937): 278–282.
Bourgoin, Adrien Paul, and Charles E. Munroe. "Projectiles Containing Explosives." Annual Report of the Board of Regents of the Smithsonian Institution (1917).
Brandes, Stuart D. *Warhogs: A History of War Profits in America*. Lexington: University Press of Kentucky, 1997.
Bruce, Robert V. *Lincoln and the Tools of War*. New York: The Bobbs-Merrill Company, 1956.
Buchanan, Brenda J., ed. *Gunpowder: The History of an International Technology*. Claverton Down: Bath University Press, 1996.
Bukowick, Peter A. "Fuze Reliability." Keynote Speech, 43rd Annual Fuze Conference, April 7, 1999.
Colby, Gerard. *Du Pont Dynasty*. Secaucus, NJ: L. Stuart, 1984.
Colley, David. "Deadly Accuracy." *American Heritage of Invention & Technology* (Spring 2001): 44–50.
Cooling, Benjamin Franklin, ed. *War, Business, and American Society: Historical Perspectives on the Military-Industrial Complex*. Port Washington, NY: National University Press, 1977.
Courtney-Green, P. R. *Ammunition for the Land Battle*. London: Brassey's, 1991.

Crosby, Alfred W. *Thowing Fire: Projectile Technology Through History*. Cambridge: University Press, 2002.
Dastrup, Boyd L. *The Field Artillery*. Westport, CT: Greenwood Press, 1994.
Davis, Carl L. *Arming the Union*. Port Washington, NY: Kennikat Press, 1973.
deTreville, John R. "Development of Point Detonating Fuzes." *Field Artillery Journal* (March–April 1979): 21–26.
Deyrup, Felicia Johnson. *Arms Making in the Connecticut Valley*. York, PA: George Shumway, 1970.
Dillon, Lester R. *American Artillery in the Mexican War, 1846–1847*. Austin: Presidial Press, 1975.
Dobyns, Kenneth W. *The Patent Office Pony*. Fredericksburg, VA: Sergeant Kirkland's, 1997.
Dupuy, Trevor N. *The Evolution of Weapons and Warfare*. Indianapolis, IN: The Bobbs-Merrill Company, 1980.
Edwards, Kenneth G. ed. *The Inventors, Andrew and Berkeley*. Sharon, CN: Sharon Historical Society, 1989.
Farley, James. *Making Arms in the Machine Age: Philadelphia's Frankford Arsenal, 1816–1870*. University Park: Pennsylvania State University Press, 1994.
Flagler, D. W. *A History of the Rock Island Arsenal*. Washington, D.C.: Government Printing Office, 1877.
Fox, Arthur B. *Pittsburgh During the American Civil War, 1860–1865*. Chicora, PA: Mechling Bookbindery, 2002.
Fuller, J. F. C. *Armament and History*. London: Eyre & Spottiswoode, 1946.
Gleick, James. *Chaos: Making a New Science*. New York: Penguin Books, 1987.
Goldman, Emily O., and Leslie C. Eliason, eds. *The Diffusion of Military Technology and Ideas*. Stanford, CA: Stanford University Press, 2003.
Gordon, Robert B. "Who Turned the Mechanical Ideal into Mechanical Reality?" *Technology and Culture* (October 1998), Vol. 29, No. 4: 744–778.
Goss, John H. "War-Time Manufacture of Fuzes." *Army Ordnance*, Vol. IX, No. 52: 224–227.
Grabau, Warren E. *Ninety-Eight Days*. Knoxville: University of Tennessee Press, 2000.
Gudmundsson, Bruce I. *On Artillery*. Westport, CT: Praeger, 1993.
Guilmartin, John F. "Ballistics in the Black Powder Era: A Cursory Examination of Technical Factors Influencing the Design of Ordnance and of the Emergence of Ballistics as an Applied Science." *Royal Armouries, Conference Proceedings 1*, Robert D. Smith, ed. (H.M. Tower of London, England, 1989): 73–98.
Hamilton, John D. *The Ames Sword Company, 1829–1935*. Providence, RI: Mowbray Company, 1983.
Hayes, Thomas J. *Elements of Ordnance*. New York: John Wiley & Sons, 1938.
Hogg, O.F.G. *Artillery: Its Origin, Heyday and Decline*. Hamden, CT: Archon Books, 1970.
_____. *The Royal Arsenal*. London: Oxford University Press, 1963.
Hughes, B.P. *Open Fire: Artillery Tactics from Marlborough to Wellington*. Chichester, Sussex: Antony Bird Publications, 1983.
Huston, James A. *The Sinews of War: Army Logistics 1775–1953*. Washington, D.C.: Office of the Chief of Military History, U.S. Army, 1966.
James, William. *The Naval History of Great Britain*. Vol. 4. London: Macmillan, 1902.
Jensen, Geoffrey, and Andrew Wiest, eds. *War in the Age of Technology*. New York: New York University Press, 2001.
Jobé, Joseph, ed. *Guns: An Illustrated History of Artillery*. Greenwich, CT: New York Graphic Society, 1971.
Jones, Wilbur D. *Arming the Eagle*. Fort Belvoir, VA: Defense Systems Management Col-

lege Press, 1999.
Keegan, John. *The Face of Battle*. New York: Viking Press, 1976.
Koistinen, Paul A. C. *Beating Plowshares into Swords: The Political Economy of American Warfare, 1606–1865*. Lawrence: University Press of Kansas, 1996.
Kuhn, Thomas S. *The Structure of Scientific Revolutions*. Vol. 2. Chicago: University of Chicago Press, 1970.
Ley, William. *Shells and Shooting*. New York: Modern Age Books, 1942.
Lorber, Azriel. *Misguided Weapons*. Washington, D.C.: Brassey's, 2002.
Lynn, John A. *Tools of War: Instruments, Ideas, and Institutions of Warfare, 1445–1871*. Chicago: University of Illinois Press, 1990.
_____, ed. *Feeding Mars: Logistics in Western Warfare from the Middle Ages to the Present*. Boulder, CO: Westview Press, 1993.
Macconochie, Arthur F. *Modern Shell Production*. Cleveland: Penton Publishing, 1941.
Malinowski, Bronislaw. *A Scientific Theory of Culture*. New York, Oxford University Press, 1960.
Manucy, Albert. *Artillery Through the Ages*. Washington, D.C.: Government Printing Office, 1949.
McConnell, David. *British Smooth-Bore Artillery: A Technological Study*. Ottawa: Minister of Supply and Services Canada, 1988.
McGuire, Randy R. *St. Louis Arsenal, Armory of the West*. Chicago: Arcadia Publishing, 2001.
McNeill, William H. *The Pursuit of Power*. Chicago: University of Chicago Press, 1982.
Mendelsohn, Everett, Merritt Roe Smith, and Peter Weingart, eds. *Science, Technology and the Military*. Boston: Kluwer Academic Publishers, 1988.
Moten, Matthew. *The Delafield Commission and the American Military Profession*. College Station: Texas A&M University Press, 2000.
Murray, James V., and John Swantek, eds. *The Watervliet Arsenal, 1813–1997*. Watervliet, NY: Watervliet Arsenal Public Affairs Office, 1993.
Nagle, James F. *A History of Government Contracting*. Washington, D.C.: George Washington University, 1997.
Nealey, J. B. "Artillery Fuzes." *Army Ordnance* (May–June 1942): 961–964.
O'Brien, Michael J., ed. *Evolutionary Archaeology*. Salt Lake City: University of Utah Press, 1996.
Palucka, Time. "Doing the Impossible." *American Heritage of Invention & Technology* (Winter 2004): 22–31.
Peck, Taylor. *Round-Shot to Rockets*. Annapolis, MD: United States Naval Institute, 1949.
Petroski, Henry. *Design Paradigms*. Cambridge: Cambridge University Press, 1994.
_____. *The Evolution of Useful Things*. New York: Alfred A. Knopf, 1992.
Potter, E. B., and Chester W. Nimitz, eds. *Sea Power: A Naval History*. Englewood Cliffs, NJ: Prentice-Hall, 1960.
Robbins and Lawrence Armory and Machine Shop/American Precision Museum, National Register Nomination Information, December 2, 1974.
Roberts, William H. *Civil War Ironclads*. Baltimore: Johns Hopkins University Press, 2002.
_____. "The Name of Ericsson: Political Engineering in the Union Ironclad Program, 1861–1863." *The Journal of Military History* (October 1999): 823–844.
_____. USS *New Ironsides in the Civil War*. Annapolis, MD: Naval Institute Press, 1999.
Rothenberg, Gunther E. *The Art of Warfare in the Age of Napoleon*. Bloomington: Indiana University Press, 1980.
Rove, Gene. "Mechanical Time Fuzes." *Ordnance* (March–April 1955): 831–833.
Schreier, Konrad F. "U.S. Army Field Artillery Weapons, 1866–1918." *Military Collector & Historian* (Summer 1968): 40–45.
Scranton, Philip. *Endless Novelty*. Princeton, NJ: Princeton University Press, 1997.
Scott, H. L. *Military Dictionary*. New York: Greenwood Press, 1968.

Simonds, Thomas C. *History of South Boston*. New York: Arno Press, 1974.
Skelton, William B. *An American Profession of Arms: The Army Officer Corps, 1784–1861*. Lawrence: University Press of Kansas, 1992.
Smith, Merritt Roe. *Harpers Ferry Armory and the New Technology*. Ithaca, NY: Cornell University Press, 1977.
_____, ed. *Military Enterprise and Technological Change*. Cambridge, MA: MIT Press, 1985.
U.S. Ordnance Department. *Fuzes for use in Mountain, Field, Siege, and Seacoast Projectiles and in Detonating Fuzes*. Washington, D.C.: Government Printing Office, 1914.
van Creveld, Martin. *Technology and War*. New York: The Free Press, 1991.
Viall, Ethan. *United States Artillery Ammunition*. New York: McGraw-Hill, 1917.
Vincenti, Walter G. *What Engineers Know and How They Know It*. Baltimore: Johns Hopkins University Press, 1990.
Whisker, James Biser. *The United States Armory at Springfield, 1795–1865*. Lewiston, Canada: Edwin Mellen Press, 1997.
White, Lynn. *Medieval Technology and Social Change*. Oxford: Clarendon Press, 1963.

Periodicals

American Mechanics' Magazine, New York.
Army and Navy Journal, New York.
Military Collector & Historian, Journal of the Company of Military Historians, Washington, D.C.
Scientific American, Munn & Co., New York.
The Monthly Chronicle of Events, Discoveries, Improvements, and Opinions, Boston.

Unpublished Sources

Biemeck, John F. *Identification, Deactivation and Preservation of Black Powder Artillery Projectiles: 1761–1865*.
Day, John. E-mail dated 31 May, 2002, reference British fuze patents.
Wirtgen, Rolf, Chief Curator, Bundesant für Wehrtechnik und Beschaffung, letter dated 30 June 2000.

Index

Numbers in ***bold italics*** indicate pages with photographs.

Abbot, Gen. Henry 30–31, 56, 72, 77, 95, 101–103, 106; biography 177
Absterdam, John 92, 94–95; biography 177; percussion fuze 95
Adams, John 85
CSS *Alabama* 3–4, ***4***
Alderson, Capt. H.J. 70, 80
Alexander, Gen. E. Porter 3, 55–56, 74–75, 79
Alger, Cyrus 21–23, 92, 112; biography 178; *see also* Naval Fuze
Alger, Francis 23, 92, 95, 112; biography 178; *see also* Naval Fuze
Antietam, Battle of 69, 72–74
Archer, Junius 107; fuze 128
armories 47; Harpers Ferry 46, 49, 52, 54–55, 185–186; Springfield 46, 49, 52, 56, 185
Army of Northern Virginia 56, 74, 79–80
Army of Tennessee (CSA) 76
Army of the Potomac 25, 29, 42–43, 62, 69–71, 74, 80, 84, 97
Army of the Tennessee (USA) 78–79
arsenal, CSA: Richmond 53
arsenals, British: Woolwich 32
arsenals, USA: 14, 47, 51; Allegheny 14, 47, 186; Augusta 186; Baton Rouge 186; Benicia 186–187; Champlain 48, 187; Charleston 187; Detroit 187; Fayetteville 187; Fort Monroe 23, 28, 34, 40, 48, 55, 187; Frankford 48–49, 91, 98, 121, 123, 187; Kennebec 187–188; Little Rock 188; Mount Vernon 188; New York 188; St. Louis 188; San Antonio 49, 188; Washington 28, 54–55, 92, 97, 189; Watertown 70, 189; Watervliet 49–50, 70, 97–98, 189

Artillery Branch 33
artillery projectiles: canister 8, 26, 38–39, 44, 62, 95; case shot 8, 23, 25–28, ***26***, ***27***, 40, 62, 66, 82, 95, 103, 111–112, 127; grape shot 8; shell 7–8, 23, 26–27, 38, 62, 66, 82, 95, 103; solid shot 5, 7–8, 24, 38, 40, 62, 66, 95; *see also* Hotchkiss; James, Charles; Parrott, Robert J.; Schenkl, John
Atlanta Campaign 44–45

Barry, Gen. William F. 43–44, 71, 80, 91, 98; biography 178
Benton, Col. James 26, 64, 97; biography 178–179
Bormann, Gen. Charles 3, 19, 25, 28, 43, 83; biography 179; fuze 17, 20, 28–30, ***29***, 35, 40, 55, 85, 94, 96–100, 102, 123, 128
Böttcher fuze 28
Boxer, Col. Edward M. 31–32; fuze 31–32, ***32***
Breckinridge, Gen. John 68
Breithaupt Fuze 36
Brice's Cross Roads, Battle of 63
Bristol Firearms Company 192
British fuzes: Armstrong 93–94; Lancaster 94
USS *Brooklyn* 80
Broun, Lt. Col. William Le Roy 53; fuze 128
Bukowick, Dr. Peter A. 122
Bull Run, 1st Battle of 77

Chancellorsville, Battle of 58, 63, 117
Charleston, Siege of 56, 64, ***65***, 67
Cleburne, Gen. Patrick 63

215

Cochran, John 91, 93–94; biography 179
Colt *see* Samuel Colt
Corps of Engineers 33
Corse, Gen. John 44

Dahlgren, Adm. John 19, 30, 33, 52, 91, biography 179; fuze 91; gun 7, 42, *81*
Dilger, Capt. Hubert 44
Du Pont, Lammot 12, gunpowder mill 14
Dyer, Gen. Alexander 32, 34, 122; biography 179; paper fuze 30, 92; shell 40

E. Remington & Sons 52,192

Forrest, Gen. Bedford 63
Fort Fisher 64
Fort Pulaski 58–61, *59, 60, 61*, 64
Fort Sumter 58, 61, 64
Foster, Gen. John G. 58
Foundries: Bellona 51–52, 55, 107, 191; Chicopee 51, 190–191; Fort Pitt 51, 70, 191; Philadelphia (Phoenixville, PA) 70, 190–191; South Boston 21, 52, 92, 112, 191; Tredegar 51–52, 55, 191; West Point 9, 51–52, 70, 92, 191–192
Frankford Arsenal Combination Fuze 123, 125–126, *125*
Franklin, Battle of 76–77
fratricide 62–63
Fredericksburg, Battle of 42, 63, 73–74
Fuller, Gen. J.F.C. 46

Gallwey, Lt. Col. T.L. 70, 80
Ganster, George 92, 94–95; biography 179
Gettysburg, Battle of 44, 56, 63–64, 74–76, 79–80
Gibbon, Gen. John 11, 24, 26–27, 31, 34–36, biography 179
Gilmore, Gen. Quincy 59–60, 64–65, 105
Grant, Pres. Ulysses S. 38, 80
gunpowder 5–7, 11–18, 21, 27, 30, 57, 66, 74, 119; fuze composition 15, 17, 19–20, 24, 29; mammoth 15; mealed 16–17, 19–20, 30; musket 30; rifled 30

Hagner, Maj. P.V. 27–28, 47
Harwood, Lt. A.A. 22
Henry, J.D. 88
Hood, Gen. John B. 76
Hooker, Gen. Joseph 42
Hotchkiss: combination fuze 101–102, 111; patents 114; percussion fuze (front) 71, 111, *113*, 123–125, *124*; percussion fuze (base) 123–125, *124*; projectile 84, 98–99, 103, 105–106, 110
Hotchkiss, Andrew 110, *111*; biography 180

Hotchkiss, Benjamin 92, 94–95, 99–100, *112*, 110–122; biography 180
Hubbell, William 93; biography 180
Huger, Gen. Benjamin 23; biography 180
Hunt, Gen. John 42, 75, 84, 117, 119; biography 180
Hunter, Gen. David 58

industrial district 8, 52–56, 87, *89*

Jackson, Gen. Thomas J. 63, 72–74
James, Charles 93, 95; biography 180–181; fuze 92; projectile 71, 84; rifled artillery 35

USS *Kearsarge* 3–4, *4*

laboratory, arsenal 14, 19–20, 48, *50*
Lee, Gen. Robert E. 64, 67, 72, 76
Lee, Gen. Stephen 68–69
USS *Lexington* 66–67
Lyon, Col. Theodore 62

Majendie, Gen. Vivian 37
Malinowski, Dr. Bronislaw 57, 128
Mallet, J.W. 53
Malvern Hill, Battle of 67–68
Manigault, Maj. Edward 56–67
Mattocks, Capt. Charles 58
McClellan, Gen. George B. 70–73
McIntyre, James: biography 181
McLaws, Gen. Lafayette 73
Mendenhall, Capt. John 68
Merriam Delayed-action Fuze 123, 126–127, *126*
Mexican War 21, 23, 28, 37–38, 45
Milliken's Bend, Battle of 67
Mordecai, Maj. Alfred 28, 33, 40; biography 181
Mordecai, Capt. Alfred, Jr. 72

Napoleon, 12-pounder (light 12-pounder) 7–8, 24–25, 42–44, 84
Naval Fuze 21–23, *22*, 32, 34, 82, 92–94, 97
navy yards: Boston 52, 189; Mare Island 52, 189; Memphis 52; New York 52, 189–190; Norfolk 52, 54–55, 190; Pensacola 52, 190; Philadelphia 52, 190; Portsmouth 52, 190; Washington 22, 33, 52–55, 82, 91, 98, 190
North & Savage 52, 192

Ordnance Department: Army 1, 15, 19–20, 28–29, 32–35, 40, 47–49, 72, 94–95,

97, 120, 123; Navy 1, 32–33, 51–52, 91, 94–95
Osborn, Maj. Thomas W. 77, 79

Paixhan, Gen. Henri-Joseph 7, 24, 35; shell gun 7, 24
paper timed fuze 17, 20–24, 26–28, 30–31, 56, 71, 82, 94–96, 98–99, 123
Parrott, Robert J. 9, 16, 71–72, 92, 94–95, 110–122, **119**; artillery 16, 43, **66**, **68**, 80, 92; biography 181; paper fuze 30, 114; percussion fuze 9, 71–72, 95, 103, 105, **107**, 112, 114, **118**; projectile 9, 72, 84, 92, 103
Patent Office, British: fuze related patents 86, **86**, 173–176; see also names of patentees
Patent Office, U.S.: 34, 85, 87, 94–95, 99, 102–103; fuze related patents 84–87, **86**, **89**, 131–172; see also names of patentees
Peninsula Campaign 70
Perryville, Battle of 63
Petersburg, Siege of 30–31, 77, 95, 101
Petroski, Dr. Henry 84
Polk, Gen. Leonidas 77, **78**
Porter, Adm. David Dixon 96
Prince, Lt. William 97
USS *Princeton* 33

Ramsey, George 28
Reed, Dr. John 107; biography 181–182
Remington see E. Remington & Sons
Rice, Edmund 24
Ripley, Gen. James W. 56, 71–72, 98
Rodman, Gen. Thomas 15, 33; biography 182; gun 7, 81–82
Rollins, J.P. 90; fuze and projectile **90**
Russell, Samuel R. 87–88

sabot 5, 57, 62, 99, 112, 117
Samuel Colt 52, 192
Sawyer, Addison 91–92, 95; biography 182
Sawyer, Sylvanus 91–92, 95; biography 182
Sawyer Combination Fuze 85, 95, 101–102

Schenkl, John 71–72, 92–95, 110–122, **116**; biography 182–183; combination fuze 85, 95, 101, **102**; operation of a Schenkl percussion fuze **104**; percussion fuze 71–72, 95, 104–105, **106**, **114**, 123; projectile 84, sabot 112; table of fuze patents 117
Semmes, Adm. Raphael 3
Seven Days Campaign 72
Sharps Rifle Manufacturing Company 192
Sherman, Gen. William T. 43, 77
Shiloh, Battle of 66–67
Shrapnel, Gen. Henry 25, 35
Simpson, Edward 12
Sinope, Battle of 24
Slocum, Gen. Henry 63
Smoot, W.S. 87
Stones River, Battle of 68
Sturtevant, Benjamin 87, 93

Talcott, Lt. Col. George 49
Tice, Issac 92, 95; biography 183; concussion fuze 95, 106–107, **108**
Toggenburger, Frederic 100–101
Trent Affair 12–13
Trumbull, Maj. Thomas 73–74
Turner, Gen. John 105, 112
USS *Tyler* 66–67

United States Military Academy (West Point) 33–34
United States Naval Academy 24, 33

Variable Time (VT) Fuze 4, 103, 121, 127
Vicksburg, Siege of 64

Wainwright, Col. Charles 42, 96, 116–117
Weapon System Pyramid 1, 56, 83, 127–129, **128**
West Point Percussion Fuze **34**, 91, 105, 114
windage 5, 31, 40
wooden fuze 17, 19–21, 23–24, 26–27, 30–31, 95, 123
Woolwich Gun 81–82
Wright, George 99

www.ingramcontent.com/pod-product-compliance
Ingram Content Group UK Ltd.
Pitfield, Milton Keynes, MK11 3LW, UK
UKHW041954140426
5217IPUK00015B/795